The International Dictionary of Artificial Intelligence

William J. Raynor, Jr.

Glenlake Publishing Company, Ltd.
Chicago • London • New Delhi

AMACOM
American Management Association
New York • Atlanta • Boston • Chicago • Kansas City
San Francisco • Washington, D.C.
Brussels • Mexico City • Tokyo • Toronto

This book is available at a special discount when ordered in bulk quantities.
For information, contact Special Sales Department,
AMACOM, a division of American Management Association, 1601 Broadway, New York, NY 10019.

This publication is designed to provide accurate and authoritative information in regard to the subject matter covered. It is sold with the understanding that the publisher is not engaged in rendering legal, accounting, or other professional service. If legal advice or other expert assistance is required, the services of a competent professional person should be sought.

© 1999 The Glenlake Publishing Company, Ltd.
All rights reserved.
Printed in the Unites States of America

ISBN: 0-8144-0444-8

This publication may not be reproduced, stored in a retrieval system, or transmitted in whole or in part, in any form or by any means, electronic, mechanical, photocopying, recording, or otherwise, without the prior written permission of the publisher.

AMACOM
American Management Association
New York • Atlanta • Boston • Chicago • Kansas City •
San Francisco • Washington, D.C.
Brussels • Mexico City • Tokyo • Toronto

Printing number
10 9 8 7 6 5 4 3 2 1

Table of Contents

About the Author iii

Acknowledgements v

List of Figures, Graphs, and Tables vii

Definition of Artificial Intelligence (AI) Terms 1

Appendix: Internet Resources 315

About the Author

William J. Raynor, Jr. earned a Ph.D. in Biostatistics from the University of North Carolina at Chapel Hill in 1977. He is currently a Senior Research Fellow at Kimberly-Clark Corp.

Acknowledgements

To Cathy, Genie, and Jimmy, thanks for the time and support. To Mike and Barbara, your encouragement and patience made it possible.

This book would not have been possible without the Internet. The author is indebted to the many WWW pages and publications that are available there. The manuscript was developed using Ntemacs and the PSGML esxttension, under the Docbook DTD and Norman Walsh's excellent style sheets. It was converted to Microsoft Word format using JADE and a variety of custom PERL scripts. The figures were created using the vcg program, Microsoft Powerpoint, SAS and the netpbm utilities.

List of Figures, Graphs, and Tables

Figure A.1—Example Activation Functions .3

Table A.1—Adjacency Matrix 6

Figure A.2—An Autoregressive Network 21

Figure B.1—A Belief Chain 28

Figure B.2—An Example Boxplot 38

Graph C.1—An Example Chain Graph 44

Figure C.1—Example Chi-Squared Distributions 47

Figure C.2—A Classification Tree For Blood Pressure 52

Graph C.2—Graph with (ABC) Clique 53

Figure C.3—Simple Five-Node Network 55

Table C.1—Conditional distribution 60

Figure D.1—A Simple Decision Tree 77

Figure D.2—Dependency Graph 82

Figure D.3—A Directed Acyclic Graph 84

Figure D.4—A Directed Graph 84

Figure E.1—An Event Tree for Two Coin Flips 98

Figure F.1—Simple Four Node and Factorization Model 104

List of Figures, Graphs, and Tables viii

Figure H.1—Hasse Diagram of Event Tree 129

Figure J.1—Directed Acyclic Graph 149

Table K.1—Truth Table 151

Table K.2—Karnaugh Map 152

Figure L.1—Cumulative Lift 163

Figure L.2—Linear Regression 166

Figure L.3—Logistic Function 171

Figure M.1—Manhattan Distance 177

Table M.1—Marginal Distributions 179

Table M.2—A 3 State Transition Matrix 180

Figure M.2—A DAG and its Moral Graph 192

Figure N.1—Non-Linear Principal Components Network 206

Figure N.2—Standard Normal Distribution 208

Figure P.1—Parallel Coordinates Plot 222

Figure P.2—A Graph of a Partially Ordered Set 225

Figure P.3—Scatterplots: Simple Principal Components Analysis .235

Figure T.1—Tree Augmented Bayes Model 286

Figure T.2—An Example of a Tree 292

Figure T.3—A Triangulated Graph 292

Figure U.1—An Undirected Graph 296

A

A* Algorithm
A problem solving approach that allows you to combine both formal techniques as well as purely heurisitic techniques.
See Also: Heuristics.

Aalborg architecture
The Aalborg architecture provides a method for computing marginals in a join tree representation of a belief net. It handles new data in a quick, flexible matter and is considered the architecture of choice for calculating marginals of factored probability distributions. It does not, however, allow for retraction of data as it stores only the current results, rather than all the data.
See Also: belief net, join tree, Shafer-Shenoy Architecture.

abduction
Abduction is a form of nonmonotone logic, first suggested by Charles Pierce in the 1870s. It attempts to quantify patterns and suggest plausible hypotheses for a set of observations.
See Also: Deduction, Induction.

ABEL
ABEL is a modeling language that supports Assumption Based Reasoning. It is currently implemented in MacIntosh Common Lisp and is available on the World Wide Web (WWW).
See Also: http://www2-iiuf.unifr.ch/tcs/ABEL/ABEL/.

ABS
An acronym for Assumption Based System, a logic system that uses Assumption Based Reasoning.
See Also: Assumption Based Reasoning.

ABSTRIPS

Derived from the STRIPS program, the program also was designed to solve robotic placement and movement problems. Unlike STRIPS, it orders the differences between the current and goal state by working from the most critical to the least critical differnce.
See Also: Means-Ends analysis.

AC²

AC² is a commercial Data Mining toolkit, based on classification trees.
See Also: ALICE, classification tree, http://www.alice-soft.com/products/ac2.html.

accuracy

The accuracy of a machine learning system is measured as the percentage of correct predictions or classifications made by the model over a specific data set. It is typically estimated using a test or "hold out" sample, other than the one(s) used to construct the model. Its complement, the error rate, is the proportion of incorrect predictions on the same data.
See Also: hold out sample, Machine Learning.

ACE

ACE is a regression-based technique that estimates additive models for smoothed response attributes. The transformations it finds are useful in understanding the nature of the problem at hand, as well as providing predictions.
See Also: additive models, Additivity And Variance Stabilization.

ACORN

ACORN was a Hybrid rule-based Bayesian system for advising the management of chest pain patients in the emergency room. It was developed and used in the mid-1980s.
See Also: http://www-uk.hpl.hp.com/people/ewc/list-main.html.

Activation functions

Neural networks obtain much of their power throught the use of activation functions instead of the linear functions of classical regression models. Typically, the inputs to a node in a neural networks are weighted and then summed. This sum is then passed through a nonlinear activation function. Typically, these functions are sigmoidal (monotone increasing) functions such as a logistic or Gaussian function, although output nodes should have activation functions matched to the distribution of the output variables. Activation functions are closely related to link functions in statistical generalized linear models and have been intensively studied in that context.

Figure A.1 plots three example activations functions: a Step function, a Gaussian function, and a Logistic function.
See Also: softmax.

Figure A.1—Example Activation Functions

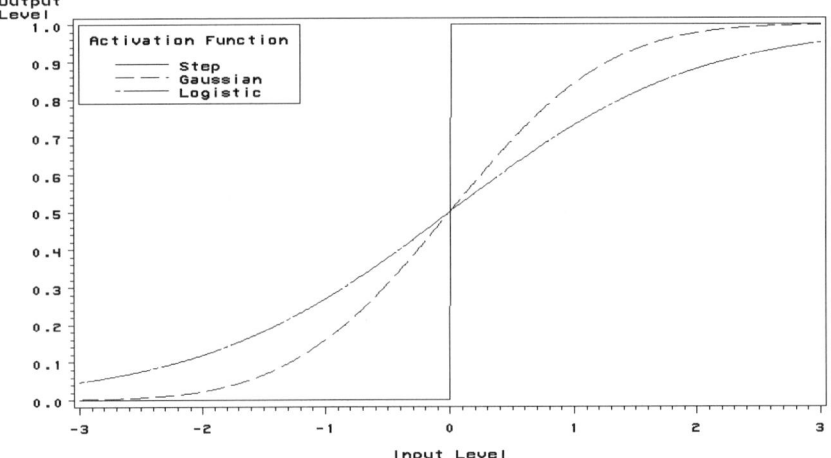

active learning

A proposed method for modifying machine learning algorithms by allowing them to specify test regions to improve their accuracy. At any point, the algorithm can choose a new point x, observe the output and incorporate the new (x,y) pair into its training base. It has been applied to neural networks, prediction functions, and clustering functions.

Act-R

Act-R is a goal-oriented cognitive architecture, organized around a single goal stack. Its memory contains both declarative memory elements and procedural memory that contains production rules. The declarative memory elments have both activation values and associative strengths with other elements.
See Also: Soar.

Acute Physiology And Chronic Health Evaluation (APACHE III)

APACHE is a system designed to predict an individual's risk of dying in a hospital. The system is based on a large collection of case data and uses 27 attributes to predict a patient's outcome. It can also be used to evaluate the effect of a proposed or actual treament plan.
See Also: http://www-uk.hpl.hp.com/people/ewc/list-main.html, http://www.apache-msi.com/.

ADABOOST

ADABOOST is a recently developed method for improving machine learning techniques. It can dramatically improve the performance of classification techniques (e.g., decision trees). It works by repeatedly applying the method to the data, evaluating the results, and then reweighting the observations to give greater credit to the cases that were misclassified. The final classifier uses *all* of the intermediate classifiers to classify an observation by a majority vote of the individual classifiers.

It also has the interesting property that the generalization error (i.e., the error in a test set) can continue to decrease even after the error in the training set has stopped decreasing or reached 0. The technique is still under active development and investigation (as of 1998).
See Also: arcing, Bootstrap AGGregation (bagging).

ADABOOST.MH

ADABOOST.MH is an extension of the ADABOOST algorithm that handles multi-class and multi-label data.
See Also: multi-class, multi-label.

adaptive

A general modifer used to describe systems such as neural networks or other dynamic control systems that can learn or adapt from data in use.

Adaptive Fuzzy Associative Memory (AFAM)

An fuzzy associative memory that is allowed to adapt to time varying input.

Adaptive Resonance Theory (ART)

A class of neural networks based on neurophysiologic models for neurons. They were invented by Stephen Grossberg in 1976. ART models use a hidden layer of ideal cases for prediction. If an input case is sufficiently close to an existing case, it "resonates" with the case; the ideal case is updated to incorporate the new case. Otherwise, a new ideal case is added. ARTs are often represented as having two layers, referred to as an F1 and F2 layers. The F1 layer performs the matching and the F2 layer chooses the result. It is a form of cluster analysis.
See Also: ftp://ftp.sas.com/pub/neural/FAQ2.html, http://www.wi.leidenuniv.nl/art/.

adaptive vector quantization

A neural network approach that views the vector of inputs as forming a state space and the network as quantization of those vectors into a smaller number of ideal vectors or regions. As the network "learns," it is adapting the location (and number) of these vectors to the data.

additive models

A modeling technique that uses weighted linear sums of the possibly transformed input variables to predict the output variable, but does not include terms such as cross-products which depend on more than a single predictor variables. Additive models are used in a number of machine learning systems, such as boosting, and in Generalized Additive Models (GAMs).
See Also: boosting, Generalized Additive Models.

Additivity And Variance Stabilization (AVAS)

AVAS, an acronym for Additivity and Variance Stabilization, is an modification of the ACE technique for smooth regression models. It adds a variance stabilizing transform into the ACE technique and thus eliminates many of ACE's difficulty in estimating a smooth relationship.
See Also: ACE.

ADE Monitor

ADE Monitor is a CLIPS-based expert system that monitors patient data for evidence that a patient has suffered an adverse drug reaction. The system will include the capability for modification by the physicians and will be able to notify appropriate agencies when required.
See Also: C Language Integrated Production System (CLIPS), http://www-uk.hpl.hp.com/people/ewc/list-main.html.

adjacency matrix

An adjacency matrix is a useful way to represent a binary relation over a finite set. If the cardinality of set A is n, then the adjacency matrix for a relation on A will be an nxn binary matrix, with a one for the i,j-th element if the relationship holds for the i-th and j-th element and a zero otherwise. A number of path and closure algorithms implicitly or explicitly operate on the adjacency matrix. An adjacency matrix is *reflexive* if it has ones along the main diagonal, and is symmetric if the i,j-th element equals the j,i-th element for all i,j pairs in the matrix.

Table A.1 below shows a symmetric adjacency matrix for an undirected graph with the following arcs (AB, AC, AD, BC, BE, CD, and CE). The relations are reflexive.

Table A.1—Adjacency Matrix

	A	B	C	D	E
A	1	1	1	1	0
B	1	1	1	0	1
C	1	1	1	1	1
D	1	0	1	1	0
E	0	1	1	0	1

A generalization of this is the *weighted adjacency matrix*, which replaces the zeros and ones with ∞ and costs, respectively, and uses this matrix to compute shortest distance or minimum cost paths among the elements.
See Also: Floyd's Shortest Distance Algorithm, path matrix.

Advanced Reasoning Tool (ART)
The Advanced Reasoning Tool (ART) is a LISP-based knowledge engineering language. It is a rule-based system but also allows frame and procedure representations. It was developed by Inference Corporation. The same abbreviation (ART) is also used to refer to methods based on Adaptive Resonance Theory.

ADVANCED SCOUT
A specialized system, developed by IBM in the mid-1990s, that uses Data Mining techniques to organize and interpret data from basketball games.

Advice Taker
A program proposed by J. McCarthy that was intended to show commonsense and improvable behavior. The program was represented as a system of declarative and imperative sentences. It reasoned through immediate deduction. This system was a forerunner of the Situational Calculus suggested by McCarthy and Hayes in a 1969 article in *Machine Intelligence*.

AFAM
See: Adaptive Fuzzy Associative Memory.

Agenda Based Systems
An inference process that is controlled by an agenda or job-list. It breaks the system into explicit, modular steps. Each of the entries, or tasks, in the job-list is some specific task to be accomplished during a problem-solving process.
See Also: AM, DENDRAL.

Agent_CLIPS
Agent_CLIPS is an extension of CLIPS that allows the creation of intelligent agents that can communicate on a single machine or across

the Internet.
See Also: CLIPS, http://users.aimnet.com/~yilsoft/softwares/agent-clips/agentclips.html.

AI
See: Artificial Intelligence.

AIC
See: Akaike Information Criteria.

AID
See: Automatic Interaction Detection.

AIM
See: Artificial Intelligence in Medicine.

AI-QUIC
AI-QUIC is a rule-based application used by American International Groups underwriting section. It eliminates manual underwriting tasks and is designed to change quickly to changes in underwriting rules.
See Also: Expert System.

airty
The airty of an object is the count of the number of items it contains or accepts.

Akaike Information Criteria (AIC)
The AIC is an information-based measure for comparing multiple models for the same data. It was derived by considering the loss of precision in a model when substituting data-based estimates of the parameters of the model for the correct values. The equation for this loss includes a constant term, defined by the true model, -2 times the likelihood for the data given the model plus a constant multiple (2) of the number of parameters in the model. Since the first term, involving the unknown true model, enters as a constant (for a given set of data), it can be dropped, leaving two known terms which can be evaluated.

Algebraically, AIC is the sum of a (negative) measure of the errors in the model and a positive penalty for the number of parameters in the model. Increasing the complexity of the model will only improve the AIC if the fit (measured by the log-likelihood of the data) improves more than the cost for the extra parameters.

A set of competing models can be compared by computing their AIC values and picking the model that has the smallest AIC value, the implication being that this model is closest to the true model. Unlike the usual statistical techniques, this allows for comparison of models that do not share any common parameters.

See Also: Kullback-Liebler information measure, Schwartz Information Criteria.

Aladdin

A pilot Case Based Reasoning (CBR) developed and tested at Microsoft in the mid-1990s. It addressed issues involved in setting up Microsoft Windows NT 3.1 and, in a second version, addressed support issues for Microsoft Word on the Macintosh. In tests, the Aladdin system was found to allow support engineers to provide support in areas for which they had little or no training.

See Also: Case Based Reasoning.

Algorithm

A technique or method that can be used to solve certain problems.

algorithmic distribution

A probability distribution whose values can be determined by a function or algorithm which takes as an argument the configuration of the attributes and, optionally, some parameters. When the distribution is a mathematical function, with a "small" number of parameters, it is often referred to as a parametric distribution.

See Also: parametric distribution, tabular distribution.

ALICE

ALICE is a Data Mining toolkit based on decision trees. It is designed for end users and includes a graphical front-end.

See Also: AC^2, http://www.alice-soft.com/products/alice.html.

allele

The value of a gene. A binary gene can have two values, 0 or 1, while a two-bit gene can have four alleles.

Alpha-Beta pruning

An algorithm to prune, or shorten, a search tree. It is used by systems that generate trees of possible moves or actions. A branch of a tree is pruned when it can be shown that it cannot lead to a solution that is any better than a known good solution. As a tree is generated, it tracks two numbers called alpha and beta.

ALVINN

See: Autonomous Land Vehicle in a Neural Net.

AM

A knowledge-based artificial mathematical system written in 1976 by Douglas Lenat. The system was designed to generate interesting concepts in elementary mathematics.

Ambler

Ambler was an autonomous robot designed for planetary exploration. It was capable of traveling over extremely rugged terrain. It carried several on-board computers and was cabaple of planning its moves for several thousand steps. Due to its very large size and weight, it was never fielded.
See Also: Sojourner, http://ranier.hq.nasa.gov/telerobotics_ page/Technologies/0710.html.

Analogy

A method of reasoning or learning that reasons by comparing the current situation to other situations that are in some sense similar.

analytic model

In Data Mining, a structure and process for analyzing and summarizing a database. Some examples would include a Classification And Regression Trees (CART) model to classify new observations, or a regression model to predict new values of one (set of) variable(s) given another set.
See Also: Data Mining, Knowledge Discovery in Databases.

ancestral ordering

Since Directed Acyclic Graphs (DAGs) do not contain any directed cycles, it is possible to generate a linear ordering of the nodes so that

any descendents of a node follow their ancestors in the node. This can be used in probability propogation on the net.
See Also: Bayesian networks, graphical models.

And-Or Graphs

A graph of the relationships between the parts of a decomposible problem.
See Also: Graph.

AND versus OR Nondeterminism

In logic programs, do not specify the order in which AND propositions and "A if B" propositions are evaluated. This can affect the efficiency of the program in finding a solution, particularly if one of the branches being evaluated is very lengthy.
See Also: Logic Programming.

ANN

See: Artificial Neural Network; *See Also:* neural network.

APACHE III

See: Acute Physiology And Chronic Health Evaluation.

apoptosis

Genetically programmed cell death.
See Also: genetic algorithms.

Apple Print Recognizer (APR)

The Apple Print Recognizer (APR) is the handwriting recognition engine supplied with the eMate and later Newton systems. It uses an artificial neural network classifier, language models, and dictionaries to allow the systems to recognize printing and handwriting. Stroke streams were segmented and then classifed using a neural net classifier. The probability vectors produced by the Artificial Neural Network (ANN) were then used in a content-driven search driven by the language models.
See Also: Artificial Neural Network.

approximation net

See: interpolation net.

approximation space

In rough sets, the pair of the dataset and an equivalence relation.

APR

See: Apple Print Recognizer.

arboART

An agglomerative hierarchial ART network. The prototype vectors at each layer become input to the next layer.
See Also: ftp://ftp.sas.com/pub/neural/FAQ2.html, http://www.wi.leidenuniv.nl/art/.

arcing

Arcing techniques are a general class of Adaptive Resampling and Combining techniques for improving the performance of machine learning and statistical techniques. Two prominent examples include ADABOOST and bagging. In general, these techniques iteratively apply a learning technique, such as a decision tree, to a training set, and then reweight, or resample, the data and refit the learning technique to the data. This produces a collection of learning rules. New observations are run through all members of the collection and the predictions or classifications are combined to produce a combined result by averaging or by a majority rule prediction.

Although less interpretable than a single classifier, these techniques can produce results that are far more accurate than a single classifier. Research has shown that they can produce minimal (Bayes) risk classifiers.
See Also: ADABOOST, Bootstrap AGGregation.

ARF

A general problem solver developed by R. R. Fikes in the late 1960s. It combined constraint-satisfaction methods and heuristic searches. Fikes also developed REF, a language for stating problems for ARF.

ARIS

ARIS is a commercially applied AI system that assists in the allocation of airport gates to arriving flights. It uses rule-based reasoning, constraint propagation, and spatial planning to assign airport gates, and provide the human decision makers with an overall view of the current operations.

ARPAbet
An ASCII encoding of the English language phenome set.

Array
An indexed and ordered collection of objects (i.e., a list with indices). The index can either be numeric (0, 1, 2, 3, ...) or symbolic ('Mary', 'Mike', 'Murray', ...). The latter is often referred to as "associative arrays."

ART
See: Adaptive Resonance Theory, Advanced Reasoning Tool.

Artificial Intelligence
Generally, Artificial Intelligence is the field concerned with developing techniques to allow computers to act in a manner that seems like an intelligent organism, such as a human would. The aims vary from the weak end, where a program seems "a little smarter" than one would expect, to the strong end, where the attempt is to develop a fully conscious, intelligent, computer-based entity. The lower end is continually disappering into the general computing background, as the software and hardware evolves.
See Also: artificial life.

Artificial Intelligence in Medicine (AIM)
AIM is an acronym for Artificial Intelligence in Medicine. It is considered part of Medical Informatics.
See Also: http://www.coiera.com/aimd.htm.

ARTMAP
A supervised learning version of the ART-1 model. It learns specified binary input patterns. There are various supervised ART algorithms that are named with the suffix "MAP," as in Fuzzy ARTMAP. These algorithms cluster both the inputs and targets and associate the two sets of clusters. The main disadvantage of the ARTMAP algorithms is that they have no mechanism to avoid overfitting and hence should not be used with noisy data.

See Also: ftp://ftp.sas.com/pub/neural/FAQ2.html, http://www.wi.leidenuniv.nl/art/.

ARTMAP-IC

This network adds distributed prediction and category instance counting to the basic fuzzy ARTMAP.
See Also: ftp://ftp.sas.com/pub/neural/FAQ2.html, http://www.wi.leidenuniv.nl/art/.

ART-1

The name of the original Adaptive Resonance Theory (ART) model. It can cluster binary input variables.
See Also: ftp://ftp.sas.com/pub/neural/FAQ2.html, http://www.wi.leidenuniv.nl/art/.

ART-2

An analogue version of an Adaptive Resonance Theory (ART) model, which can cluster real-valued input variables.
See Also: ftp://ftp.sas.com/pub/neural/FAQ2.html, http://www.wi.leidenuniv.nl/art/.

ART-2a

A fast version of the ART-2 model.
See Also: ftp://ftp.sas.com/pub/neural/FAQ2.html, http://www.wi.leidenuniv.nl/art/.

ART-3

An ART extension that incorporates then analog of "chemical transmitters" to control the search process in a hierarchial ART structure..
See Also: ftp://ftp.sas.com/pub/neural/FAQ2.html, http://www.wi.leidenuniv.nl/art/.

ASR

See: speech recognition.

assembler

A program that converts a text file containing assembly language code into a file containing machine language.
See Also: linker, compiler.

assembly language

A computer language that uses simple abbreviations and symbols to stand for machine language. The computer code is processed by an assembler, which translates the text file into a set of computer instructions. For example, the machine language instruction that causes the program store the value 3 in location27 might be STO 3 @27.

assertion

In a knowledge base, logic system, or ontology, an assertion is any statement that is defined a priori to be true. This can include things such as axioms, values, and constraints.
See Also: ontology, axiom.

association rule templates

Searches for association rules in a large database can produce a very large number of rules. These rules can be redundant, obvious, and otherwise uninteresting to a human analyst. A mechanism is needed to weed out rules of this type and to emphasize rules that are interesting in a given analytic context. One such mechanism is the use of templates to exclude or emphasize rules related to a given analysis. These templates act as regular expressions for rules. The elements of templates could include attributes, classes of attributes, and generalizations of classes (e.g., C+ or C* for one or more members of C or 0 or more members if C). Rule templates could be generalized to include a C - or A - terms to forbid specific attributes or classes of attributes. An *inclusive* template would retain any rules which matched it, while an *restrictive* template could be used to reject rules that match it. There are the usual problems when a rule matches multiple templates.
See Also: association rules, regular expressions.

association rules

An association rule is a relationship between a set of binary variables W and single binary variable B, such that when W is true then B is true with a specified level of confidence (probability). The statement that the set W is true means that all its components are true and also true for B.

Association rules are one of the common techniques is data mining and other Knowledge Discovery in Databases (KDD) areas. As an example, suppose you are looking at point of sale data. If you find that a person shopping on a Tuesday night who buys beer also buys diapers about 20 percent of the time, then you have an assoication rule that {Tuesday,beer} ⇒ {diapers} that has a confidence of 0.2. The support for this rule is the proportion of cases that record that a purchase is made on Tuesday and that it includes beer.

More generally, let **R** be a set of **m** binary attributes or items, denoted by $I_1, I_2, ..., I_m$. Each row r in a database can constitute the input to the Data Mining procedure. For a subset **Z** of the attributes **R**, the value of **Z** for the **i**-th row, $t(Z)_i$ is 1 if all elements of **Z** are true for that row. Consider the association rule **W** ⇒ **B**, where B is a single element in **R**. If the proportion of all rows for which both **W** and **B** holds is ≥ **s** and if **B** is true in at least a proportion **g** of the rows in which **W** is true, then the rule **W** ⇒ **B** is an (s,g) association rule, meaning it has support of at least s and confidence of at least g. In this context, a classical if-then clause would be a **(e,1)** rule, a truth would be a **(1,1)** rule and a falsehood would be a **(0,0)** rule.

See Also: association templates, confidence threshold, support threshold.

Associative Memory

Classically, locations in memory or within data structures, such as arrays, are indexed by a numeric index that starts at zero or one and are incremented sequentially for each new location. For example, in a list of persons stored in an array named persons, the locations would be stored as person[0], person[1], person[2], and so on. An associative array allows the use of other forms of indices, such as names or arbitrary strings. In the above example, the index might become a relationship, or an arbitrary string such as a social security number, or some other meaningful value. Thus, for example, one could look up person["mother"] to find the name of the mother, and person["OldestSister"] to find the name of the oldest sister.

associative property

In formal logic, an operator has an associative property if the arguments in a clause or formula using that operator can be regrouped without changing the value of the formula. In symbols, if the operator O is associative then aO (b O c) = (a O b) O c. Two common examples would be the + operator in regular addition and the "and" operator in Boolean logic.

See Also: distributive property, commutative property.

ASSOM

A form of Kohonen network. The name was derived from "Adaptive Subpace SOM."
See Also: Self Organizing Map, http://www.cis.hut.fi/nnrc/new_book.html.

Assumption Based Reasoning

Asumption Based Reasoning is a logic-based extension of Dempster-Shafer theory, a symbolic evidence theory. It is designed to solve problems consisting of uncertain, incomplete, or inconsistent information. It begins with a set of propositional symbols, some of which are assumptions. When given a hypothesis, it will attempt to find arguments or explanations for the hypothesis.

The arguments that are sufficient to explain a hypothesis are the **quasi-support** for the hypothesis, while those that do not contradict a hypothesis comprise the **support** for the hypothesis. Those that contradict the hypothesis are the **doubts**. Arguments for which the hypothesis is possible are called **plausibilities**. Assumption Based Reasoning then means determining the sets of supports and doubts. Note that this reasoning is done qualitatively.

An Assumption Based System (ABS) can also reason quantitatively when probabilities are assigned to the assumptions. In this case, the degrees of support, degrees of doubt, and degrees of plausibility can be computed as in the Dempster-Shafer theory. A language, ABEL, has been developed to perform these computations.
See Also: Dempster-Shafer theory, http://www2-iiuf.unifr.ch/tcs/ABEL/reasoning/.

asymptotically stable

A dynamic system, as in a robotics or other control systems, is asymptotically stable with respect to a given equilibrium point if, when the systems starts near the equilibrium point, it stays near the equilibrium point and asymptotically approaches the equilibrium point.
See Also: Robotics.

ATMS

An acronym for an Assumption-Based Truth Maintenance System.

ATN

See: Augmented Transition Network Grammer.

atom

In the LISP language, the basic building block is an atom. It is a string of characters beginning with a letter, a digit, or any special character other than a (or). Examples would include "atom", "cat", "3", or "2.79".
See Also: LISP.

attribute

A (usually) named quantity that can take on different values. These values are the attribute's domain and, in general, can be either quantitative or qualitative, although it can include other objects, such as an image. Its meaning is often interchangable with the statistical term "variable." The value of an attribute is also referred to as its feature. Numerically valued attributes are often classified as being nominal, ordinal, integer, or ratio valued, as well as discrete or continuous.

Attribute-Based Learning

Attribute-Based Learing is a generic label for machine learning techniques such as classification and regression trees, neural networks, regression models, and related or derivative techniques. All these techniques learn based on values of attributes, but do not specify relations between objects parts. An alternate approach, which focuses on learning relationships, is known as Inductive Logic Programming.
See Also: Inductive Logic Programming, Logic Programming.

Attribute extension

See: Extension of an attribute.

Augmented Transition Network Grammer

Also known as an ATN. This provides a representation for the rules of languages that can be used efficiently by a computer. The ATN is an extension of another transition grammer network, the Recursive Transition Network (RTN). ATNs add additional registers to hold partial parse structures and can be set to record attributes (i.e., the speaker) and perform tests on the acceptablility of the current analysis.

autoassociative

An autoassociative model uses the same set of variables as both predictors and target. The goal of these models to usually to perform some form of data reduction or clustering.
See Also: Cluster Analysis, Nonlinear Principal Components Analysis, Principal Components Analysis.

AutoClass

AutoClass is machine learning program that performs unsupervised classification (clustering) of multivariate data. It uses a Bayesian model to determine the number of clusters automatically and can handle mixtures of discrete and continuous data and missing values. It classifies the data probabilistically, so that an observation be classified into multiple classes.
See Also: Clustering, http://ic-www.arc.nasa.gov/ic/projects/bayes-group/autoclass/.

Autoepistemic Logic

Autoepistemic Logic is a form of nonmonotone logic developed in the 1980s. It extends first-order logic by adding a new operator that stands for "I know" or "I believe" something. This extension allows introspection, so that if the system knows some fact A, it also knows that it knows A and allows the system to revise its beliefs when it receives new information. Variants of autoepistemic logic can also include default logic within the autoepistemic logic.
See Also: Default Logic, Nonmonotone Logic.

autoepistemic theory

An autoepistemic theory is a collection of autoepistemic formulae, which is the smallest set satifying:

1. A closed first-order formula is an autoepistemic formula,
2. If A is an autoepistemic formula, then L A is an autoepistemic formula, and
3. If A and B are in the set, then so are !A, A ∨ B, A ∧ B, and A ⇒ B.

See Also: autoepistemic logic, Nonmonotone Logic.

Automatic Interaction Detection (AID)

The Automatic Interaction Detection (AID) program was developed in the 1950s. This program was an early predecessor of Classification And Regression Trees (CART), CHAID, and other tree-based forms of "automatic" data modeling. It used recursive significant testing to detect interactions in the database it was used to examine. As a consequence, the trees it grew tended to be very large and overly agressive.

See Also: CHAID, Classification And Regression Trees, Decision Trees and Rules, recursive partitioning.

automatic speech recognition

See: speech recognition.

Autonomous Land Vehicle in a Neural Net (ALVINN)

Autonomous Land Vehicle in a Neural Net (ALVINN) is an example of an application of neural networks to a real-time control problem. It was a three-layer neural network. Its input nodes were the elements of a 30 by 32 array of photosensors, each connected to five middle nodes. The middle layer was connected to a 32-element output array. It was trained with a combination of human experience and generated examples.

See Also: Artificial Neural Network, Navlab project.

autoregressive

A term, adapted from time series models, that refers to a model that depends on previous states.

See Also: autoregressive network.

autoregressive network

A parameterized network model in ancestral order so that the value of a node depends only on its ancestors. (See Figure A.2)

Figure A.2—An Autoregressive Network

AVAS

See: Additivity And Variance Stabilization; *See Also:* ACE.

axiom

An axiom is a sentence, or relation, in a logic system that is assumed to be true. Some familiar examples would be the axioms of Euclidan geometry or Kolmogorov's axioms of probability. A more prosaic example would be the axiom that "all animals have a mother and a father" in a genetics tracking system (e.g., BOBLO).
See Also: assertion, BOBLO.

B

backpropagation

A classical method for error propagation when training Artificial Neural Networks (ANNs). For standard backpropagation, the parameters of each node are changed according to the local error gradient. The method can be very slow to converge although it can be improved through the use of methods that slow the error propagation and by batch processing. Many alternate methods such as the conjugate gradient and Levenberg-Marquardt algorithms are more effective and reliable.

Backtracking

A method used in search algorithms to retreat from an unacceptable position and restart the search at a previously known "good" position. Typical search and optimization problems involve choosing the "best" solution, subject to some constraints (for example, purchasing a house subject to budget limitations, proximity to schools, etc.) A "brute force" approach would look at all available houses, eliminate those that did not meet the constraint, and then order the solutions from best to worst. An incremental search would gradually narrow in the houses under consideration. If, at one step, the search wandered into a neighborhood that was too expensive, the search algorithm would need a method to back up to a previous state.

Backward chaining

An alternate name for backward reasoning in expert systems and goal-planning systems.
See Also: Backward Reasoning, Forward Chaining, Forward Reasoning.

Backward Reasoning

In backward reasoning, a goal or conclusion is specified and the knowledge base is then searched to find sub-goals that lead to this conclusion. These sub-goals are compared to the premises and are either falsified, verified, or are retained for further investigation. The reasoning process is repeated until the premises can be shown to support the conclusion, or it can be shown that no premises support the conclusions.

See Also: Forward Reasoning, Logic Programming, resolution.

bagging

See: Bootstrap AGGregation.

bag of words representation

A technique used in certain Machine Learning and textual analysis algorithms, the bag of words representation of the text collapses the text into a list of words without regard for their original order. Unlike other forms of natural language processing, which treats the order of the words as being significant (e.g., for syntax analysis), the bag of words representation allows the algorithm to concentrate on the marginal and multivariate frequencies of words. It has been used in developing article classifiers and related applications.

As an example, the above paragraph would be represented, after removing punctuation, dumplicates, and abbreviations, converting to lower-case and sorting as the following list:

> a algorithm algorithms allows analysis and applications article as bag been being certain classifier collapses concentrate developing for forms frequencies has in into it language learning list machine marginal multivariate natural of on order original other processing regard related representation significant syntax technique text textual the their to treats unlike used which without words

See Also: feature vector, Machine Learning.

BAM

See: Bidirectional Associative Memory.

basin of attraction
The basin of attraction B for an attractor A in a (dynamic) state-space S is a region in S that will always bring the system closer to A.

batch training
See: off-line training.

Bayes classifier
See: Bayes rule.

Bayes factor
See: likelihood ratio.

Bayesian belief function
A belief function that corresponds to an ordinary probability function is referred to as a Bayesian belief function. In this case, all of the probability mass is assigned to singleton sets, and none is assigned directly to unions of the elements.
See Also: belief function.

Bayesian hierarchical model
Bayesian hierarchical models specify layers of uncertainty on the phenomena being modeled and allow for multi-level heterogeneity in models for attributes. A base model is specified for the lowest level observations, and its parameters are specified by prior distributions for the parameters. Each level above this also has a model that can include other parameters or prior distributions.

Bayesian Knowledge Discover
Bayesian Knowledge Discoverer is a freely available program to construct and estimate Bayesian belief networks. It can automatically estimate the network and export the results in the Bayesian Network Interchange Format (BNIF).
See Also: Bayesian Network Interchange Format, belief net, http://kmi.open.ac.uk/projects/bkd.

Bayesian learning
Classical modeling methods usually produce a single model with fixed parameters. Bayesian models instead represent the data with

distribution of models. Depending on technique, this can either be as a posterior distribution on the weights for a single model, a variety of different models (e.g., a "forest" of classification trees), or some combination of these. When a new input case is presented, the Bayesian model produces a distribution of predictions that can be combined to get a final prediction and estimates of variability, etc. Although more complicated than the usual models, these techniques also generalize better than the simpler models.

Bayesian Methods

Bayesian methods provide a formal method for reasoning about uncertain events. They are grounded in probability theory and use probabilistic techniques to assess and propagate the uncertainty.
See Also: Certainty, fuzzy sets, Possibility theory, probability.

Bayesian Network (BN)

A Bayesian Network is a graphical model that is used to represent probabilistic relationships among a set of attributes. The nodes, representing the state of attributes, are connected in a Directed Acyclic Graph (DAG). The arcs in the network represent probability models connecting the attributes. The probability models offer a flexible means to represent uncertainty in knowledge systems. They allow the system to specify the state of a set of attributes and infer the resulting distributions in the remaining attributes. The networks are called Bayesian because they use the Bayes Theorem to propagate uncertainty throughout the network. Note that the arcs are not required to represent causal directions but rather represent directions that probability propagates.
See Also: Bayes Theorem, belief net, influence diagrams.

Bayesian Network Interchange Format (BNIF)

The Bayesian Network Interchange Format (BNIF) is a proposed format for describing and interchanging belief networks. This will allow the sharing of knowledge bases that are represented as a Bayesian Network (BN) and allow the many Bayes networks to interoperate.
See Also: Bayesian Network.

Bayesian Updating

A method of updating the uncertainty on an action or an event based on new evidence. The revised probability of an event is P(Event given new data)=P(E prior to data)*P(E given data)/P(data).

Bayes rule

The Bayes rule, or Bayes classifier, is an ideal classifier that can be used when the distribution of the inputs given the classes are known exactly, as are the prior probabilities of the classes themselves. Since everything is assumed known, it is a straightforward application of Bayes Theorem to compute the posterior probabilities of each class. In practice, this ideal state of knowledge is rarely attained, so the Bayes rule provides a goal and a basis for comparison for other classifiers.
See Also: Bayes Theorem, naïve bayes.

Bayes' Theorem

Bayes Theorem is a fundamental theorem in probability theory that allows one to reason about causes based on effects. The theorem shows that if you have a proposition H, and you observe some evidence E, then the probability of H after seeing E should be proportional to your initial probability times the probability of E if H holds. In symbols, P(H|E)µP(E|H)P(H), where P() is a probability, and P(A|B) represents the conditional probability of A when B is known to be true. For multiple outcomes, this becomes

$$\Pr(H_i | E) = \frac{\Pr(H_i)\Pr(E|H_i)}{\sum_j \Pr(H_j)\Pr(E|H_j)}.$$

Bayes' Theorem provides a method for updating a system's knowledge about propositions when new evidence arrives. It is used in many systems, such as Bayesian networks, that need to perform belief revision or need to make inferences conditional on partial data.
See Also: Kolmogorov's Axioms, probability.

beam search

Many search problems (e.g., a chess program or a planning program) can be represented by a search tree. A beam search evaluates the tree similarly to a breadth-first search, progressing level by level down the tree but only follows a best subset of nodes down the tree, prun-

ing branches that do not have high scores based on their current state. A beam search that follows the best current node is also termed a best first search.
See Also: best first algorithm, breadth-first search.

BELIEF

A freely available program for the manipulation of graphical belief functions and graphical probability models. As such, it supports both belief and probabilistic manipulation of models. It also allows second-order models (hyper-distribution or meta-distribution). A commercial version is in development under the name of GRAPHICAL-BELIEF.
See Also: belief function, graphical model.

belief chain

A belief net whose Directed Acyclic Graph (DAG) can be ordered as in a list, so that each node has one predecessor, except for the first which has no predecessor, and one successor, except for the last which has no successor (See Figure B.1.).

Figure B.1—A Belief Chain

See Also: belief net.

belief core

The core of a set in the Dempster-Shafer theory is that probability is directly assigned to a set but not to any of its subsets. The core of a belief function is the union of all the sets in the frame of discernment which have a non-zero core (also known as the focal elements).

Suppose our belief that one of Fred, Tom, or Paul was responsible for an event is 0.75, while the individual beliefs were B(Fred)=.10, B(Tom)=.25, and B(Paul)=.30. Then the uncommitted belief would be 0.75-(0.1+0.25+0.30) = .10. This would be the core of the set {Fred, Tom, Paul}.
See Also: belief function, communality number.

belief function

In the Dempster-Shafer theory, the probability certainly assigned to a set of propositions is referred to as the belief for that set. It is a lower probability for the set. The upper probability for the set is the probability assigned to sets containing the elements of the set of interest and is the complement of the belief function for the complement of the set of interest (i.e., $P^u(A)=1-Bel(\text{not } A)$.) The belief function is that function which returns the lower probability of a set.

Belief functions that can be compared by considering that the probabilities assigned to some repeatable event are a statement about the average frequency of that event. A belief function and upper probability only specify upper and lower bounds on the average frequency of that event. The probability addresses the uncertainty of the event, but is precise about the averages, while the belief function includes both uncertainty and imprecision about the average.

See Also: Dempster-Shafer theory, Quasi-Bayesian Theory.

belief net

Used in probabilistic expert systems to represent relationships among variables, a belief net is a Directed Acyclic Graph (DAG) with variables as nodes, along with conditionals for each arc entering a node. The attribute(s) at the node are the head of the conditionals, and the attributes with arcs entering the node are the tails. These graphs are also referred to as Bayesian Networks (BN) or graphical models.

See Also: Bayesian Network, graphical model.

belief revision

Belief revision is the process of modifying an existing knowledge base to account for new information. When the new information is consistent with the old information, the process is usually straightforward. When it contradicts existing information, the belief (knowledge) structure has to be revised to eliminate contradictions. Some methods include expansion which adds new "rules" to the database, contraction which eliminates contradictions by removing rules from the database, and revision which maintains existing rules by changing them to adapt to the new information.

See Also: Nonmonotone Logic.

Belle

A chess-playing system developed at Bell Laboratories. It was rated as a master level chess player.

Berge Networks

A chordal graphical network that has clique intersections of size one. Useful in the analysis of belief networks, models defined as Berge Networks can be collapsed into unique evidence chains between any desired pair of nodes allowing easy inspection of the evidence flows.

Bernoulli distribution

See: binomial distribution.

Bernoulli process

The Bernoulli process is a simple model for a sequence of events that produce a binary outcome (usually represented by zeros and ones). If the probability of a "one" is constant over the sequence, and the events are independent, then the process is a Bernoulli process.
See Also: binomial distribution, exchangeability, Poisson process.

BESTDOSE

BESTDOSE is an expert system that is designed to provide physicians with patient-specific drug dosing information. It was developed by First Databank, a provider of electronic drug information, using the Neuron Data "Elements Expert" system. It can alert physicians if it detects a potential problem with a dose and provide citations to the literature.
See Also: Expert System.

best first algorithm

Used in exploring tree structures, a best first algorithm maintains a list of explored nodes with unexplored sub-nodes. At each step, the algorithm chooses the node with the best score and evaluates its sub-nodes. After the nodes have been expanded and evaluated, the node set is re-ordered and the best of the current nodes is chosen for further development.
See Also: beam search.

bias input

Neural network models often allow for a "bias" term in each node. This is a constant term that is added to the sum of the weighted inputs. It acts in the same fashion as an intercept in a linear regression or an offset in a generalized linear model, letting the output of the node float to a value other than zero at the origin (when all the inputs are zero.) This can also be represented in a neural network by a common input to all nodes that is always set to one.

BIC

See: Schwartz Information Criteria.

Bidirectional Associative Memory (BAM)

A two-layer feedback neural network with fixed connection matrices. When presented with an input vector, repeated application of the connection matrices causes the vector to converge to a learned fixed point.
See Also: Hopfield network.

bidirectional network

A two-layer neural network where each layer provides input to the other layer, and where the synaptic matrix of layer 1 to layer 2 is the transpose of the synaptic matrix from layer 2 to layer 1.
See Also: Bidirectional Associative Memory.

bigram

See: n-gram.

binary

A function or other object that has two states, usually encoded as 0/1.

Binary Input-Output Fuzzy Adaptive Memory (BIOFAM)

Binary Input-Output Fuzzy Adaptive Memory.

Binary Resolution

A formal inference rule that permits computers to reason. When two clauses are expressed in the proper form, a binary inference rule attempts to "resolve" them by finding the most general common clause. More formally, a binary resolution of the clauses A and B,

with literals L1 and L2, respectively, one of which is positive and the other negative, such that L1 and L2 are unifiable ignoring their signs, is found by obtaining the Most General Unifier (MGU) of L1 and L2, applying that substitute on L3 and L4 to the clauses A and B to yield C and D respectively, and forming the disjunction of C-L3 and D-L4. This technique has found many applications in expert systems, automatic theorem proving, and formal logic.
See Also: Most General Common Instance, Most General Unifier.

binary tree

A binary tree is a specialization of the generic tree requiring that each non-terminal node have precisely two child nodes, usually referred to as a left node and a right node.
See Also: tree.

binary variable

A variable or attribute that can only take on two valid values, other than a missing or unknown value.
See Also: association rules, logistic regression.

binding

An association in a program between an identifier and a value. The value can be either a location in memory or a symbol. Dynamic bindings are temporary and usually only exist temporarily in a program. Static bindings typically last for the entire life of the program.

Binding, Special

A binding in which the value part is the value cell of a LISP symbol, which can be altered temporarily by this binding.
See Also: LISP.

binit

An alternate name for a binary digit (e.g., bits).
See Also: Entropy.

binning

Many learning algorithms only work on attributes that take on a small number of values. The process of converting a continuous attribute, or a ordered discrete attribute with many values into a discrete vari-

able with a small number of values is called binning. The range of the continuous attribute is partitioned into a number of bins, and each case continuous attribute is classified into a bin. A new attribute is constructed which consists of the bin number associated with value of the continuous attribute. There are many algorithms to perform binning. Two of the most common include equi-length bins, where all the bins are the same size, and equiprobable bins, where each bin gets the same number of cases.
See Also: polya tree.

binomial coefficient

The binomial coefficient counts the number of ways n items can be partitioned into two groups, one of size k and the other of size n-k. It is computed as

$$C_k^n = \binom{n}{k} = \frac{k!}{k!(n-k)!}.$$

See Also: binomial distribution, multinomial coefficient.

binomial distribution

The binomial distribution is a basic distribution used in modeling collections of binary events. If events in the collection are assumed to have an identical probability of being a "one" and they occur independently, the number of "ones" in the collection will follow a binomial distribution.

When the events can each take on the same set of multiple values but are still otherwise identical and independent, the distribution is called a multinomial. A classic example would be the result of a sequence of six-sided die rolls. If you were interested in the number of times the die showed a 1,2,...,6, the distribution of states would be multinomial. If you were only interested in the probability of a five or a six, without distinguishing them, there would be two states, and the distribution would be binomial.
See Also: Bernoulli process.

BIOFAM

See: Binary Input-Output Fuzzy Adaptive Memory.

bipartite graph

A bipartite graph is a graph with two types of nodes such that arcs from one type can only connect to nodes of the other type.
See: factor graph.

bipolar

A binary function that produces outputs of -1 and 1. Used in neural networks.

bivalent

A logic or system that takes on two values, typically represented as True or False or by the numbers 1 and 0, respectively. Other names include Boolean or binary.
See Also: multivalent.

blackboard

A blackboard architecture system provides a framework for cooperative problem solving. Each of multiple independent knowledge sources can communicate to others by writing to and reading from a blackboard database that contains the global problem states. A control unit determines the area of the problem space on which to focus.

Blocks World

An artificial environment used to test planning and understanding systems. It is composed of blocks of various sizes and colors in a room or series of rooms.

BN

See: Bayesian Network.

BNB

See: Boosted Naïve Bayes classification.

BNB.R

See: Boosted Naïve Bayes regression.

BNIF

See: Bayesian Network Interchange Format.

BOBLO

BOBLO is an expert system based on Bayesian networks used to detect errors in parental identification of cattle in Denmark. The model includes both representations of genetic information (rules for comparing phenotypes) as well as rules for laboratory errors.
See Also: graphical model.

Boltzman Machine

A massively parallel computer that uses simple binary units to compute. All of the memory of the computer is stored as connection weights between the multiple units. It changes states probabilistically.

Boolean circuit

A Boolean circuit of size N over k binary attributes is a device for computing a binary function or rule. It is a Directed Acyclic Graph (DAG) with N vertices that can be used to compute a Boolean results. It has k "input" vertices which represent the binary attributes. Its other vertices have either one or two input arcs. The single input vertices complement their input variable, and the binary input vertices take either the conjunction or disjunction of their inputs. Boolean circuits can represent concepts that are more complex than k-decision lists, but less complicated than a general disjunctive normal form.

Boosted Naïve Bayes (BNB) classification

The Boosted Naïve Bayes (BNB) classification algorithm is a variation on the ADABOOST classification with a Naïve Bayes classifier that re-expresses the classifier in order to derive weights of evidence for each attribute. This allows evaluation of the contribution of the each attribute. Its performance is similar to ADABOOST.
See Also: Boosted Naïve Bayes Regression, Naïve Bayes.

Boosted Naïve Bayes regression

Boosted Naïve Bayes regression is an extension of ADABOOST to handle continuous data. It behaves as if the training set has been expanded in an infinite number of replicates, with two new variables added. The first is a cut-off point which varies over the range of the target variable and the second is a binary variable that indicates whether the actual variable is above (1) or below (0), the cut-off

point. A Boosted Naïve Bayes classification is then performed on the expanded dataset.
See Also: Boosted Naïve Bayes classification, Naïve Bayes.

boosting

See: ADABOOST.

Bootstrap AGGregation (bagging)

Bagging is a form of arcing first suggested for use with bootstrap samples. In bagging, a series of rules for a prediction or classification problem are developed by taking repeated bootstrap samples from the training set and developing a predictor/classifier from each bootstrap sample. The final predictor aggregates all the models, using an average or majority rule to predict/classify future observations.
See Also: arcing.

bootstrapping

Bootstrapping can be used as a means to estimate the error of a modeling technique, and can be considered a generalization of cross-validation. Basically, each bootstrap sample from the training data for a model is a sample, with replacement from the entire training sample. A model is trained for each sample and its error can be estimated from the unselected data in that sample. Typically, a large number of samples (>100) are selected and fit. The technique has been extensively studied in statistics literature.

Boris

An early expert system that could read and answer questions about several complex narrative texts. It was written in 1982 by M. Dyer at Yale.

bottom-up

Like the top-down modifier, this modifier suggests the strategy of a program or method used to solve problems. In this case, given a goal and the current state, a bottom-up method would examine all possible steps (or states) that can be generated or reached from the current state. These are then added to the current state and the process repeated. The process terminates when the goal is reached or all derivative steps exhausted. These types of methods can also be referred to as data-driven or forward search or inference.

See Also: data-driven, forward and backward chaining, goal-driven, top-down.

bottom-up pathways

The weighted connections from the F1 layer of a ART network to the F2 layer.
See Also: ftp://ftp.sas.com/pub/neural/FAQ2.html, http://www.wi.leidenuniv.nl/art/.

Bound and Collapse

Bound and Collapse is a two-step algorithm for learning a Bayesian Network (BN) in databases with incomplete data. The two (repeated) steps are bounding of the estimates with values that are consistent with the current state, followed by a collapse of the estimate bounds using a convex combination of the bounds. Implemented in the experimental program Bayesian Knowledge Discoverer.
See Also: Bayesian Knowledge Discover, http://kmi.open.ac.uk/projects/bkd/.

boundary region

In a rough set analysis of a concept X, the boundary region is the (set) difference between the upper and lower approximation for that concept. In a rough set analysis of credit data, where the concept is "high credit risk," the lower approximation of "high credit risk" would be the largest set containing only high credit risk cases. The upper approximation would be the smallest set containing all high credit risk cases, and the boundary region would be the cases in the upper approximation and not in the lower approximation. The cases in the boundary region include, by definition, some cases that do not belong to the concept, and reflect the inconsistency of the attribute tables.
See Also: lower approximation, Rough Set Theory, upper approximation.

bound variable or symbol

A variable or a symbol is bound when a value has been assigned to it. If one has not been assigned, the variable or symbol is unbound.
See Also: binding.

Box Computing Dimension

A simplified form of the Hausdorff dimension used in evaluating the fractal dimension of a collection in document and vision analysis.

Box-Jenkins Analysis

Box-Jenkins Analysis is a specific form of time series analysis, where the output is viewed as a series of systematic changes and cumulative random shocks. An alternate form of analysis would be a spectral analysis, which treats the series of events as an output of a continuous process and models the amplitude of the frequencies of that output.
See Also: spectral analysis, time series analysis.

boxplot

A boxplot is a simple device for visualizing a distribution. In its simplest form, it consists of a horizontal axis with a box above it, possibly with a spike sticking out of the two ends. The beginning and end of the box mark a pair of percentiles, such as the 25 and 75 percentile points. The ends can mark more extreme percentiles (10 and 90), and a vertical line marks the center (median or mean). (See Figure B.2.)

Figure B.2—An Example Boxplot

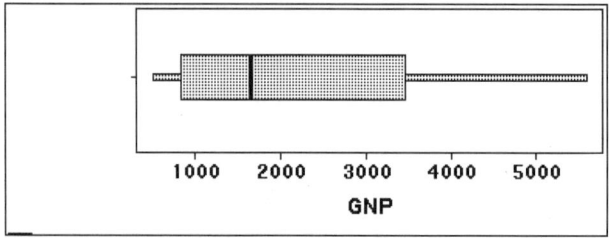

branch-and-bound search

Branch-and-Bound searches are used to improve searches through a tree representation of a solution space. As the algorithm progresses through a tree, it maintains a list of all partial paths that have been previously evaluated. At each iteration, it chooses the best (lowest cost) path that is currently known and expands that to its next level, scoring each of the new possible paths. These new paths are added to the list of possible paths replacing their common ancestor, and the process is reevaluated at the current best path. When a solution has been found, it may be improved by reevaluating the stored paths to eliminate more expensive solutions. The remaining paths can then be evaluated until they provide either a better solution or become more expensive than the best known solution.

Branching factor

Branching factor is a measure of the complexity of a problem or search algorithm. If an algorithm generates a tree with a maximum depth of D and N nodes, the branching factor is $B=N^{(1/d)}$. This measure can be used to compare various algorithms and strategies for a variety of problems. It has been shown that, for a variety of tree types, alpha-beta pruning gives the best results of any general game-searching algorithm.

breadth-first search

A search procedure in which all branches of a search tree are evaluated simultaneously, by switching from branch to branch, as each branch is evaluated to reach a conclusion or to form new branches.
See Also: depth-first search.

Brier scoring rule

This distance measure is the squared Euclidean distance between two categorical distributions. It has been used as a scoring rule in classification and pattern recognition.
See Also: mean square error criterion.

brute force algorithm

Algorithms that exhaustively examine every option are often referred to as brute force algorithms. While this approach will always lead to the "best" solution, it can also require unreasonable amounts of time or other resources when compared to techniques that use some other property of the problem to arrive at a solution, techniques that use a greedy approach or a limited look-ahead. An example would be the problem of finding a maximum of a function. A brute force step would divide the feasible region into small grids and then evaluate the results at every point over the grid. If the function is "well-behaved," a smarter algorithm would evaluate the function at a small

number of points and use the results of those evaluations to move toward a solution iteratively, arriving at the maximum quicker than the brute force approach.
See Also: combinatorial explosion, greedy algorithm, look-ahead.

bubble graph

A bubble graph is a generalization of a Directed Acyclic Graph (DAG), where the nodes represent groups of variables rather than a single variable, as in a DAG. They are used in probabilistic expert systems to represent multivariate head tail relationships for conditionals.
See Also: belief net, directed acylic graph, graphical model.

bucket brigade algorithm

An algorithm used in classifier systems for adjusting rule strengths. The algorithm iteratively applies penalties and rewards to rules based on their contributions to attaining system goals.

BUGS

BUGS is a freely available program for fitting Bayesian models. In addition to a wide array of standard models, it can also fit certain graphical models using Markov Chain Monte Carlo techniques. The Microsoft Windows version, called WinBUGS, offers a graphical interface and the ability to draw graphical models for later analysis.
See Also: Gibbs sampling, graphical model, Markov Chain Monte Carlo methods, http://www.mrc-bsu.cam.ac.uk/bugs/.

C

C

A higher-level computer language designed for general systems programming in the late 1960s at Bell Labs. It has the advantage of being very powerful and somewhat "close" to the machine, so it can generate very fast programs. Many production expert systems are based on C routines.
See Also: compiler, computer language.

CAD

See: Computer-Aided Design.

Caduceus

An expert system for medical diagnosis developed by H. Myers and H. Pople at the University of Pittsburgh in 1985. This system is a successor to the INTERNIST program that incorporates causal relationships into its diagnoses.
See Also: INTERNIST.

CAKE

See: CAse tool for Knowledge Engineering.

car

A basic LISP function that selects the first member of a list. It accesses the first, or left, member of a CONS cell.
See Also: cdr, cons. LISP.

cardinality

The cardinality of a set is the number of elements in the set. In general, the cardinality of an object is a measure, usually by some form of counting, of the size of the object.

CART
See: Classification And Regression Trees.

Cascade Fuzzy ART
A hierarchial Fuzzy ART network that develops a hierarchy of analogue and binary patterns through bottom-up learning guided by a top-down search process.
See Also: ftp://ftp.sas.com/pub/neural/FAQ2.html, http://www.wi.leidenuniv.nl/art/.

case
An instance or example of an object corresponding to an observation in traditional science or a row in a database table. A case has an associated feature vector, containing values for its attributes.
See Also: feature vector, Machine Learning.

Case Based Reasoning (CBR)
Case Based Reasoning (CBR) is a data-based technique for automating reasoning from previous cases. When a CBR system is presented with an input configuration, it searches its database for similar configurations and makes predictions or inferences based on similar cases. The system is capable of learning through the addition of new cases into its database, along with some measure of the goodness, or fitness, of the solution.
See Also: Aladdin, CLAVIER.

CAse tool for Knowledge Engineering (CAKE)
CAse tool for Knowledge Engineering (CAKE) can act as a front end to other expert systems. It is designed to allow domain experts to add their own knowledge to an existing tool.

CASSIOPEE
A troubleshooting expert system developed as a joint venture between General Electric and SNECMA and applied to diagnose and predict problems for the Boeing 737. It used Knowledge Discovery in Databases (KDD) based clustering to derive "families" of failures.
See Also: Clustering, Knowledge Discovery in Databases.

categorical variable

An attribute or variable that can only take on a limited number of values. Typically, it is assumed that the values have no inherent order. Prediction problems with categorical outputs are usually referred to as classification problems.
See Also: Data Mining, ordinal variable.

category proliferation

The term refers to the tendancy of ART networks and other machine learning algorithms to generate large numbers of prototype vectors as the size of input patterns increases.
See Also: ART, ftp://ftp.sas.com/pub/neural/FAQ2.html, http://www.wi.leidenuniv.nl/art/.

category prototype

The resonating patterns in ART networks.
See Also: ART, ftp://ftp.sas.com/pub/neural/FAQ2.html, http://www.wi.leidenuniv.nl/art/.

cautious monotonicity

Cautious monotonicity is a restricted form of monotone logic that allows one to retain any old theorems whenever any new information follows from an old premise.
See Also: monotone logic.

CBR

See: Case Based Reasoning.

C-Classic

A C language version of the CLASSIC system. No longer being developed.
See Also: CLASSIC, Neo-Classic.

cdr

A basic LISP function that selects a sublist containing all but the first member of a list. It accesses the second member of a CONS Cell.
See Also: car, Cons cell, LISP.

CHAID

An early follow-on to the Automatic Interaction Detection (AID) technique, it substituted the Chi-Square tests on contingency tables for the earlier techniques' reliance on normal theory techniques and measurements, like t-tests and analyses of variance. The method performs better on many n-ary attributes (variables) than does the AID technique. But the method still suffers due to its reliance on repeated statistical significance testing, since the theory that these tests rely on assumes such things as independence of the data sets used in repeated testing (which is clearly violated when the tests are performed on recursive subsets of the data).
See Also: Automatic Interaction Detection, Classification And Regression Trees, decision trees, recursive partitioning.

chain graph

An alternate means of showing the multivariate relationships in a belief net. This graph includes both directed and undirected arcs, where the directed arcs denote head/tail relationships as in a belief graph and the undirected arcs show multivariate relationships among sets of variables. (See Graph C.1.)

Graph C.1—An Example Chain Graph

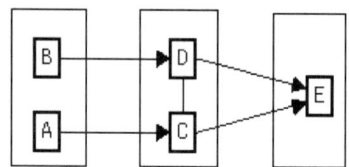

See Also: belief net, bubble graph.

chain rule

The chain rule provides a method for decomposing multi-variable functions into simpler univariate functions. Two common examples are the backpropagation in neural nets, where the prediction error at a neuron is broken into a part due to local coefficients and a part due to error in incoming signals, which can be passed down to those nodes, and in probability-based models which can decompose complex probability models into products of conditional distributions. An

example of the latter would be a decomposition of P(A,B,C) into the product of P(A|B,C), P(B|C), and P(C), where P(X|Y) is the conditional probability of X given Y. This latter decomposition underlies much of belief nets.
See Also: backpropagation, belief net.

CHAMP
See: Churn Analysis, Modeling, and Prediction.

Character Recognition
The ability of a computer to recognize the image of a character as a character. This has been a long-term goal of AI and has been fairly successful for both machine- and hand-printed material.

Checkers Playing Programs
The best checkers playing programs were written by Samuels from 1947 to 1967 and can beat most players. Game-playing programs are important in that they provide a good area to test and evaluate various algorithms, as well as a way to test various theories about learning and knowledge representation.

CHEMREG
CHEMREG is a knowledge-based system that uses Case Based Reasoning to assist its owner in complying with regulatory requirements concerning health and safety information for shipping and handling chemical products.

Chernoff bound
The Chernoff bound is a result from probability theory that places upper and lower limits on the deviation of a sample mean from the true mean and appears repeatedly in the analyses of machine learning algorithms and in other areas of computer science. For a sequence of m independent binary trials, with an average success rate of p, the probability that the total number of heads is above (below) $(p+g)m$ $[(p-g)m]$ is less than e^{-2mg^2}.

Chess, Computer
The application of AI methods and principles to develop machines that can play chess at an intelligent level. This area has been a

continual test bed of new algorithms and hardware in AI, leading to continual improvement. This has culminated in the recent match between A. Kasporov and Deep Blue.

CHESS 4.5 (and above)

A chess program that uses a brute force method called interactive deepening to determine its next move.

Chinook

Chinook is a checkers playing program and currently holds the man-machine checkers championship. Chinook won the championship in 1994 by forfeit of the reigning human champion, Marion Tinsely, who resigned due to health problems during the match and later died from cancer. The program has since defended its title. Chinook uses an alpha-beta search algorithm and is able to search approximately 21 moves ahead, using a hand-tuned evaluation function. It has an end-game database of over 400 billion positions, as well as a large database of opening sequences.
See Also: Deep Blue, http://www.cs.ualberta.ca/~chinook.

Chi-Squared Distribution

The Chi-Squared distribution is a probability distribution, indexed by a single parameter n, that can be generated as a sum of independent squared gaussian values. Its density is given by the formula

$$f(x\,|\,v) = \frac{1}{2^{v/2}\Gamma(v/2)} x^{(v-2)/w} e^{-x/2}, x > 0.$$

The parameter n is commonly referred to its degrees of freedom, as it typically is a count of the number of independent terms in the above sum, or the number of unconstrained parameters in a model. Figure C.1 plots Chi-Square densities for several different values of the degrees of freedom parameter.
See Also: Chi-Squared statistic.

Figure C.1—Example Chi-Squared Distributions

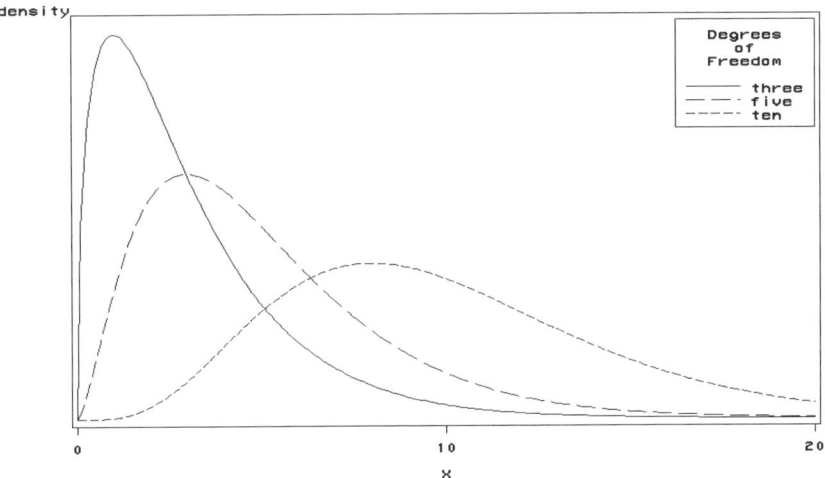

Chi-Squared Statistic

A Chi-Squared Statistic is test statistic that is used to measure the difference between a set of data and a hypothesized distribution. Large values of this statistic occur when the data and the hypothesis differ. Its values are usually compared to a Chi-Squared distribution. It is commonly used in contingency tables (cross-classifications) as a measure of independence. In this context, the sum of the squared differences between the observed counts in a cell and the expected number of counts, divided by the expected count (i.e., observed-expected^2/expected).
See Also: Chi-Squared Distribution, Data Mining, dependence rule.

choice parameter

An ART parameter that controls the ability of a a network to create new categories.
See Also: ftp://ftp.sas.com/pub/neural/FAQ2.html, http://www.wi.leidenuniv.nl/art/.

Chomsky hierarchy

A hierachial classification of the complexity of languages. The levels are, in order of increasing complexity:

Type	Label	Description
3	Regular	A regular expression or a deterministic finite automata can determine if a string is a member of the language.
2	Context Free	Computable by a context-free grammer or a push down automata.
1	Context Sensitive	Computable by linear bounded automata.
0	Recursive	A Turing machine can compute whether a given string is a member of the language.

Choquet Capability

Used in Quasi-Bayesian models for uncertainty, a positive function $v(x)$ is a (2-monotone) Choquet Capability if v(empty set) = 0, v(universe)=1, and v(X or Y) = v(X) + v(Y) - upper(v(X and Y)). A lower probability that is also 2-monotone Choquet is also a lower envelope, and can be generated from a convex set of probability distributions. A n-monotone Choquet Probability is also a Dempster-Shafer belief function.
See Also: belief function, lower/upper probability, lower envelope, Quasi-Bayesian Theory.

chromosome

In genetic algorithms, this is a data structure that holds a sequence of task parameters, often called genes. They are often encoded so as to allow easy mutations and crossovers (i.e., changes in value and transfer between competing solutions).
See Also: Crossover, Gene, Genetic Algorithm, Mutations.

chunking

Chunking is a method used in programs such as Soar to represent knowledge. Data conditions are chunked together so that data in a state implies data b. This chunking allows Soar to speed up its learning and goal-seeking behavior. When Soar solves an impasse, its algorithms determine which working elements allowed the solution of the impasse. Those elements are then chunked. The chunked results can be reused when a similar situation is encountered.
See Also: Soar.

Church Numerals

Church Numerals are a functional representation of non-negative numerals, allowing a purely logical manipulation of numerical relationships.
See Also: Logic Programming.

Church's Thesis

An assertion that any process that is algorithmic in nature defines a mathematical function belonging to a specific well-defined class of functions, known as recursive functions. It has made it possible to prove that certain problems are unsolvable and to prove a number of other important mathematical results. It also provides the philosophical foundation for the ideas that AI is possible and can be implemented in computers. It essentially implies that intelligence can be reduced to the mechanical.

Churn Analysis, Modeling, and Prediction (CHAMP)

Churn Analysis, Modeling, and Prediction (CHAMP) is a Knowledge Discovery in Databases (KDD) program under development at GTE. Its purpose is to model and predict cellular customer turnover (churn), and thus allow them to reduce or affect customer turnover.
See Also: http://info.gte.com.

CIM

See: Computer Integrated Manufacturing.

circumspection

Circumspection is a form of nonmonontone logic. It achieves this by adding formulae to that basic predicate logic that limit (circumscribe) the predicates in the initial formulae. For example, a formula with a p-ary predicate symbol can be circumscribed by replacing the p-ary symbol with a predicate expression of arity p. Circumscription reaches its full power in second-order logic but has seen limited application due to current computational limits.
See Also: Autoepistemic logic, Default Logic, Nonmonotone Logic.

city block metric

See: Manhattan metric.

CKML

See: Conceptual Knowledge Markup Language.

class

A class is an abstract grouping of objects in a representation system, such as the class of automobiles. A class can have sub-classes, such as four-door sedans or convertibles, and (one or more) super-classes, such as the class of four-wheeled vehicles. A particular object that meets the definitions of the class is called an instance of the class. The class can contain slots that describe the class (own slots), slots that describe instances of the class (instance slots) and assertions, such as facets, that describe the class.
See Also: facet, slot.

CLASSIC

A knowledge representation system developed by AT&T for use in applications where rapid response to queries is more important than the expressive power of the system. It is object oriented and is able to express many of the characteristics of a semantic network. Three versions have been developed. The original version of CLASSIC was written in LISP and is the most powerful. A less powerful version, called C-Classic, was written in C. The most recent version, Neo-Classic, is written in C++. It is almost as powerful as the lisp version of CLASSIC.
See Also: Knowledge Representation, Semantic Memory, http://www.research.att.com/software/tools/.

classification

The process of assigning a set of records from a database (observations in a dataset) into (usually) one of "small" number of pre-specified disjoint categories. Related techniques include regression, which predicts a range of values and clustering, which (typically) allows the categories to form themselves. The classification can be "fuzzy" in several senses of the word. In usual sense, the classification technique can allow a single record to belong to multiple (disjoint) categories with a probability (estimated) of being in each class. The categories can also overlap when they are developed either through a hierarchical model or through an agglomerative technique. Finally, the classification can be fuzzy in the sense of using "fuzzy logic" techniques.
See Also: Clustering, fuzzy logic, regression.

Classification And Regression Trees (CART)

Classification And Regression Trees (CART) is a particular form of decision tree used in data mining and statistics.

Classification Methods

Methods used in data mining and related areas (statistics) to develop classification rules that can categorize data into one of several pre-specified categories. A specialized form of regression, the output of the rules can be a form of membership function. It provides some measure of the likelihood that an observation belongs to each of the classes. The membership may be crisp or imprecise. An example of a crisp assignment would be a discriminant function that identifies the most likely class, implicitly setting the membership of that class to one and the others, too. An example of an imprecise membership function would be a multiple logistic regression or a Classification And Regression Trees (CART) tree, which specifies a probability of membership for many classes.
See Also: Data Mining, Knowledge Discovery in Databases.

classification tree

A classification tree is a tree-structured model for classifying dates. An observation is presented to the root node, which contains a splitting rule that sub-classifies the observation into one of its child nodes. The process is recursively repeated until the observation "drops" into a terminal node, which produces the classification.

Figure C.2 on page 52 shows a partial classification tree for blood pressure.
See Also: decision tree, recursive partitioning.

classifier ensembles

One method of improving the performance of machine learning algorithms is to apply ensembles (e.g., groups) of classifiers to the same data. The resulting classifications from the individual classifiers are then combined using a probability or voting method. If the individual classifiers can disagree with each other, the resulting classifications can actually be more accurate than the individual classifiers. Each of the individual classifiers needs to have better than a 50 percent chance of correct classifications.

Figure C.2—A Classification Tree For Blood Pressure

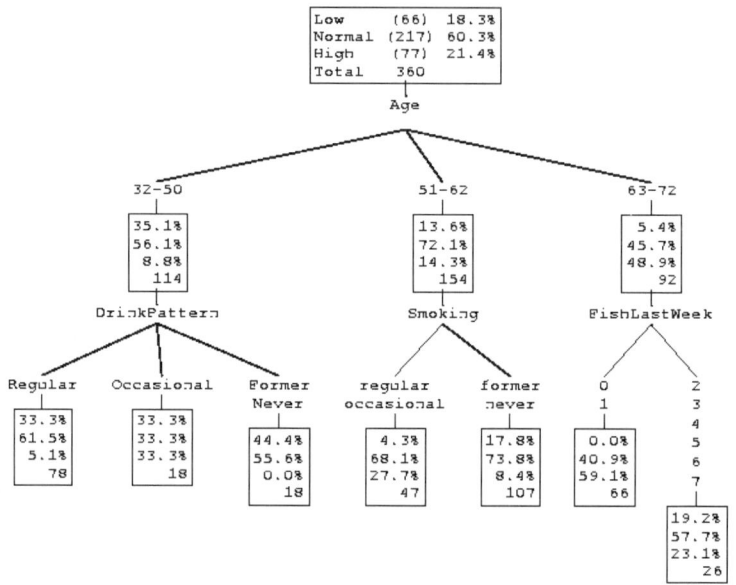

clause

A fact or a rule in PROLOG.

CLAVIER

The CLAVIER system is a commercially developed and fielded case reasoning system used at Lockheed to advise autoclave operators in the placement of parts in a load. The initial system was built from the records of expert operators, annotated with comments and classified as being either valid or invalid. When presented with a new set of parts to be cured in the autoclaves, the system can search previous loads and retrieve similar previous runs. The operators can accept or modify the system's suggestions. The system will also critique the suggested modification by comparing past runs. After the run is made, the results of the run can be entered into the study and become part of the basis for future runs.

CLIPS

CLIPS is a widely used expert system development and delivery tool. It supports the construction of rule and/or object-based expert systems. It supports rule-based, object-oriented and procedural programming. It is written in the C language and is widely portable. By design, it can be either integrated in other systems or can be extended by multiple programming languages. It has been developed by NASA and is freely available as both source code and compiled executables. Numerous extensions and variations are also available. CLIPS uses the Rete Algorithm to process rules.
See Also: Expert System, Rete Algorithm, http://www.ghg.net/clips/CLIPS.html.

clique

A set of nodes C from a graph is called complete if every pair of nodes in C shares an edge. If there is no larger set complete set, then C is maximally complete and is called a clique. Cliques form the basis for the construction of Markov trees and junction trees in graphical models.

In Graph C.2, (ABC) forms a clique, as do the pairs AE and CD.
See Also: graphical model, junction graph, Markov tree.

Graph C.2—Graph with (ABC) Clique

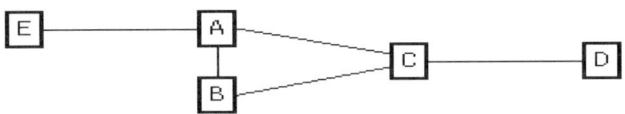

CLOS

CLOS is the name of an object-oriented extension to Common LISP, a Common Lisp Object System.

closed world assumption

The closed world model or assumption is a method used to deal with "unknown" facts in data and knowledge bases with restricted domains. Facts that are not known to be true are assumed to be false.

closure

If R is a binary relationship and p is some property, then the closure of R with respect to p is the smallest binary relation that contains R and satisfies p. For example, with a set A={a,b,c,d} and a relationship R={<a,a>,<b,c>,<c,d>}, the transitive closure of R adds the three pairs {<a,c>,<a,d>,<b,d>} to R.

Closures

A generalization of anonymous functions that assigns values to functional expressions. The function retains the binding context that was current at the time it was created. That context can then be used for references to free variables within the function.

Clustering

Clustering is a technique used in Data Mining, OnLine Analytical Processing (OLAP), and similar activities to group observations. A clustering procedure attempts to identify and extract "similar" groups of observations from a data set. Unlike classification procedures, the number and memberships in the groups are not known a priori.

The observations are grouped on the same set of attributes as is used to assess their homogeneity. In contrast, classification and regression techniques use one group of variables to obtain homogeneity on a second set. The clustering process can either be agglomerative, where each record starts as its own cluster and is merged with other clusters, or divisive, where all the data starts in a single large cluster and is gradually broken down into smaller, more homogeneous clusters. While the clustering is often of interest in its own right, it can also be used to pick out interesting subgroups for further analysis.

The clusters can be disjoint, so that each observation falls in one and only one cluster, hierarchical, where the higher level clusters are further split into sub-clusters recursively, or overlapping, so that an individual data point can have membership into more than one cluster.

See Also: Classification Procedures, Data Mining, Knowledge Discovery in Databases, regression.

cluster tree

A cluster tree of variables is a tree of clusters of the variables. Any cluster tree corresponding to a Bayesian Network is a representation of the probability distribution of the variables and the probability of the network can be computed from products and divisions of the probabilities of the clusters.

Figure C.3 shows a simple five-node network and its cluster tree representation. The arcs in the latter are labeled with the separating variables, which consist of the intersection of the adjacent nodes.

Figure C.3—Simple Five-Node Network

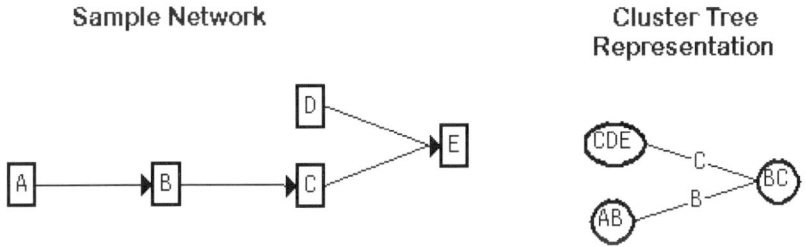

See Also: Bayesian Network, junction tree.

CMI

See: Compatibility Modification Inference.

CNF

See: Conjunctive Normal Form.

codebook vector

A codebook vector is the centroid of cluster in a Kohonen neural network.
See Also: Kohonen network.

COG project

The COG project is an on-going endeavor at MIT to build a humanoid robot that can exhibit humanoid intelligence. It is embodied in a vaguely human-like robot that has a trunk, an arm, a head, and eyes. Ears and fingers are in development.
See Also: Kismet, http://www.ai.mit.edu/projects/cog.

COGSYS

COGSYS is a generic knowledge-based system development environment designed specifically to address real-time problems and is marketed by Cogsys, Ltd.
See Also: http://www.cogsys.co.uk/.

combinatorial explosion

When a program begins looking at combinations of choices, as in a look-ahead procedure, or a planning problem, the number of possible choices grows as the product of the number of choices for each element in the search. This grows much faster than the number of individual choices, and can lead to an extremely large number of combinations to evaluate, can prevent the program from reaching a solution in a reasonable time. As an example, consider a program that wishes to find the optimal combination of a number of two-level factors. When there is only one factor, there are only two "combinations" to evaluate. When there are five factors, the program needs to consider 25 or 32 combinations, and when there are 10 factors, there are 210 or 1024 combinations.
See Also: greedy algorithm, look-ahead.

comma strategy

The comma strategy is a method that can be used in evolutionary algorithms. At each generation, the parents generate offspring and are discarded ("die"), leaving only the offspring to compete in the next generation.
See Also: plus strategy.

committee of experts methods

Committee of experts methods apply multiple models (experts) to the same data and produce a result by either averaging the multiple predictions or by finding the majority or most predicted outcome.
See Also: ADABOOST, arcing, Bootstrap AGGregation (bagging), hierarchical mixtures of experts.

Common LISP

A set of common specifications for all the various LISP dialects. Defined in the book *Common Lisp: the Language*.

communality number
>The sum of all cores of sets that contain a set A is the communality number for A. It is a measure of the probability that could flow freely to every point in A from the entire belief function. In contrast, the core of A is that probability that is assigned directly to the set A and not to any of its members. The difference between the two numbers measures the probability that could inherit from all of its supersets.
>*See Also:* belief core, belief function.

commutative property
>In formal logic, an (binary) operator is commutative if the order of the arguments does not change the value of the result. In ordinary arithmetic, addition and multiplication are both commutative as a+b = b+a and a*b = b*a. This does not hold for example in matrix multiplication where multiplication is not commutative.

Compatibility Modification Inference (CMI)
>A class of methods for performing inference using fuzzy logic. Given a fuzzy rule, a CMI system first determines the degrees to which the antecedent of a rule is matched and uses that value to determine the strength of the consequence.

compiler
>A program that translates text files in one computer language into another, usually lower level, language. For example, a C compiler will translate a set of C files and headers into an object (machine language) or an assembler file. A compiler might also resolve cross-references, macros, and macro directives in the process of compiling.

compliment coding
>An input encoding scheme sometimes used for ART networks. In order to prevent category proliferation, both the original input and its complement are presented to the network.
>*See Also:* ART, ftp://ftp.sas.com/pub/neural/FAQ2.html, http://www.wi.leidenuniv.nl/art/.

composition
>A composition is a function or relationship that can be constructed from other functions or relationships. For example, the function

"Grandparent(X)" is a recursive composition of the Parent() function, Grandparent(X) = Parent(Parent(X)).

Compositional Rule of Inference (CRI)

See: fuzzy associative memory.

Computer-Aided Design (CAD)

The process of using a computer to aid in the design and (CADCAM) manufacture of objects or systems. The complexity of these systems range from basic drawing systems through systems that can warn you about basic dimensional constraints to systems that understand and implement constraints based on other properties of the objects in the system. It is used for the design of mechanical, electronic, construction, and other systems.

Computer-Aided Education

The use of computers to aid in the education of personnel.

Computer-Aided Instruction, Intelligent

See: Intelligent Computer-Aided Instruction.

Computer Integrated Manufacturing (CIM)

Computer Integrated Manufacturing refers to the integration of computer sensors and controllers into a manufacturing process. This includes three types of functions. First the computers provide programmable and flexible automation of the manufacturing process. This leads to the ability to optimize the process flexibly to react to current variations in the process. Finally, the various sensors and controllers can be integrated into a comprehensive system.

Concept

A symbol with meaning or interpretation in an application domain.
See Also: Extension of a concept, intension of a concept.

concept drift

Systems that classify or predict a concept (e.g., credit ratings or computer intrusion monitors) over time can suffer performance loss when the concept they are tracking changes. This is referred to as concept drift. This can either be a natural process that occurs without a reference to the system, or an active process, where others are reacting to the system (e.g., virus detection).

concept language

A language used to construct concepts, such as a first-order or propositional language. The choice of language determines the concepts that are expressible in a particular system.
See Also: Concept, concept space, Knowledge Discovery in Databases.

concept lattice

A concept space that is partially ordered by the concept's extensions and intensions forms a concept lattice. Extensions are related by a subset relation among concepts and by the greater generality of the concept intensions. The orderings are only partial as not all subsets or clusters will satisfy a less than or greater than relationship. Two subsets may both contain a given subset and be contained in another subset but not have any ordering between themselves, or they may share nothing more that the empty set as a subset and the universe as a superset.
See Also: partially ordered set.

concept learning

In machine learning, a concept is exemplified by a set of positive examples (cases that are examples of the concept) and a set of negative examples (cases that are not examples of the concept). In concept learning, the learner is attempting to construct a rule or algorithm that allows it to completely separate the positive and negative examples.
See Also: equivalence query, Machine Learning, membership query.

concept space

Consider the set of all concepts that can be formed with a particular language and attribute set. If these concepts can be ordered or partially ordered, they form a concept space.
See Also: concept language, concept lattice.

Conceptual dependency

A theory of natural language processing.

Conceptual Knowledge Markup Language (CKML)

Conceptual Knowledge Markup Language (CKML), like Ontology Markup Language (OML) and Simple HTML Ontology Expression (SHOE), is a knowledge representation language designed for use on the WWW. It is also an XML application and extends OML. OML and SHOE both provided means to ontologies and objects within those ontologies. CKML also adds the ability to specify attributes, conceptual scales, and conceptual views of the information.
See Also: Ontology Markup Language(OML), Simple HTML Ontology Expression (SHOE), http://asimov.eecs.wsu.edu/WAVE/Ontologies/CKML/.

conditional

In probabilistic expert systems, a collection of conditional distributions for the same group of variables (referred to as the head) over all of the states of a conditioning set of variables (referred to as the tail). The conditional distribution of height and weight for various mutually exclusive groupings of age and sex would be a conditional, with height and weight as the head variables and age and sex the tail variables.
See Also: slice.

conditional distribution

When you start with a given multivariate distribution and then constrain the variables or attributes to a subset of the possible states, the resulting (renormalized) probability distribution is conditional with respect to the original multivariate distribution. For example, Table C.1 shows an original multivariate distribution on Age and Sex and two sex-specific conditional distributions (of the 31 possible conditionals that can be derived from this distribution).

Table C.1—Conditional Distributions

	Female	Male	Female Conditional	Male Conditional
Young	.1	.1	.2	.2
Middle	.3	.2	.6	.4
Old	.1	.2	.2	.4

Conditional distributions are important in manipulating probabilistic expert systems.

conditional embedding

See: Smet's rule.

conditional independence

Conditional independence is a fundamental notion in probability models and in the construction of a belief network and a Bayesian Network. Two attributes or groups of attributes are said to be conditionally independent with respect to a third group when the two attributes are unrelated or independent for fixed values of the third. When the third attribute is "free" or unmeasured, the two attributes can appear to be dependent.

condition attribute

In the theory of Rough Sets, attributes are broken into condition attributes and decision attributes. A condition attribute is one that is used as a predictor or classification attribute for the decision attribute (i.e., the output of the model). The decision attribute(s) is(are) conditioned on the condition attributes.
See Also: Rough Set.

condition number

When manipulating numerical values, a modeling system can be led awry if the magnitudes of the numbers are far apart, possibly leading to numerical instabilities. The condition number is a measure of the potential for problems and is formed as a ratio of the largest number to the smallest non-zero number. The meaning of this number is related to the machine precision of the system on which it is implemented.
See Also: machine precision.

confidence interval

A technique for quantifying the uncertainty of a calculated value. Using some assumptions (i.e., models) about the data collection and the variations in the data values, an interval can be constructed that will contain the "true" value in a given proportion of the repeated uses of the rule. A single observed interval is called a confidence interval and the proportion is called the confidence level. Many cases can be covered with "simple" parametric assumptions while more

complicated cases can be handled by approximations and simulation techniques.
See Also: bootstrapping, Gibbs sampling.

confidence threshold

Confidence thresholds are used in association rules to describe a lower bound on the probability that the consequence of an association is true when the antecedent is true. The confidence threshold is chosen to eliminate "uninteresting" or low probability consequences when searching for associations in a database.
See Also: association rules, support threshold.

configuration

The term configuration is used to refer to the particular values of a subset of attributes in a model, such as a Bayesian Network or neural network. These are usually being treated in this context as inputs or constraints on the model.

confusion matrix

A square table summarizing the number or proportion of times items from known categories are classified into various categories by a classification program. The entry in the i-th row and j-th column typically describes the likelihood of classifying an item from the i-th class into the j-th class.

Conjunctive Normal Form (CNF)

A conjunction of binary functions on attributes. A Conjunctive Normal Form (CNF) of a Boolean equation is obtained by swapping the disjunctions in a Disjunctive Normal Form (DNF) with conjunctions. Any Boolean function can be represented as a CNF and a DNF.
See Also: Disjunctive Normal Form.

connected graph

A graph is connected if there is at least one path between every pair of nodes in the graph. A connected undirected graph is a tree if it has no cycles.
See Also: path, undirected graph.

Connectionism

This is the name of a highly parallel model for "intelligent" computing. Rather than use a single high-speed processor to compute an algorithm, the process is broken among many smaller, but specialized processes that compute simultaneously. An example would be a neural network process where each "neuron" in the network is assigned to a single processor.

CONNIVER

The successor to the PLANNER program. This program attempted to overcome limitations in the PLANNER backtracking algorithm.

cons cell

A cons cell is a basic data structure in LISP; a cons cell holds two pointers, or a pointer and a value. It is used to construct many more complex structures, such as lists and trees, by linking the cons cells. The cons operator joins together two objects.
See Also: car, cdr, LISP.

constraint propagation

Many systems have a series of constraints on the values or properties. If these can be represented by a network of relationships, the systems can propagate the local constraints throughout the system to achieve global consistency. Generally, when a stable system is updated with new data or a query, the constraints can be iteratively fired to cascade through the system until the values of the system reach a stable state.
See Also: relaxation procedures.

constraint reasoning

See: Constraint Satisfaction.

Constraint Satisfaction

A general term for a variety of techniques used in AI and other areas of computation. Constraint solving systems work with a knowledge base of constraints and include an engine to search for solutions that meet these constraints. A constraint solving system will cycle through the constraints, changing the free values in the system to meet some maximization or minimization criteria.

constraint solving
See: Constraint Satisfaction.

construction sequence
An ordered sequence of conditionals that fulfill the conditions needed to compute a probability distribution. These sequences allow probabilistic expert systems to compute probabilities based on a multiplication series, rather than computing and saving an entire multivariate distribution and its associated marginals and/or conditionals. Construction sequences are often represented by a Directed Acylic Graph (DAG) or their multivariate generalizations called bubble graphs.
See Also: conditional, probabilistic expert systems.

continuer
A function, usually a conditional, that allows one to expand a marginal to a complete multivariate distribution. When the marginal is non-zero, the continuer must be a conditional, and when the marginal is non-negative, the continuer can be chosen to be a conditional but may not be unique. Used in probabilistic expert systems, these allow one to construct probability distributions given the appropriate marginal and conditional distributions.

continuous attribute
A continuously valued attribute is one that can take on values from the (bounded) real line. The attribute may be nominal, ordinal, interval, or ratio in nature. In the first two cases, the numeric values are immaterial.
See Also: interval attribute, Machine Learning, nominal (attribute type), ordinal attribute, ratio attribute.

continuous training
See: on-line training.

contrast enhancement
The general function of a F2 layer in an ART network. The most common version is a winner-take-all function.
See Also: ART, ftp://ftp.sas.com/pub/neural/FAQ2.html, http://www.wi.leidenuniv.nl/art/.

Control Theory

In Robotics, Control theory underlies robot control. It includes such concepts as dynamics, feedback control, kinematics, task encoding. The control problem associated with a robotics arm is to specify a series of impulse in time so that a series of motions or events occur.
See Also: Robotics.

core

In Rough Set Theory, the core attributes are those attributes that are in the intersection of all reducts. Neither the reducts nor the minimal reducts of a set of attributes are necessarily unique. The core attributes are those that appear in all reducts of an attribute set and must be contained in any reduced table. The remaining attributes in the set of (minimal) reducts must be selected on other criteria (e.g., smallest total number of attributes in the reduced table or best upper and lower approximations to some concept(s)).
See Also: indiscernable, lower approximation, reduct, Rough Set Theory, upper approximation.

coreference resolution

In natural language processing, this is the process of determining which phrases in a body of text refer to the same thing. In the text, "Frank went to the store. It was a nice day and he bought a loaf of bread. It was rye", the program needs to determine that the first "it" refers to the particular time when the event occurred, the second "it" refers to the load of bread, and that "he" refers to Frank. In the text, "John got a Saturn. He needed the car for work", the phrase "a Saturn" and "the car" are coreferences.

Coroutines

A set of programs that communicate with related programs as peers. Each program interacts with the other programs via input and output routines. These are typically used in such systems as operating systems, simulation, and language parsing.

correlation

Correlation is a statistical measure of the association between two attributes or types of events. It typically ranges from -1 to 1, with a -1 indicating a complete negative association (e.g., if one type of event occurs the other cannot), and a +1 indicating a complete posi-

tive association. For continuous attributes, the *Pearson correlation coefficient* is computed as the ratio of the covariance between two attributes to the product of the attributes' standard errors.
See Also: covariance.

cost

See: utility.

Cottrel-Munro-Zipser technique

See: Principal Components Analysis.

Coulter FACULTY

Coulter FACULTY is an operating knowledge-based system that acts as an assistant in laboratory hematology. It can also assist in scheduling workflow.
See Also: http://ourworld.compuserve.com/homepages/VMishka/, http://www-uk.hpl.hp.com/people/ewc/list-main.html.

counterpropagation

A Kohonen Learning Vector Quantization (LVQ) network performs classification by a nearest-neighbor classification on the codebook vectors. Similarly, counterpropagation performs a nearest-neighbor regression on the codebook vectors.
See Also: learning vector quantization, nearest-neighbor.

covariance

The covariance between two attributes or events is a statistical measure of their association. For two continuous attributes, the covariance is computed as $\Sigma(x-\mu_X)(y-\mu_Y)/(n-1)$, the average cross-product of the deviations of the individual values from their average or expectation.
See Also: correlation, expectation.

covering

A set of binary attributes is said to be covering with respect to a database and a support threshold s if the proportion of records in a database for which each of the attributes is true is $\geq$ s.
See Also: association rules, confidence threshold, support threshold.

C++

An extension of the C language that implements many ideas taken from object-oriented languages, such as classes, instances, methods, and inheritance. The syntax of the Java language is derived from the syntax of C and C++.
See Also: C, Computer Language, Java.

C5.0/See5

C5.0 is the commercial successor (http://www.rulequest.com/) to the decision tree software program C4.5. A Windows version is available as the product See5. It produces rulesets, can use boosting, and calculates variable misclassification costs.
See Also: ADABOOST, boosting, C4.5, cubist, ruleset.

C4.5

A program for generating classification trees for data with discretely classified attributes. It uses a recursive partitioning (divide-and-conquer) algorithm to find "good" splits for predicting the target classification (or class variable). The resulting trees can either be used directly or re-expressed as a series of production rules.

credal set

Quasi-Bayesian methods for representing and manipulating uncertainty extend the notion of a probability distribution to represent uncertainty about a set of propositions using a set of distributions. Because of the nature of these operations, this set is often extended to include the convex set enclosing the set of distributions (e.g., all mixtures of the original distributions). This convex set is called the credal set.
See Also: Quasi-Bayesian Theory.

credible interval

See: credible set.

credible set

In Bayesian and Quasi-Bayesian models, a p-level credible set is any set of events for which the total probability is p. If the events are ordered on an interval (e.g., predicted values of a stock), then the interest is usually on a p-level credible interval, in particular the highest posterior density interval, which is the shortest interval with the specified probability.

Crews_NS

Crews_NS is scheduling system used to schedule drivers and guards for the Dutch Railways. The Crews_NS system accommodates changes in plans and resource availability. It uses state-space searches and constraint propagation to guide the system and operate in automatic, semi-automatic, and manual modes.

CRI

See: Compositional Rule of Inference.

cross entropy

See: Kullback-Liebler information measure.

crossover

In (biologic) genetics, the blueprint for future offspring is stored in an organism's genes. During reproduction, these genes can become tangled. The tangles are broken by repair mechanisms, which can glue the wrong pieces together. This is referred to as a "crossover." Genetic algorithms mimic this exchange in order to generate new varieties of solutions or models. The model's behavior is encoded in a (fixed-length) string, called a chromosome, which can allow for crossovers during reproduction, a state in a genetic algorithm that propagates the successful members of the current generation.
See Also: Chromosome, Gene, Genetic Algorithm, mutation.

Cross-validation

An improvement on the split-sample validation method for estimating the error associated with a modeling technique. Typically, the data is split into k-sub-samples of the same size, and the model is fit k times, each time removing one of the k sub-samples from the data, and estimating the error from the holdout sample. The k error measures can then be combined to estimate the true error of a technique. Bootstrapping can be a better, but more expensive means of estimating the error associated with a model.

CRYSALIS

A blackboard-based system to determine the spatial location of a protein's atoms. It uses a listing of the ordered amino acids and an electron density map, a three-dimensional "snapshot" of a protein.
See Also: blackboard.

Cubist

Cubist is a commercial program that adapts the C5.0 algorithms to continuous responses. It produces a regression tree.
See Also: C5.0/See5, Classification And Regression Trees, http://www.rulequest.com.

cumulative probability distribution

For an ordered variable (e.g., age) or set of states, the cumulative probability distribution is a function that returns the probability of being less than or equal to a given value in the ordering. When the attribute is continuous, the derivative of this function is referred to as a probability density function.

curse of dimensionality

As the number of dimensions in a predictive model increases, the "size" of the data space being modeled increases in an exponential fashion. As the number of predictors increases for a given sample size, the coverage of the 'data space' becomes increasingly sparse, so that any new observation becomes "further" away from any previously observed data point. This leads to problem of variable selection often encountered in many statistical techniques.

cut

In PROLOG, a cut is an operator that is used to terminate backtracking.
See Also: PROLOG.

Cybenko's theorem

This theorem proved that it was possible to approximate any continuous function to any desired degree of accuracy using a neural network with a sigmoidal transfer function and two hidden layers. This is important, as it demonstrates that neural networks can "learn" arbitrary continuous functions to whatever accuracy is required. It does

not state the size of the network that would be required to achieve the specified error rate.
See Also: neural network.

Cybernetics

A term, coined by Norman Weiner, used to signify the study of control mechanisms in machines and biological organisms. It is derived from the Greek word for steersman. Its Latin equivalent gave rise to such terms as governor and government.

Cyc

Cyc is a very large general knowledge base and associated inference engine under development since 1984 by Douglas Lenant. The goal of the project is to build a very deep layer of "commonsense" knowledge about things and their relationships that can be used to make other programs more knowledgeable.

The Cyc knowledge base consists of tens of thousands of individual terms and assertions that relate those terms. The knowledge base is currently divided into hundreds of "microtheories," all of which share common assumptions, but which may disagree with the assertions of other "microtheories." The Cyc program is now also adding its own assertions as part of its inferencing process.

This technology has begun to be applied in a number of areas. Given its large common sense capabilities, it has been successfully applied to natural language processing and in Data Mining involving large heterogeneous and multimedia databases.
See Also: CycL.

CycL

CycL is the knowledge representation language used by the Cyc system. It is essentially an extension of a first-order predicate calculus.
See Also: http://www.cyc.com/.

Cycle (cyclic)

A graph contains a cycle if there is a path of directed arcs that returns through its originating node without using any directed arc more than once.
See Also: directed acyclic graph, directed graph.

D

DADO
A parallel machine architecture optimized for AI. The multiple processing elements are structured into a binary tree.

daemon
A daemon is a term for a autonomous computer process that can (appear) to run simultaneously with other processes on a computer. The daemon can interact with other processes or handle external (user) requests. A common example is a mail transport daemon that waits for mail to arrive and handles local delivery.

DAG
See: Directed Acyclic Graph.

DAI
See: Distributed Artificial Intelligence.

Dante
Dante I and Dante II were ambitious experimental semi-autonomous robots designed to work in hostile environments, such as volcanoes and extraterrestrial environments. Dante I was developed to explore Mt. Eusibius in the Antarctic, but failed due to the extreme cold. Dante II was more successful in exploring another volcano, but eventually slipped, rolled over, and was unable to right itself.

dART and dARTMAP
See: Distributed ART and ARTMAP.

database marketing

A Data Mining technique that uses customer databases and Data Mining tools to select potential customers in precisely targeted fashion. Also known as mailshot response.

data cleaning

The process of validating data prior to a data analysis or Data Mining. This includes both ensuring that the values of the data are valid for a particular attribute or variable (e.g., heights are all positive and in a reasonable range) and that the values for given records or set of records are consistent. Some examples include insuring that age increases in time, or that age and weight values are in agreement (no seven-foot person weighs less than 100 pounds). Care must be exercised when handling anomalous values to insure that valid outliers are not improperly removed. These outliers can be quite informative.

Data cleaning is an important initial step in the construction of data warehouses and in Data Mining. Failure to properly clean the data can lead to invalid conclusions, driven by outliers and/or impossible values, or missed relationships.

See Also: Data Mining, data warehouse.

data dictionary

A data dictionary is a database of information about variables in other data tables. A data dictionary is contains the "meta-data" about the structure, contents and relationships among other databases and their attributes in a data warehouse.

See Also: Data Mining, data warehouse, Knowledge Discovery in Databases.

data mart

A data warehouse that has been specialized to address certain analyses. The data is typically a subset of some larger data warehouse that addresses a special question or is structured for a particular toolset.

See Also: Data Mining, data warehouse.

Data Mining

A term used in statistics and Knowledge Discovery in Databases fields to describe the application of automatic or semi-automatic procedures to data with the aim of discovering previously unknown patterns in the data. There are a variety of methods, each discussed fur-

ther in other entries. These procedures include *classification procedures* which attempt to learn how to classify objects into previously defined classes and *regression procedures* which attempt to predict or assign a value to designated output from designated input fields. They also include *clustering methods* which attempt to find groups of similar data points, dependency models (both quantitative and structural), such as *graphical models*, which attempt to model the interrelationships of a set of data, and deviation methods which attempt to extract the most significant deviations from a set of normative cases or values.
See Also: http://www.kdnuggets.com/.

Data Mining Query Language (DMQL)

A query language developed for Data Mining applications. It is derived from Structured Query Language (SQL), a standard language used in database applications.

data navigation

In Data Mining and OnLine Analytical Processing (OLAP), the analyst is typically working with many data attributes simultaneously. Data navigation tools provide a means to view particular slices (subset of the full attribute set) and subsamples (subsets of the rows) and the means to switch among them.
See Also: Data Mining, OnLine Analytical Processing.

data preprocessing

Prior to performing Data Mining, the data have to be preprocessed to normalize their structure. This can include the data cleaning, data selection or sampling, and data reduction and mapping.
See Also: data cleaning, data reduction.

data reduction

A term primarily used in scientific data analysis referring to the extraction of important variables or functions of variables from a large number of available attributes.

data visualization

Complex data structures and relationships are often difficult to grasp. Data visualization tools attempt to represent these relationships and information graphically. Data visualization tools can range from the

prosaic histogram and scatter plot, through network graphs and into complex 3-D structures, such as a Virtual Reality Modeling Language (VRML) representation.
See Also: Data Mining, statistics.

data warehouse

This term refers to a large centralized collection of corporate or other organizational data, usually collected from multiple sources. The databases are expected to have been cleaned and the attribute names, values, and relationships regularized. These large collections typically include meta-data, data containing information about the data collection itself. These data warehouses can offer economies of scale but must also tradeoff ease of access with organizational security concerns, as well as privacy concerns.
See Also: Data Mining, OnLine Analytical Processing.

Data warehousing

A term from the business and database field which refers to the collection and cleaning of transactional data to support online analysis methods such as online analytical processing, and "decision support." The formation of a data warehouse is an essential first step in the related field of Knowledge Discovery in Databases (KDD).
See Also: Knowledge Discovery in Databases, OnLine Analytical Processing.

datalog

See: deductive database.

DataLogic/R

DataLogic/R is a database "mining" system that uses Rough Set Theory and inductive logic to analyze data at different levels of knowledge representation. The vendor is Reduct Systems, Inc.
See Also: Rough Set Theory.

d-connection

See: d-separation.

DDB

See: Deductive DataBase.

DEC

A form of Kohonen network. The name was derived from "Dynamically Expanding Content."
See Also: http://www.cis.hut.fi/nnrc/new_book.html.

decision attribute

Decision attributes are the output or target variables in a Rough Set Data Analysis. The predictor or classification attributes are called condition attributes, as the decision is conditioned on the values of these attributes.
See Also: condition attributes, Rough Set.

decision list

A k-decision list is an ordered sequence of k if-then-else rules. Each rule in the sequence is tested until one of the rules is satisfied. When the rule is satisfied, the action associated with that rule is taken, Both the k term Conjunctive Normal Form (CNF) and the k-term Disjunctive Normal Form (DNF) can be represented by k-decision lists, which are Probably Approximately Correct (PAC) learnable
See Also: Machine Learning, Probably Approximately Correct learning model.

decision problem

A decision problem may be represented by three elements: a set of valid actions A, a set of states S, and a utility or payoff function u(A,s) >0 for elements in A and S. The problem is to choose the action A when the state S is uncertain.

Decision Support System (DSS)

A data modeling and reporting system that has been structured to answer specific ongoing business questions or issues. It is usually distinguished from classical IS systems by its emphasis on "real-time", or interactive analysis, where the business analyst can use multiple tools on the data to provide answers "now." It should be distinguished from Data Mining and Knowledge Discovery in Databases (KDD), where the emphasis is on discovering "new" relationships to expand the current data model.
See Also: data mart, Data Mining, data warehouse.

decision table

A decision table is an alternate form of decision tree that can be represented as a dimension-stacked two-dimensional or three-dimensional table. In the typical decision tree or classification tree, a single attribute is chosen to form the split, and the attribute is chosen independently of the attributes chosen at other nodes. A decision table instead chooses pairs of attributes at each level and applies the same split to all nodes at a given level on the tree. Although this can result in a classifier that does not perform as well as the general tree model, it has the advantage that it is easy to present and explain to an unsophisticated user. Data Mining programs, such as MineSet, can place an interactive front-end in front of the table and allow users to "drill-down" into the table, exploring the results or advice of the tree building process.
See Also: dimension stacking, generalized logic diagrams, Karnaugh map.

Decision Theory

Decision Theory is a formal mathematical theory describing the methods of making logical choices when the outcomes are uncertain. The theory places heavy reliance on Bayesian methods for combining data and is sometimes referred to as Bayesian decision theory.

Decision Tree

One method of representing a decision sequence or a regression or classification function is through a decision tree. The tree represents the decision-making process or a regression/classification process as a series of nested choices or questions. At each step in the process, a single binary or multinomial question is posed, and the answer determines the next set of choices to be made. In a regression or classification context, this method is sometimes referred to as recursive partitioning. The process of generating the tree is similar to clustering, in that the objective is to find homogeneous groups of cases. However, it differs in that it focuses on partitioning on a specified set of predictors in order to achieve a homogeneous value of the dependent variable, while clustering techniques form partitions of the dataset on the same set of variables in which it measures the homogeneity criterion. Currently, most partitioning algorithms are orthogonal, splitting on one predictor at a time, although some algorithms are oblique, partitioning on multiple variables simultaneously. The tree can be repre-

sented as a collection of rules (IF condition1 THEN condition$_2$). (See Figure D.1.) Some examples of Decision Tree methods include Classification And Regression Trees (CART) methods, OC1, C4.5, and a commercial programs such as Knowledge Seeker.
See Also: Classification And Regression Trees, Data Mining, OC1, C4.5, Knowledge Discovery in Databases, KnowledgeSeeker, recursive partitioning.

Figure D.1—A Simple Decision Tree

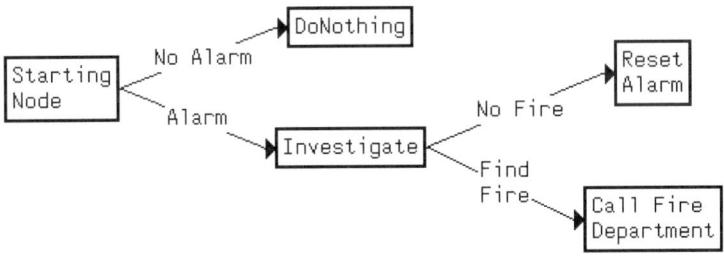

declarative language

A computer language, such as PROLOG, where the programming sets the goals, boundary conditions and constraints, and lets a computer determine how to reach a solution (e.g., via an inference engine).
See Also: procedural language.

Declarative Representation

A form in which knowledge could be represented in a knowledge base. The knowledge base contains declarations of facts (and, optionally, truth-values) such as "All persons are mortal" and "Socrates was a person", etc. The inference engine can then deduce properties of Socrates, including the fact that he was mortal. This form of representation has the advantage that it is modular and easy to update, in contrast to a procedural representation. However, this representation lacks the search control provided by a procedural representation.
See Also: Knowledge Base, Knowledge Representation.

Deduction

A form of inference from general principles to specific conclusions.
See Also: Induction, Inference, Logic, Reasoning.

Deductive Database (DDB)

A generalization of the common relational database. A DDB treats the items in a database as a set of ground assertions, and has a set of axioms, referred to as an Intensional DataBase (IDB). This database can be viewed as a function-free logic program.
See Also: Logic Programming.

Deep Blue

A chess playing system developed by IBM. This combination of general-purpose workstation hardware and special computer chips was rated as chess grandmaster and lost to Gary Kasparov, the reigning World Champion, in a series of six games played in 1995.

Deep Structure

See: Grammer, Transformational.

Default Logic

See: Reasoning, Default.

Default Reasoning

See: Reasoning, Default.

defuzzification

The process of converting a fuzzy response into a single, usually scalar, valued response. There are a variety of ways of doing this. Two approaches include rounding for binary outputs, and centroids (e.g., weighted means) for continuous outputs.
See Also: fuzzy logic.

degrees of freedom

In Robotics, degrees of freedom are used to describe the number of "dimensions" in which a robot can move its control arms. A one-degree of freedom "arm" can move back and forth along a line, or sweep out an arc (e.g., a pendulum). A two-degree of freedom arm can sweep out a plane or circle, while a three-degree of freedom arm can move within a (partial) sphere. These arms can have higher degrees of freedom, corresponding to multiple sub-arms. For example, a unit consisting of a three-degree of freedom arm attached to a three-degree of freedom "hand" would have six degrees of freedom. The latter three degrees of freedom would correspond to the ability to control the yaw, pitch, and roll of an object "held" by the "hand".

In Machine Learning and statistical contexts, the degrees of freedom for a statistic are the count of unconstrained numbers in that statistic. For example, in a five-category multinomial, there are four degrees of freedom in the counts, as the total of the counts has to add up to the sample size. Thus, a Chi-Square Statistic on that table would have four degrees of freedom.

See Also: Chi-Square Distribution, Chi-Square statistic, Robotics.

demon

See: daemon.

demon procedures

Many frame-based and object-based systems have a collection of associated automatic procedures, sometimes called demon procedures, such as "when-requested" procedures or "when-read" procedures. These refer to procedures that are automatically triggered when a particular event occurs. The procedures can be generic to a type of object or specific to a particular instance. A more prosaic example would be a program that watches a mail file and notifies the recipient that new mail has arrived.

de Morgan's Laws

de Morgan's Laws are two standard relationships in logic:
1. The negation of a conjunction is the disjunction of the negations; and
2. The negation of a disjunction is the conjunction of the negations.

Dempster's rule of combination

Dempster's rule of combination provides a method for combining different belief functions over the same frame of discernment. The core for a set from a combination of two belief functions Bel1 and Bel is computed from the cores of the two functions. The product set of the two cores is first computed, and values associated with non-

intersecting sets are discarded. The remaining products are normalized to one, and are assigned to the sets that form the intersections of the two sets in the product. The core of a set is the probability that is assigned precisely to that set.
See Also: belief function, Dempster-Shafer theory.

Dempster-Shafer theory

A. Dempster and G. Shafer (his student) proposed an extension to standard probability methods that have been adapted to many areas of reasoning about uncertainty. Classical probability assumes that probability is associated with the elements of a set, and calculates probabilities associated with sets of these by combining the probabilities associated with the elements in a set. A Dempster-Shafer probability allows probability to be assigned directly to sets of elements, rather than be derived from their elements. As an example, consider a group of experts that are asked to choose from among four courses of actions. While some experts might choose a single action, some may also indicate a pair or some other set of actions as being desirable. This latter group has assigned weight directly to a set of the actions rather than to the elements that the first group did. The Dempster-Shafer theory supports reasoning from evidence such as this.
See Also: belief function, frame of discernment, probability, Quasi-Bayesian Theory.

demodulation

Demodulation is used in automated reasoning systems to rewrite clauses and eliminate redundant information. For example, the rule that 0+(0+x)=x can be rewritten as 0+x=x, eliminating the extra terms.
See Also: OTTER.

DENDRAL

A rule-based expert system that can identify molecules based on data on their spectral and nuclear magnetic resonance data.

dependence

A set of attributes is said to be dependent if the state of a subset of the attributes affects the (distribution of) the state of the remaining attributes. For two variables, the attributes X and Y are dependent if $Pr(X \cup Y) \neq Pr(X)Pr(Y)$, where $Pr(.)$ is a probability measure. If the converse holds (Pr(X∪Y)=Pr(X)Pr(Y)), then the attributes are said to be independent.

dependence rule

A dependence rule is a generalization of the concept behind an association rule, used in Data Mining. Association rules are designed to find positive associations between attributes (e.g., people who buy tea also buy coffee with support S and confidence C). However, these rules will not pick up negative associations, such as "People who buy coffee usually do not buy tea." Dependency rules use the same binary attributes as association rules but use a statistical measure, the Chi-Squared Statistic, that detects both positive and negative associations.
See Also: association rules, Data Mining.

Dependency Directed Backtracking

A specialized form of backtracking that examines the dependencies of previous solutions and backtracks to a state that is "above" the current state, rather than any one that occurred "before" the current state.

Dependency Models

A statistical technique used in Data Mining and similar areas to describe the interrelationships between a set of measurements. Unlike regression techniques, which treat one group of variables (the dependent or output variables) differently from another set (the independent or input variables), dependency modeling tends to treat all variables as being interrelated, although the methods does support directed relationships. The models can be thought of on two levels, a structural model and a quantitative model. At the structural level, the model specifies which variables are directly or locally interrelated with one another, often via a dependency graph (as illustrated below) or by a transition matrix. At the quantitative level a numeric value is assigned to each of the linkages allowed in the structural model. One such measure for a pair of continuous measurements might be partial correlation between the two variables, given all the other variables. The structural graph shown in Figure D.2 illustrates the relationships among five variables: A, B, C, D, and E. In this example, the variable C is affected by all the remaining variables. Variables A and B are related to each other and to C, but conditional on controlling C are unaffected by D and E. Similarly, D and E are related to each other and to C, but, conditional on controlling C are unaffected by A and

B. This would imply that if you can control C, you could manipulate A without regard to D and E.
See Also: Data Mining, Knowledge Discovery in Databases, Knowledge Representation.

Figure D.2—Dependency Graph

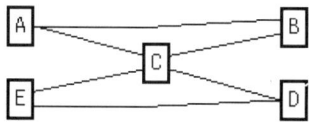

dependent variable

In regression analysis and other machine-learning methods, the objective of the analysis is to predict the value of an attribute correctly, either as a continuous response or as a classification. That target variable can be referred to as a dependent variable.
See Also: regression, regressor.

depth-first search

A search procedure in which each possibility is completely evaluated before beginning to evaluate other searches. When the search can be represented as a tree, a depth-first search would completely explore one branch before moving to other branches at that level.
See Also: breadth-first search.

DESSY

See: DEcision Support SYstem.

Devisor

A planning system for spacecraft activities.

dimension

Typically, the number of variables or attributes used to describe a case is termed its dimension. In general, the dimension of a problem refers to the number of free (unspecified) values in a specification of a problem.

dimension stacking

This technique reduces the dimensionality of a set of categorical attributes, often for visualization. The attributes are collected into groups, and, within each group, are embedded with each other to form a new, multi-level aggregate variable. For example, suppose there are two attributes, sex, with levels F and M, and age, with three levels Y, M, and O, and you wished to stack age within sex. The new attribute would have the ordered values:

F, Y
F, M
F, O
M, Y
M, M
M, O

Note that the order of age is maintained with each level of sex. If there were further attributes stacked within age, they would also maintain their order and stacking relationship across levels of sex.
See Also: decision table, Karnaugh map.

Dirac Delta Function

In Robotics and control theory, a Dirac Delta Function is used to represent an infinitely large amount of energy (or torque) delivered by an actuator in an infinitesimally short time. The function is named for the physicist Paul Dirac.
See Also: Robotics.

directed acyclic graph (DAG)

A graph (or network) is a directed acyclic graph if there are no "loops" or cycles (A->B->...->A) and each arc or link has a single direction associated with it (A->B or B->A, but not A<->B). These are often used in the representation of knowledge networks. Figure D.3 on page 84 depicts a DAG. It differs from the one shown in Figure D.4. The direction of the AB arc breaks the cycles in the directed graph.

directed graph

A graph (or network) is a directed graph if all the arcs have directions, usually represented as arrowheads. Figure D.4 on page 84

depicts a directed graph with two cycles: (ACBA, and ADCBA).
See Also: undirected graph.

Figure D.3—A Directed Acyclic Graph

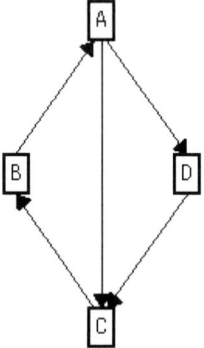

Figure D.4—A Directed Graph

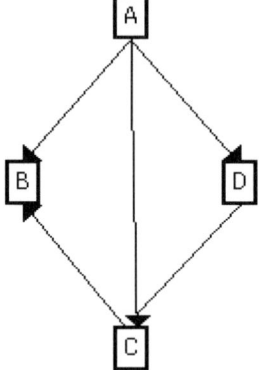

direction strategies

Direction strategies are used in automated reasoning systems to decide which of the available clauses will be pursed next. A first-in, first-out strategy (level saturation) chooses the first (oldest) clause in the list of retained clauses while a last-in, first-out strategy chooses

the newest clauses. Other rules might choose, for example, the simplest clause available, or some other weighting.
See Also: OTTER.

discounting

Discounting is a method for combining or de-emphasizing belief and probability functions, either by weighted averages of a set of functions or combining a single function with a vague or vacuous function. As an example of the latter, a belief function could be averaged with a belief function that assigns all of its mass to the entire frame of discernment. It can also be used to combine multiple experts belief functions that conflict with each other, unlike Dempster's rule of combination, which discards the probability mass assigned to conflicting subsets of the frame.
See Also: Dempster's rule of combination, frame of discernment.

Discourse Reasoning

A term from natural language processing referring to methods that attempt to understand a text or a dialogue.

discretely valued attribute

A discretely valued attribute is one which can only take on a finite number of values and that can be encoded onto the set of integers, such as sex, race, state of birth, counts, etc.
See Also: continuous attribute, Machine Learning.

disjoint

Two sets in a universe are disjoint if they do not share any elements.
See Also: partition.

Disjunctive Normal Form (DNF)

A Boolean function defined for a set of variables $X=\{x_1, x_2, ...\}$, which are combined in conjunctions of literals (x_i or ! x_i), called terms. The function is in Disjunctive Normal Form if the function can be written as a disjunction of terms.
See also: Conjunctive Normal Form.

disjunctive syllogism

A disjunctive syllogism would be (p or q), -p therefore q.

distinct variables restriction

Distinct variables restriction is a form of weighting restriction in automated reasoning systems. Clauses that contain more than k terms, where k is the restriction limit, are not considered by the system.
See Also: OTTER.

Distriubuted ART and ARTMAP (dART and dARTMAP)

ART and ARTMAP models can learn distributed code representations in the F2 layer. When the F2 layers used a winner-takes-all selection they are equivalent to Fuzzy ART and ARTMAP, respectively.
See Also: ftp://ftp.sas.com/pub/neural/FAQ2.html, http://www.wi.leidenuniv.nl/art/.

Distributed Artificial Intelligence (DAI)

Distributed Artificial Intelligence primarily refers to distributed sensory and control networks such as traffic control and robotic systems. A major distinction in this field is between a Distributed Problem Solving (DPS) system and a MultiAgent System (MAS). The former uses networks to solve a single problem, and the latter emphasizes coordination and information-sharing across a network of possibly heterogeneous agents.

Distributed Problem Solving (DPS)

This term refers to the use of multiple systems to solve a particular problem. The problem is typically partitioned into a number of separate sub-problems which are distributed to other systems for solution, and the results gathered back to form the solution. In certain stochastic systems several systems may work simultaneously to solve the same problem, each following randomly chosen paths.
See also: Distributed Artificial Intelligence.

distributive property

In formal logic, an operator is distributive if the result of applying the operation to a single and compound argument is the same as applying the operation to each member of the compound argument and collecting the results in a compound argument. Symbolically, the operator O is distributive with respect to another operator | when O (b|c) =

(aOb)|(aOc), where a, b, and c are elements in the logic.
See Also: commutative property.

DISXPERT

DISXPERT is a rule-based system tool that assists social service caseworkers in referring disability recipients to vocational rehabilitation services. The system mixes rules derived by machine learning techniques (ID3 and Linear Discriminant Analysis) and rules derived from expert vocational rehabilitation counselors to generate a large knowledge base of rules. The system has both improved the productivity of the caseworkers and decreased the dropout rate in the referred cases.
See Also: Linear Discriminant Analysis.

divide and conquer

Divide and conquer is the name of a general technique for solving complex problems. The basic idea is to solve the larger problem by first solving simpler problems and then to combine the smaller solutions into larger solutions. For example, a sorting algorithm might use network sorts to sort small groups of data quickly and then use a merge algorithm to combine progressively large subsets.

DMQL

See: Data Mining Query Language.

DNF

See: Disjunctive Normal Form.

Domain Knowledge

The facts, procedures, and relationships specific to a particular area of knowledge (i.e., a domain) that an expert system must manipulate to demonstrate mastery of a particular "domain." This differs from the general strategies and heuristics that can apply to many different knowledge domains. For example, a mathematics expert system would need to understand the rules of mathematics, (i.e., the mathematics domain) that a medical expert system could ignore, although both systems might share certain common inference techniques.

domain of attraction

The region around an equilibrium point of a dynamic system where the system will approach the equilibrium point.
See Also: Robotics.

domain theory

An organized system of claims about a particular application domain. These are distinct from hypotheses, which are conjectures about relationships that might hold in the domain.

DoseChecker

DoseChecker is a CLIPS-based expert system used for monitoring drug doses for patients with renal impairment. It monitors attributes of individual patients and compares their drug orders to these values, and will issue alerts/advisories on suspicious drug orders.
See Also: CLIPS, http://www-uk.hpl.hp.com/people/ewc/list-main.html.

Dot Pattern Analysis

A low-level technique used in visual processing, where similar regions are chunked together to form higher level structures, such as blobs, lines, and curves.

doubts

See: Assumption Based Reasoning.

downward closure

A collection of sets is downwardly closed with respect to a property if when a set P has the property, all subsets of P also have that property. An example would be in a market basket analysis. If the set of items "Coffee", "Pizza", and "Bread" were known to be independent, then by the nature of independence, the set of "Coffee" and "Pizza" would be independent, as would the set of "Coffee" and "Bread", and the set of "Bread" and "Pizza".
See Also: dependence rule, Market Basket data, upward closure.

DPN

See: Dynamic Probabilistic Network.

DPS

See: Distributed Problem Solving.

drift

See: concept drift.

d-separation

Two nodes in a directed graphical model are *d-separated* if all the paths from A to B through common ancestors pass through known (instantiated) ancestors and all of the paths through descendents are not instantiated. Nodes that are not d-separated are *d-connected*. An equivalent condition is that the disjoint subsets A and B are separated by a third subset C in the moral graph of the smallest sub-graph of graph G containing $A \cap B \cap C$.
See Also: graphical model, moral graph.

DSS

See: Decision Support System.

dummy variables

When an attribute is categorical ("red", "green", "blue") it often needs to be recoded into a group of stand-in variables that are commonly referred to as dummy variables. In the above example, you could encode the single three-level categorical variable into three indicator variables called red, green, and blue. Each of the three variables would be a 0/1 variable, where a 1 indicates that item is in the appropriate category. There are multiple forms of encodings in common use. Their value depends on the objective of the model.

DXplain

DXplain is a commercial expert system that uses clinical findings to produce a ranked list of diagnoses to be associated with those clinical findings. It can use over 5000 attributes to diagnose over 2000 diseases. It uses a Bayesian Network to generate and update the probabilities associated with the diagnoses.
See Also: Bayesian Network, http://www.lcs.mgh.harvard.edu/lcs-dome/dxplain.htm.

DYANCLIPS

DYNACLIPS, an extension of CLIPS, is an implementation of a framework for dynamic knowledge exchange among intelligent agents. Each intelligent agent is a CLIPS shell and runs a separate process under a SunOS operating system. Intelligent agents can exchange facts, rules, and CLIPS commands at run time. Knowledge exchange among intelligent agents at run time does not effect execution of either sender.
See Also: blackboard, CLIPS, http://users.aimnet.com/~yilsoft/softwares/dynaclips/dynaclips.html.

dynamic belief network

See: Dynamic Probabilistic Network.

Dynamic Probabilistic Network (DPN)

This type of network is a special case of a Hidden Markov Model (HMM). The hidden states of the HMM are decomposed into the product of several different subspace of states, and changes in the product space are assumed to occur along exactly one dimension at time. As an example, suppose we wish to model the views of a robot moving through a plant with 15 possible locations and 4 possible views through its cameras. Then, a general HMM would consider only 15*4 or 60 states, while a DPN might assume that, at each time step, the robot could change either its location or viewpoint, and attempt to model it as a two-dimension (location x viewpoint) walk. These models are also known as dynamic belief networks or factorial hidden markov models (HMMs).
See Also: Hidden Markov Model.

E

EA

See: Evolutionary Algorithm.

Eager Evaluation

See: Greedy Evaluation.

early stopping

A technique to avoid overfitting in neural network and other adaptive data modeling tools. Essentially the data is divided into a training and validation set and the modeling technique is "detuned" to learn very slowly. As the model learns on the training set, the error in the validation set is monitored, and the learning (maximization) process is stopped when the error in the validation set starts to go up. In practice, the validation error can vary while it is still decreasing overall (and likewise can appear to decrease when the overall trend is upward). One approach to avoid this problem is to store the intermediate models while training the system to convergence and then back out to the true minimum (i.e., overshoot and correct). Elaboration of this technique are available.

EASE

EASE is a knowledge-based system for assessing workplace exposure to potentially hazardous new substances. It is an extension of the C Language Integrated Production System (CLIPS) expert system, using wxCLIPS for the user interface.
See Also: C Language Integrated Production System, wxCLIPS, http://www.aiai.ed.ac.uk/~rhr/winease.html.

edge coloring

Similar to node coloring, edge coloring provides a visual means to highlight information in a graphical model. Edge coloring empha-

sizes the flow of information through the model, coloring the edges according to some measure of the information flowing through each edge. One such measure might be the weight of evidence.
See Also: graphical model, node coloring, weight of evidence.

Edge Detection

A group of techniques in image and vision system for determining the edges of an object when presented with an image of the objects. Generally, this involves comparing the intensities of neighboring regions in the image and looking for a "sharp" change.

EDR project

See: Electronic Dictionary Research project.

Effectors

In Robotics, effectors are a general term for a motor-driven device that a robot can use to have an effect upon the world. This could include such things as hands, arms, legs, and attached tools.

Electronic Dictionary Research (EDR) project

The Japanese Electronic Dictionary Research (EDR) project is a long-term project to build a Japanese-English dictionary. It includes a bilingual word dictionary, a concept classification dictionary and concept description dictionary, and a co-occurrence dictionary, which can assist computers in understanding natural phrasing as well as a large corpus of textual material.

elementhood

In fuzzy logic, elementhood is the membership of a particular item in a fuzzy set.
See Also: fuzzy logic, membership function.

ELI

See: English Language Interpreter.

ElimBel

A simple belief propagation algorithm designed for a Bayesian Network. It can be generally applied to both singly connected and multiple-connected networks. However, it requires that the entire net-

work be recomputed every time new evidence is added to the network and requires as many passes as there are outcome notes. The algorithm requires that nodes be ordered and produces updates for the last node in the ordering.
See Also: http://www.spaces.uci.edu/thiery/elimbel.

Eliza

A famous program that mimics a "Rogerian" psychotherapist. Although it has no understanding of the conversation, it is able give the appearance of intelligence by repeating back earlier assertions that contain key words in the form of questions.

elliptical basis function networks

Radial basis function networks typically compute the Euclidean distance of their inputs essentially finding the radius of the distance from the inputs from to the center (the node). When the inputs are filtered through a linear layer, which scales and rotates its inputs, the Euclidean distance on the filtered inputs is equivalent to an elliptical distance on the original (pre-linear inputs) and is referred to as an elliptical basis function.
See Also: linear layer, radial basis function.

EM algorithm

See: Expectation-Maximization algorithm.

Embedded Systems

Refers to a computer that is integral to some other device, such as a car, a dishwasher, or a camera. These systems act as intelligent controllers and attempt to perform a function such as optimizing performance (as in a car), or meeting a target specification, such as adjusting the exposure in a camera to guarantee a "good" picture. These systems are generally far simpler and more robust than the typical computer most persons are familiar with. They typically include a specialized CPU, ROM to hold the operating system and program code, some RAM to allow computation and temporary storage, and some I/O devices to determine the device state and control some functions. The system's parameters are usually set at the time the program is written to ROM, although some systems include FlashRAM or some similar form of dynamic memory that allows the system to be adjusted or to "learn" after the system has been built. Such systems could be viewed as very specialized expert systems although they usually lack the ability to interact with their owners or to explain their actions.

empirical natural language processing

Classical "rationalist" natural language processing is based on hand-coded rules to understand languages. It has been quite successful in understanding restricted areas such as questions about specific databases (e.g., moon rocks or airplane maintenance) or in special worlds, such as Winograd's "blocks" world. Empirical methods are much more data driven and can be partially automated by using statistical (stochastic) and other machine learning methods. These methods tend to focus on the distribution of words and word clusters within a large body of related text. These are often based on approaches such as a Hidden Markov Model (HMM) and Probalistic Context Free Grammar (PCFG).

These techniques can be roughly categorized as being either supervised or unsupervised. The supervised techniques require that the text be annotated by experts to indicate the parts of speech and semantic senses of the words. Unsupervised training is more difficult, and requires that the data are "proper" sentences in the target language. Although the latter is preferable in terms of the amount of preparation, the supervised techniques generally provide better performance.

See Also: Hidden Markov Model, natural language processing, Probabilistic Context Free Grammar.

EMYCIN

A derivative of the MYCIN program, this system could be used to construct rule-based expert systems.
See Also: MYCIN.

English Language Interpreter (ELI)

An English Language Interpreter (ELI) converts English sentences into contextual dependency forms. C. Riesbeck wrote the ELI, in 1975, for the Yale AI project.

ensemble learning

See: committee of experts methods.

entropy

Entropy is a measure of the disorganization or information within a system. The entropy is lowest when there is a certain outcome or state, and highest when all the possible states are equally likely. For a discrete system with k states, it is defined as

$$-\sum_i p_i \log(p_i),$$

where p_i is the probability of being in state i.
See Also: fuzzy entropy, maximum entropy principle.

EP

See: Evolutionary Programming.

EPAM

An early (1963) program that simulated human learning of nonsense syllables. It also exhibited many of the behaviors of human subjects.

EPILEPTOLOGIST'S ASSISTANT

EPILEPTOLOGIST'S ASSISTANT is an expert system developed by the Department of Veterans Affairs. It guides nurses in gathering specialized patient histories that were formerly collected by the epileptologist (a neurologist specializing in epilepsy).
See Also: Expert System.

epistatasis

In a Genetic Algorithm, a gene is said to be epistatic when it has a strong interaction with another gene. This is contrary to usual biologic interpretation, where a gene is said to be epistatic if some of its alleles can suppress another gene. The presence of interaction among the parameters indicates that the problem will be more difficult to solve, as the effect of changing one gene will depend on the state of others.

EPISTLE

A recent (1981) expert assistant system that was designed to check spelling, grammar, and style in business correspondence.

Epistomology
The field of philosophy that deals with the nature and sources of knowledge.

epoch
An epoch is an iteration in a procedure. It is commonly used in discussion of neural net algorithms.

EQP
EQP is an automated theorem proving program for first-order equational logic. Its strengths are good implementations of associative-commutative unification and matching a variety of strategies for equational reasoning and fast search. It seems to perform well on many problems about lattice-like structures. It is freely available on the WWW.
See Also: http://www.mcs.anl.gov/AR/eqp/.

equilibrium state
In Robotics, a point in a dynamic system is an equilibrium point if, when the system is at that point, it stays at that point. Further, the system is (asymptotically) stable if, when the system is at a nearby point, the system remains nearby and (asymptotically) will enter the equilibrium point.
See Also: Robotics.

equivalence class
A set of objects that share a common value for an attribute or a relation on (a subset of) their attributes.
See Also: Extension of a concept, Extension of an attribute.

equivalence query
In Machine Learning the learning program sometimes needs to test the validity of a rule with an external teacher, such as asking "Are all winged animals birds?" This type of question is called an equivalence query, as it is asking if the concept of birds is equivalent to the rule "Winged animals are birds."
See Also: concept learning, Machine Learning, membership query.

equivalence relation

A transitive, reflexive, and symmetric binary relation on a set U. Equivalent members of U (with respect to a specific relation) are indiscernible with respect to that relation. They are in the same equivalence class.
See Also: indiscernible, rough set.

ERMA

A 1974 natural language program that attempted to mimic the thought and speech patterns of a patient in psychotherapy.

estimation

The process of generating a score or scoring function for a dataset. This can refer to either the process of fitting the model where you would be estimating the coefficients of the equations (e.g., the parameters of a regression function or the split points in a decision tree) or the process of assigning scores to individual observations using the model (e.g., credit ratings). This usually refers to a prediction or scoring function, as opposed to a classification function, but can also be used in the latter context.
See Also: classification, statistics.

ETPS

See: Theorem Proving System.

Euclidean distance

The Euclidean distance is a simple measure of the distance between two objects, as in nearest neighbor techniques. It is computed as the square root of the sum of the squared differences between the two objects over each attribute. This distance is the multi-attribute generalization of the measure of distance in plane geometry.
See Also: Mahalanobis distance, Manhattan distance.

EURISKO

A learning program that used heuristic to develop new heuristics. Douglas Lenat, et al., developed EURISKO in 1981.

evaluator

The name for the part of a LISP interpreter or compiler that attempts to evaluate a symbol or token from its input queue.
See Also: compiler, interpreter.

event tree

A decision tree without any costs or probabilities or other weights is sometimes referred to as an event tree. It shows the possible paths or options available, without reference to the costs or probabilities of following those paths. (See Figure E.1.)
See Also: decision tree.

Figure E.1—An Event Tree for Two Coin Flips

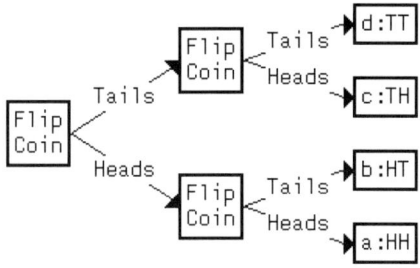

evidence flows

In belief networks, evidence flows are used to demonstrate how a particular piece of data alters the weights or probabilities for other conclusions.

evidence theory

See: belief functions, Dempster-Shaefer theory.

Evolutionary Algorithm (EA)

An Evolutionary Algorithm (EA) is a general class of fitting or maximization techniques. They all maintain a pool of structures or models that can be mutated and evolve. At every stage in the algorithm, each model is graded and the better models are allowed to reproduce or mutate for the next round. Some techniques allow the successful models to crossbreed. They are all motivated by the biologic process of evolution. Some techniques are asexual (so, there is no crossbreeding between techniques) while others are bisexual, allowing successful models to swap "genetic" information. The asexual models allow a wide variety of different models to compete, while sexual methods require that the models share a common "genetic" code.

Evolutionary Programming (EP)

Evolutionary Programming (EP) is a Machine Learning (model estimation) technique that generalizes the Genetic Algorithm (GA) by keeping the evolutionary behavior and dropping the tight link to biologic genetics. It is essentially similar to asexual reproduction, in that each generation is evaluated and the most fit are most likely to reproduce. During reproduction, each "child" model is allowed to mutate. This method focuses less on the internal representation of the model and more on the behavior of the models. It becomes easier to mix diverse types of models in the same mix. Note that this technique usually selects the "winners" stochastically rather than deterministically.

exchangeability

A sequence is said to be exchangeable with respect to some measure P(.) if the measure of the sequence has the same value whenever any two of the elements of the sequence are exchanged. This concept is important in the analysis and manipulation of probabilistic belief networks.
See Also: Bayesian Network.

existential quantifier

The "existential quantifier" in logic is a quantifier of a proposition that implies there is at least one case in which a particular proposition is true. It is usually represented by a backward capital E.
See Also: universal quantifier.

expectation (ART)

The top-down prototype vector of the selected F2 category in an ART network.
See Also: ART, ftp://ftp.sas.com/pub/neural/FAQ2.html, http://www.wi.leidenuniv.nl/art/.

expectation (mathmatical)

The expectation of an attribute is a measure of a "typical" location of an attribute. It is the arithmetic mean or average value of an attribute with respect to a specified probability distribution. It is calculated by multiplying each possible value for the attribute by its respective probability (or density) and summing. The common arithmetic average of a set of k numbers is an expectation with respect to a probability distribution that assigns probability 1/k to each of the elements in the set.

Expectation-Maximization (EM) Algorithm

The Expectation-Maximization (EM) algorithm is a technique for estimating Machine Learning techniques. It can be employed when the model meets certain technical constraints. If the model can be simplified by the assumption that certain hidden values exist, the model learns by first guessing the hidden values and then cycling through a series of maximizations given the current hidden values, and then estimating the hidden values given the current maximized values. It has been successfully used in a wide variety of Machine Learning and statistical models; one example being the AutoClass class clustering program.

expected value

See: expectation.

Expert System

An expert system is a computer system that attempts to model the domain knowledge on a human expert. These systems can then be used in place of, or to assist, human experts in forming decisions.

explanation

An important aspect of building trust in a computer-based system lies in its ability to provide compelling justification for the decisions or conclusions that it provides.

exploratory data analysis

This refers to the use of "simple" tabular and graphical displays to gain a better understanding of the structure of a dataset. Originally introduced by Tukey to describe a collection of techniques that could quickly characterize a batch of data without recourse to "heavy" statistical modeling, it has since become an alternate approach to modeling, concentrating on intuitive and visual techniques for rapidly summarizing data, rather than classical statistical estimation and testing techniques.

Some of the commonly used techniques include "five-number summaries" (median, upper and lower quartiles, and upper and lower "fences"), box and whisker plots, and various smoothed histograms and scatter-plots. These can be linked in computer animations to allow various types of brushing to explore the linkage between various views. More complex techniques allow "grand tours" of high dimensional data, which may be either guided or run in a projection pursuit mode, where the program hunts for "interesting" views of the data.

See Also: Data Mining.

Extension of a concept

The set of objects which are referred to by a concept in an application domain.

See Also: Concept, intension of a concept.

Extension of an attribute

The set of objects which have a particular value for an attribute is the extension of an attribute. The objects that share a particular value of an attribute form an equivalence class.

See Also: equivalence class.

F

facet

In class-based ontologies, a facet represents information about a slot, such as a constraint on the values of an instance slot. Some examples would be an assertion about the permissible value types (all mothers must be of type female) or information about the cardinality of the slot.
See Also: class.

fact

In PROLOG, a fact is a statement about the relationship between objects.

factor graph

A factor graph is a bipartate graph with one set of nodes representing the variables in the model and a second set of nodes representing the local (probability) functions representing relationships between the variable nodes. Each function nodes is connected to the variable nodes on which it depends. Likewise, each variable node is connected to the variables it influences or is influenced by. Factor graphs may contain directed edges. Factor graphs are more general than either Markov Random Fields or Bayesian networks in terms of expressing the factorization of multivariate distribution. Figure F.1 on the following page shows a simple four node graphical model as well as a particular factorization of that model.

factorial hidden Markov model

See: Dynamic Probabilistic Network.

factorial recognition network

See: Helmholtz machine, naïve Bayes.

Figure F.1—Simple Four Node and Factorization Model

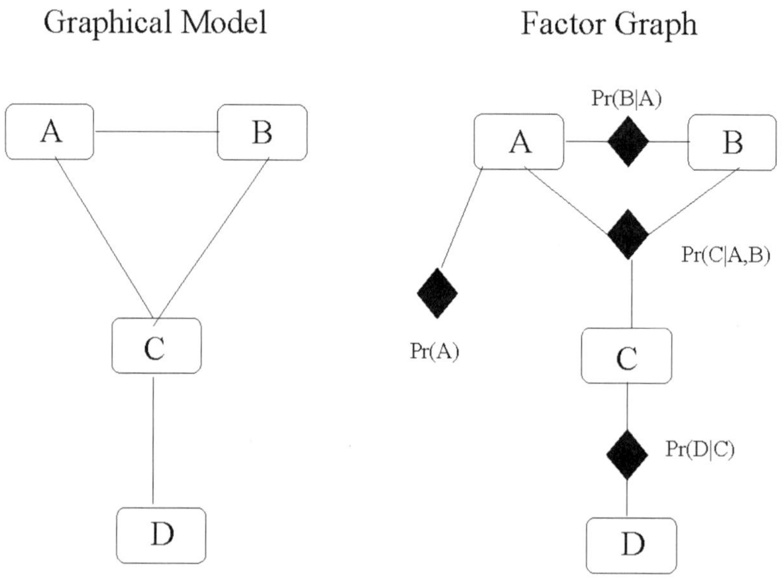

Graphical Model | Factor Graph

fail

A PROLOG operator that causes backtracking to occur.

FAIS

A fraud detection system developed for the U.S. Treasury's Financial Crimes Enforcement Network. It monitors financial transactions to identify potential money-laundering schemes. It was developed using Knowledge Discovery in Databases (KDD) techniques.
See Also: Knowledge Discovery in Databases.

FAM

See: Fuzzy Associative Memory.

fan-in

A term used in describing neural networks and other network models. It is the number of incoming connections for a node. The corresponding number of outgoing connections is termed the fan-out.

fan-out

See: fan-in.

FASSOM

A form of Kohonen network. The name was derived from "Feedback Controlled Supspace SOM."
See Also: ASSOM, SOM, http://www.cis.hut.fi/nnrc/new_book.html.

FASTRAK-APT

FASTRAK-APT is a project scheduling expert system developed by Hyundai Engineering and Construction. It is used for generation, verifying, and modifying construction project PERT-CPM networks. It uses Case Based Reasoning and constraint-based reasoning to assist human project planners.
See Also: Case Based Reasoning.

fault tree

A fault tree is an event tree that is used to represent the possible faults in a process. It can be used as a simple analysis tool or as a control or diagnosis structure for an automated system. For example, a diagnosis system could use fault tree and associated probabilities to propose checks or repairs for a computer system or a medical condition.
See Also: decision tree, event tree, probability tree.

FCM

See: Fuzzy Cognitive Map.

FDS

FDS is a program designed to solve certain mathematical programs using Means-Ends analysis.
See Also: Means-Ends analysis.

feature (attribute)

See: attribute.

Feature Analysis

An image analysis technique that decomposes the image into easily recognized parts (horizontal, vertical, or diagonal lines, curves, etc.).

The image can then be classified or recognized by comparing the feature list with those of various standards.

Feature Extraction

Feature Extraction is used in speech recognition and image processing to refer to the reduction of the input signal into a collection of broader features that can be used for further analysis. It is used more generally as term for the process of variable reduction.
See Also: data reduction.

feature points

In image analysis, the feature points are a list of identifiable places observed in an image.

feature vector

A feature vector is one method used to represent a textual or visual object in a form suitable for numeric processing and machine learning. As an example, a block of text (e.g., an article in a newspaper) could be collapsed into a (sorted) list of words. This list could be compared against a standard glossary of, say, 50,000, words and represented by a 50,000-element binary vector with ones (1s) for the words that occurred in the document and zeros (0s) for those that did not. This vector could then be used to classify the document or in further analysis. This type of representation, which ignores the word order in the document, is sometimes called a bag of words representation.

A feature vector is also a general term used in Machine Learning and related areas to describe a vector or list containing the values of attributes for a case. It typically has a fixed length (dimension). It can also be referred to as a record or a tuple.
See Also: attribute, Machine Learning, Wise Wire.

feedback

In general, this term is used to describe systems or inputs where the current output or state can modify the effect of input. A positive feedback acts as an amplifier or magnifier on the output (e.g., the rich get richer and the poor get poorer). A negative feedback acts to diminish large inputs and magnify small inputs. This becomes important in keeping a system in control or "on target." Error-driven feedback systems use the deviation of the system from the current set point or

target point to generate a corrective term. This concept is fundamental in the discussion of Robotics and control theory.
See Also: Robotics.

feedback network

A neural network is a feedback network if its graph contains any cycles.

feedforward network

A neural network is a feedforward network if the graph representing the network is acyclic (e.g., contains no cycles).

FFOIL

FFOIL is a specialization of the FOIL program specialized to learn functional relationships. In empirical trials on functions such as a greatest common denominator or an Ackermann's function, it has successfully been able to learn the function much faster than FOIL.
See Also: FOIL, Inductive Logic Programming.

Fifth Generation Computing

A term used by the Japanese to refer to their initiative to build a new generation of computers specially tuned for logic programming and logical inferences.

first-order learning

First-order learning is the process of learning a relationship from a database of positive and negatives examples. It differs from the more common Machine Learning procedures, which learn attributes and values, in that it attempts to learn a generalizable relation. An example is the program FOIL.
See Also: FOIL, Inductive Logic Programming.

fitness

In evolutionary and genetic algorithms, the fitness of a solution is a measure of how well the individual solution solves the task at hand. It can be used to select individual solutions for reproduction.

Floyd's Shortest Distance Algorithm

This is one of several algorithms that can be used to find the shortest distance or lowest cost paths between nodes in graph. The connections and costs between the nodes are represented in an adjacency matrix. Floyd's algorithm constructs a cost matrix in n^3 steps. Other algorithms can be used when this number is too large, when only a few paths are needed, or when the costs are dynamic.
See Also: adjacency matrix, graph.

FOG

See: FOrecast Generator.

FOIL

FOIL is an inductive logic program that can learn first-order relationships. It uses a restricted form of Prolog, omitting cuts, fails, disjunctive goals and functions other than constants. It learns by using a divide-and-conquer technique to expand clauses until no more examples can be absorbed, and can simplify definitions by pruning.
See Also: first-order learning, Logic Programming, Inductive Logic Programming, Prolog.

FOL

A program to check proofs stated in first order logic. Weyhrauch and Filman developed FOL at Stanford University in 1975.

F1 layer

The initial resonating layer of an ART network.
See Also: ARTftp://ftp.sas.com/pub/neural/FAQ2.html, http://www.wi.leidenuniv.nl/art/.

FOrecast Generator (FOG)

FOrecast Generator (FOG) is a Canadian natural language generation system. It can translate weather forecasts from a database into either French or English.
See Also: generation, Natural Language Understanding.

forest

A forest is a collection of trees. This term is sometimes used in discussion of techniques such as mixtures of experts, generalized addi-

tive models, and boosting, that combine the results of a collection of decision trees to form a final decision.
See Also: boosting, generalized additive models, mixture-of-experts models.

FOR_RAIL

FOR_RAIL is a neural network-based crossing guard system under development by Nestor. It uses video sensors to collect input.
See Also: Artificial Neural Network.

FORTH

A low-level extensible stack-based programming language. It uses a reverse polish (or, postfix) syntax, so that the addition of two numbers would be described by the command sequence a b +, which would leave the resultant sum (a+b) on the top of the stack. Although basic FORTH is rather low-level, the language includes operations that allow the programmer to easily define new operations, as well as redefining existing operations. Charles Moore designed FORTH for machine control in Astronomy, and has spread to numerous other areas, particularly in embedded systems. It has been used in mobile robots.
See Also: Mobile Robot.

Forward Chaining

A method of solving logic problems by working forward from the known data or previously proven inferences towards a goal or solution to a problem.
See Also: Backward Chaining.

forward propagation

Used in neural networks to mean prediction.
See Also: Artificial Neural Network.

Forward Reasoning

The process of reasoning from premises to conclusions. In automated logic systems, this can result in a rapid growth of conclusions that are irrelevant to the desired conclusion.
See Also: Backward Reasoning, logic programming, resolution.

fractal

A fractal is a compound object that contains multiple subobjects, each of which has some locally measurable characteristic similar to the same characteristic measured on the whole object. The ideas of fractals and fractal dimension are used in document and vision analysis.
See Also: Hausdorff dimension.

frame of discernment

The set of propositions that are of interest in Dempster-Shafer theory is referred to as the frame of discernment. This differs from the standard Universe that probability theory uses in that a frame of discernment can include sets whose members are not in the frame of discernment. A frame of discernment can be refined by splitting apart its sets and can be coarsened by aggregating them. Two frames of discernment are compatible if they are equivalent after a process of refinement and/or coarsening.

Frame Representation Language (FRL)

Roberts and Goldstein of MIT developed the Frame Representation Language (FRL) in the late 1970s. The frame templates (classes) are organized into a hierarchy where the relationship between two objects is described as "a kind of". For example, persons would be a kind of mammal, which in turn might be a kind of mortal. Socrates would be an instance of the person class.
See Also: Frames.

Frames

A form of knowledge representation introduced by M. Minsky in 1975. Objects are represented by a complex data structure that contains a series of named slots that describe that type of object and its relationships to other objects in the knowledge base. The templates for an object can have default values. The slots can be further constrained by generic relationship (e.g., the age of a person is less than the age of the person's parents) and specific constraints for a particular object. The slots can also contain actions (functions) and goals. The frame for an object contains named "slots" for information about that object. The information in these slots can then be referred to in order to determine valid actions and goals. Minsky introduced frames as a form of organizing knowledge in 1975.

See Also: Knowledge Base, Knowledge Representation, Semantic Memory.

Franz LISP

A LISP dialect implemented on the VAX machines. It was written in C and was, thus, portable to many UNIX machines.

Fredkin Prize

The Fredkin Prize was $100,000 prize for the first computer program to beat a reigning world chess champion. MIT Computer Science Professor Edward Fredkin established the prize in 1980. The inventors of the Deep Blue Chess machine won the Fredkin Prize. Deep Blue beat Gary Kasparov, the reigning world champ.

Professor Fredkin offered the final $100,000 as the third in a series of three prizes. Two scientists from Bell Laboratories (whose program first attained a masters rating in chess) won the first prize of $5,000. Five Carnegie Mellon graduate students who built Deep Thought (the first program to achieve international master status) claimed the second prize of $10,000.
See Also: Deep Blue.

FRA

See: Fuzzy Rule Approximation.

FRL

See: Frame Representation Language.

FSI

See: Fuzzy Singleton Inference; See Also: binary input-output fuzzy adaptive memory.

F2 layer

The second layer of an ART network where pattern choice and other behaviors take place.
See Also: ARTftp://ftp.sas.com/pub/neural/FAQ2.html, http://www.wi.leidenuniv.nl/art/.

function

A function is a relationship that takes zero or more attributes and returns a single item that may be compound. In class and frame based systems, a function that takes a single term and returns a single term is sometimes called a slot. A multivariate function is a function that returns a compound object, such as a list or an array, which may be regarded as the specification of a single multi-dimensional item.
See Also: anonymous, class, function, slot.

functional programming languages

Functional programming languages are defined solely in terms of well-defined mathematical functions that take arguments and return values, with no side effects. In a pure functional language, there is no assignment; hence, the computation can be spread over many computers with reduced need for synchronization.
See Also: Logic Programming.

function, anonymous

A function that does not have a name, but is only defined inline with its use. Used in LISP as (lambda (args) (expression)), it allows for a more efficient code.

function, recursive

A function that can call itself while evaluating its arguments. A classic example is the factorial function $f(x) := x\, f(x-1)$, for $x>0$ and $f(x) = 1$ for $x <= 0$. $f(x)$ is the product of x and $f(x-1)$, so that you must evaluate $f(x-1), f(x-2),...$ to evaluate $f(x)$.
See Also: function, anonymous.

fusion and propagation

The fusion and propagation algorithm is a fundamental algorithm for producing multiple marginals from a graphical model that can be represented as a tree. It provides a rule for fusing incoming messages at each node and for propagating those messages out from a node. The fusion takes place in the local frame of discernment, so the full joint frame is never explicitly required.
See Also: graphical model, peeling.

Fuzzy ART

A network that synthesizes Adaptive Resonance Theory (ART) and Fuzzy Logic.
See Also: ftp://ftp.sas.com/pub/neural/FAQ2.html, http://www.wi.leidenuniv.nl/art/.

Fuzzy ARTMAP

A supervised Fuzzy ART network.
See Also: ftp://ftp.sas.com/pub/neural/FAQ2.html, http://www.wi.leidenuniv.nl/art/.

Fuzzy Associative Mmemory (FAM)

A fuzzy function, or model, that takes a k-dimensional fuzzy input and produces a 1-dimension fuzzy output. Comparable to a regression model or a neural network. The model can learn (estimate) from data or have its parameters set in some other fashion, e.g., by the model designer.

FuzzyCLIPS

FuzzyCLIPS is an enhanced version of C Language Integrated Production System (CLIPS) developed at the National Research Council of Canada that allows the implementation of fuzzy expert systems. It enables domain experts to express rules using their own fuzzy terms. It allows any mix of fuzzy and normal terms, numeric-comparison logic controls, and uncertainties in the rule and facts. Fuzzy sets and relations deal with fuzziness in approximate reasoning, while certainty factors for rules and facts manipulate the uncertainty. The use of the above modifications is optional and existing CLIPS programs still execute correctly.
See Also: C Language Integrated Production System, http://ai.iit.nrc.ca/fuzzy/fuzzy.html.

Fuzzy Cognitive Map (FCM)

A graph with signed and directed arcs between nodes. The arc from node i to node j is an indicator of the influence of node i on node j. Likewise, the arc from j to i is an indicator of the influence of node j on node i. These arcs do not need to be symmetric. When the nodes are initialized to some state, repeated application of the connection matrix derived from the graph can be used to determine the evolution of the system and any fixed points or limit cycles.

fuzzy complement

The fuzzy complement of a fuzzy set is a fuzzy set whose membership functions are the complements of the original set (i.e., 1-m(A,x) where x are the elements in the original fuzzy set A).

fuzzy count

A measure of the size of a fuzzy set A and defined as the sum of all membership values in A. It is the fuzzy generalization of a classic set notion of cardinality, or size of a set.

fuzzy entropy

Fuzzy entropy is a measure of the fuzziness of a set. For a set A and its fuzzy complement B, fuzzy entropy is the ratio of the underlap of A∩B to the overlap of A∪B. In classical (crisp) sets, this value is, by definition, 0, since the cardinality of A∩B is defined to be 0 and the cardinality of A∪B is similarly defined to be 1 (for a non-empty universe). The larger this value is, for a given set of elements, the fuzzier the set A (and B) becomes.
See Also: fuzzy set theory, underlap, overlap.

fuzzy intersection

In (crisp) set theory, the intersection of two sets is the set of all elements that are in both sets. In fuzzy set theory, the fuzzy intersection is the set of all elements with non-zero memberships in both sets. The membership function of an element in this new set is defined to be the minimum of its membership in the two parent sets. Thus the intersection of a set and its complement (A ∧ not-A), which is defined to be an empty set (of measure zero) in classic crisp sets, can be non-empty in fuzzy sets.
See Also: fuzzy complement, fuzzy set, fuzzy union.

fuzzy logic

A logic system based on manipulation of fuzzy sets. Some of the basic rules include definitions for intersections, unions, and complements.

fuzzy logic system

An inference system based on fuzzy logic.

fuzzy measure

The fuzzy measure of a fuzzy set is defined to be the sum of the fuzzy membership values of all elements with non-zero membership in the set. It is often denoted by m(A).

Fuzzy Rule Approximation (FRA)

A method for inference based on fuzzy logic. A given set of fuzzy rules defines a map from the input space to the output space. A FRA system attempts to replace the fuzzy rules with a neural network that approximates that rulebase.

fuzzy set

A set fuzzy set A consists of set objects X with membership values denoted by m(A,x). The relation that maps elements x in X to the membership values in (0,1) is called a membership function. A fuzzy set is a generalization of classical set theory, where each element x in the universe X has a membership of 0 or 1 in a set A, and has been proposed as a means to deal with uncertainty.
See Also: fuzzy logic.

Fuzzy Singleton Inference (FSI)

See: Binary Input-Output Fuzzy Adaptive Memory.

fuzzy union

The fuzzy union of two sets is defined to be the set of all elements with non-zero memberships in either of the two sets. The membership function of elements in the new set is defined to be the maximum of the two memberships in the parent sets.
See Also: fuzzy set.

FuzzyCLIPS

FuzzyCLIPS is an enhanced version of C Language Integrated Production System (CLIPS) developed at the National Research Council of Canada that allows the implementation of fuzzy expert systems. It enables domain experts to express rules using their own fuzzy terms. It allows any mix of fuzzy and normal terms, numeric-comparison logic controls, and uncertainties in the rule and facts. Fuzzy sets and relations deal with fuzziness in approximate reasoning, while certainty factors for rules and facts manipulate the uncertainty. The use of the above modifications is optional and existing CLIPS programs still execute correctly.

See Also: C Language Integrated Production System, http://ai.iit.nrc.ca/fuzzy/fuzzy.html.

G

GA
See: Genetic Algorithm.

gain
The figure of merit used to judge potential classification splits in ID3, defined as the change in entropy by the split. It was replaced with the gain ratio criterion in C4.5.
See Also: C4.5.

gain control
ART networks have two non-specific gain control signals, G1 and G2 for the F1 and F2 layers, respectively. G1 implements the 2/3 rule in the F1 layer, while G2 enables/disables the F2 layer.
See Also: ART, ftp://ftp.sas.com/pub/neural/FAQ2.html, http://www.wi.leidenuniv.nl/art/.

gain ratio criterion
A normalized version of the gain (entropy) criterion originally used in ID3. The latter tended to favor splits that generated many leaves. In C4.5, the gain score is divided by a split information score. This adjusts the gain from a split for the entropy of the number of splits.

GAM
See: Generalized Additive Model.

Game Trees
Many game programs choose their next move by looking ahead for several moves to evaluate the possible moves. These possibilities are often represented as a tree of possibilities.

GARI

A planning system for machining mechanical parts.

Gate Function

A gate, or mixing, function is used in mixture-of-experts or hierarchical mixture-of-experts systems to combine or select the individual experts predictions or selections for output (at that level).

As an example, consider a system to predict creditworthiness based on income and other factors. If the individual experts prediction consisted of models developed on non-overlapping partitions of the training data, the gate function would be a simple selection function that would choose the appropriate sub-model. If the sub-models were developed using overlapping regions of the data, the gate function might weight the prediction of the sub-models by each models' distance from this data point, or by their previous accuracy.

See Also: hierarchical mixtures of experts, mixture-of-experts models.

Gaussian ARTMAP

An ARTMAP network that uses Gaussian-defined receptive fields.
See Also: ftp://ftp.sas.com/pub/neural/FAQ2.html, http://www.wi.leidenuniv.nl/art/.

Gaussian distribution

See: normal distribution.

Gaussian function

The Gaussian function is the classic "bell" curve, frequently seen in statistical analysis and as a weight function for combining values in interpolation (smoothing) nets. The relevance of a reference point to a specified value is proportional to the $e^{-2(x-y)^2/s}$, where x is the value, y is the reference point, and s is a parameter that specifies the width of the bell. The Gaussian function is also used as a radial basis function.
See Also: interpolation net.

GBB

GBB is a generalized object-oriented shell for building high-performance blackboard applications.
See Also: blackboard.

gene

In biology, a section of a chromosome that encodes a single trait is referred to as a gene. By analogy, genetic algorithms refer to a section of a chromosome that encodes the value of a parameter as a gene.
See Also: Genetic Algorithm.

generalized additive model (GAM)

A Generalized Additive Model (GAM) extends the flexible learning models of additive models to generalized linear models.
See Also: generalized linear model.

generalized EM algorithim

The EM algorithm converges on an exact maximum solution to an estimation problem, such as probabilities in a partially observed network. However, this approach can be computationally or analytically infeasible. A generalized EM algorithm substitutes approximations for the E step and/or the M step. For example, one could use a Gibbs sampling method to compute an approximate expectation (the E step) or a lower bound on the maximum likelihood for the M (maximization) step.
See Also: generalized forward-backward algorithm, variational inference.

generalized forward-backward algorithm

A method for probability propagation in networks. After some rearrangement of the network, probability calculations are propagated down the network, with each node storing its state, and then back up the network to obtain final estimates of the state of the network.
See Also: generalized EM, sum-product algorithm.

generalized linear model

Classical linear regression techniques model the response as a linear function of the predictor and assume that the response attribute is normally distributed about its mean with a common error variance. The generalized linear model extends the linear model to cases, such as logistic regression on binary variables, where the observation has a mean that is a function of a linear model and whose distribution is non-normal.
See Also: Generalized Additive Model, logistic regression.

generalized list

A generalized list over some set of elements is a list whose elements are either elements of the set or generalized lists from the set. A generalized list can contain both elements and other forms of a list.
See Also: list.

Generalized Logic Diagram (GLD)

A Generalized Logic Diagram (GLD) is a generalization of a Karnaugh map. The Karnaugh map uses dimension stacking to imbed multiple binary attributes into a two-dimensional table whose entries correspond to the binary output of that combination. A GLD allows stacks multi-level attributes and allows a general response, possibly including a graphic, as the entries. Continuous attributes can be included after binning. A decision table is a special form of a GLD.
See Also: decision table, dimension stacking, Karnaugh map.

Generalized Phrase Structure Grammers

A variant of the context-free phrase structure grammer.

Generalized Upper Model

The Generalized Upper Model is a task-independent and domain-independent ontology that supports natural language processing in English, German, and Italian. It contains a hierarchy of about 250 concepts and a separate hierarchy for relationships.
See Also: ontology, http://www.darmstadt.gmd.de/publish/komet/genum/newUM.html.

General Problem Solving (GPS) inference engine

GPS sought a series of operations that would eliminate the difference between an initial state and a final goal. It used a Means-Ends analysis to determine the individual steps. Newell, Shaw, and Simon developed the GPS inference engine.
See Also: Means-Ends analysis.

General Regression Neural Network (GRNN)

A General Regression Neural Network (GRNN) is the continuous analog of Donald Specht's Probabilistic Neural Networks (PNN). Rather than return a 0-1 signal from each hidden unit that the input case matches, it returns a weight and the output associated with each matched hidden unit. The final prediction is the weighted average of the outputs.

Generate and Test Method

Generate and Test Method is a general term for a method that generates a series of answers and then tests them against the current case(s). They usually have two modules: a generator module to propose solutions and a test module that scores them. The method can be exhaustive, evaluating all possible solutions, or can continue testing until some acceptability criterion is reached. This type of technique is commonly used to identify new samples or situations presented to it.

generation

In Genetic and Evolutionary algorithms, each iteration of the algorithm is referred to as a generation. This includes the creation of new competitors and their evaluation.
See Also: Genetic Algorithm, Evolutionary Algorithm.

Generic Spacecraft Analyst Assistant (GenSAA)

A Generic Spacecraft Analyst Assistant (GenSAA) is an expert system designed to assist control personnel in monitoring spacecraft. It uses C Language Integrated Production System (CLIPS) as its inference engine.
See Also: CLIPS, http://groucho.gsfc.nasa.gov:80/Code_520/Code_522/Projects/GenSAA/.

Genetic algorithm (GA)

A technique for estimating computer models (e.g., Machine Learning) based on methods adapted from the field of genetics in biology. To use this technique, one encodes possible model behaviors into a "genes". After each generation, the current models are rated and allowed to mate and breed based on their fitness. In the process of mating, the genes are exchanged, and crossovers and mutations can occur. The current population is discarded and its offspring forms the next generation.

Also, Genetic Algorithm describes a term used to describe a variety of modeling or optimization techniques that claim to mimic some aspect of biological modeling in choosing an optimum. Typically, the object being modeled is represented in a fashion that is easy to modify automatically. Then a large number of candidate models are generated and tested against the current data. Each model is scored and the "best" models are retained for the next generation. The retention can be deterministic (choose the best k models) or random (choose the k models with probability proportional to the score.) These models are then randomly perturbed (as in asexual reproduction) and the process repeated until it converges. If the model is constructed so that they have "genes," the winners can "mate" to produce the next generation.

GenSAA

See: Generic Spacecraft Analyst Assistant.

GermAlert

GermAlert is an expert system used to monitor culture-based criteria for "significant" infections requiring immediate treatment.
See Also: http://www-uk.hpl.hp.com/people/ewc/list-main.html.

GermWatcher

GermWatcher is a CLIPS-based expert system that can monitor laboratory data for evidence of nosocomial (hospital-acquired), for reporting to the Center for Disease Control (CDC).
See Also: http://www-uk.hpl.hp.com/people/ewc/list-main.html.

Gibbs sampling

A Markov Chain Monte Carlo (MCMC) method for sampling values from belief distribution.
See Also: Markov Chain Monte Carlo method.

Gini Index

A figure of merit used in machine learning and statistical models, such as Classification And Regression Trees (CART). The Gini Index for a grouping is defined to be $1-\Sigma p_i^2$, where p_i is the proportion of cases in the i-th category. It reaches a minimum of 0 when all the cases in a node or grouping are in the same category, and its maximum when all the cases are spread out equally across all of the categories.
See Also: Classification and Regression Trees.

GLD
See: Generalized Logic Diagram.

goal
The solution that a program is attempting to reach.

goal directed
See: backward chaining.

G1
See: gain control.

GPS inference engine
See: General Problem Solving inference engine.

gradient descent
Gradient descent, or hill climbing, is a common technique for estimating parameters in Machine Learning algorithms such as neural nets or other regression style techniques. These algorithms "learn" by adjusting their parameters to minimize some error measure. At any given point in the learning process, the algorithm evaluates how a change in the parameters could decrease the current error and moves in that direction.

Typically, the algorithm determines the direction as a function of the derivative of the error function (its gradient) with respect to the parameters or a weighted derivative, where the matrix of second derivatives (the Hessian matrix) determines the weights. Once the direction has been chosen, it is multiplied by a learning rate parameter and added to the current values of the parameter vector.

See Also: learning rate, Machine Learning.

Grammer, Augmented Transition Network
See: Augmented Transition Network Grammer.

grand tour
The grand tour is a name for Data Mining and visualization techniques that are used to explore high-dimensional data spaces. The data are projected onto a series of two-dimensional and three-dimensional plots, along with measures of interest. The tour can be random

or can be directed toward finding projections that are "interesting" to the analyst directing the tour. An example could be the exploration of purchase data patterns to reveal unexpected associations.

Graph

A graph is a set of objects that have connections to other objects. The objects are often referred to as nodes and the connections as arcs or edges. If the connections have directions associated with them, the graph is referred to as a directed graph. If the connections are such that there is only one path between any two objects, then the graph is acyclic. A graph has both properties is referred to as a Directed Acyclic Graph (DAG).
See Also: Bayesian Network, belief net, Graph.

graphical model

In a graphical model, the relationships between the attributes can be represented as a (mathematical) graph. Typically, the nodes of the graph represent variables or actions, and the arcs represent dependencies or information flows.
See Also: Bayesian Network, belief net, Graph.

Gray codes

A form of binary encoding (patented by Frank Gray in 1953) which can be used to encode the integers [0, ... , 2^{N-1}] as a binary string of length N. They have the special property that adjacent integers differ by only one bit, sometimes referred to as an "adjacency property." They have been used in a Genetic Algorithm to encode numbers, as a small mutation in a Gray code encoding tends to yield a small change in the value.

greatest lower bound

In a partially ordered set, suppose that $A \geq C$ and $B \geq C$. If $C \geq D$ for any element D that also is $\leq$ both A and B then, C is the greatest lower bound for elements A and B.
See Also: least upper bound, lattice, partially ordered set.

greedy algorithm

Algorithms are often described as being greedy when they attempt to solve a larger problem by taking short steps that are locally optimum but ignoring combinations of steps that might lead to a better overall

solution. For example, decision trees are often constructed using greedy algorithms. At any particular node, the greedy program will choose the best single split as the next level in the tree, rather than looking for combinations of splits that could yield a better solution several steps later. Greedy algorithms have the advantage that they are easier to implement and can be faster than global algorithms, and often yield a result that is "good enough."
See Also: look-ahead.

Greedy Evaluation

Symbols or goals are evaluated as soon as possible. Often used in forward chaining systems.

GRNN

See: Generalized Regression Neural Network.

GROBIAN

GROBIAN is an experimental rough sets analysis program. In addition to the usual analysis offered by programs such as Rosetta, it also includes some alternate measures of the quality of the rough sets approximations and some additional statistical tests.
See Also: http://www.infj.ulst.ac.uk/~cccz23/grobian/grobian.html.

G2

See: gain control.

H

HACKER

HACKER, written by G.J. Sussman, generated plans for solving problems in the "blocks world". Modeled on human problem solving techniques, the program attempts to find a solution by looking through an "answer library". If no immediate answer is available, it attempts to modify a similar one. A "criticizer" subsystem then looks for errors in the plan and attempts to fix them.
See Also: Blocks World.

Hamming distance

Classical distance measures, such as Euclidean distance or Manhattan distance, require that the component attributes in the feature vector are on an interval level or ratio level. The Hamming distance is a distance measure appropriate for nominal or ordinal measures and counts the number of attributes on which the pair differs.
See Also: interval attribute, metric, ratio attribute.

hard selection

Selection by death in a genetic algorithm.
See Also: soft selection.

Hardy

Hardy is a hypertext-based diagramming tool. Hardy is integrated with NASA's rule-based and object-oriented language C Language Integrated Production System Version 6.0 (CLIPS 6.0) to enable users to develop diagram-related applications rapidly.
See Also: C Language Integrated Production System, http://www.aiai.ed.ac.uk/~hardy/hardy/hardy.html.

HARPY

B. Lowerre wrote HARPY, a speech understanding system, in 1975. This program contained a series of precompiled words, and the "understanding" was implemented as a series of transitions between these words.

HART-J and HART-S

Two modular hierarchial ART (HART) models. The first implements an agglomerative clustering method, while the second implements a divisive clostering method, where each ART layer learns the differences between the input and the matching prototype of the previous layer.
See Also: ftp://ftp.sas.com/pub/neural/FAQ2.html, http://www.wi.leidenuniv.nl/art/.

HASP

A blackboard-based system for the real-time interpretation of sonar signals in a specific area of the ocean. It used the inputs from several sensors in known locations to detect and identify the location and movement of ships in its region.

Hasse diagram

A Hasse diagram is a reduced representation of the complete graph of a partially ordered set. A complete representation of a partially ordered set has arcs between all nodes a and b for which a R b, where R represents the ordering relation. A Hasse diagram is a graph that eliminates all links between two nodes for which there is a longer path between the nodes. An event tree is a Hasse diagram. (See Figure H.1.)
See Also: Directed Acyclic Graph, event tree, partially ordered set, singular diagram.

Hausdorff dimension

A measure of the fractal complexity of an object. It is used in document and vision analysis.

head

The first element of a list.
See Also: car, cdr, cons cell, LISP, list, tail.

Figure H.1—Hasse Diagram of Event Tree

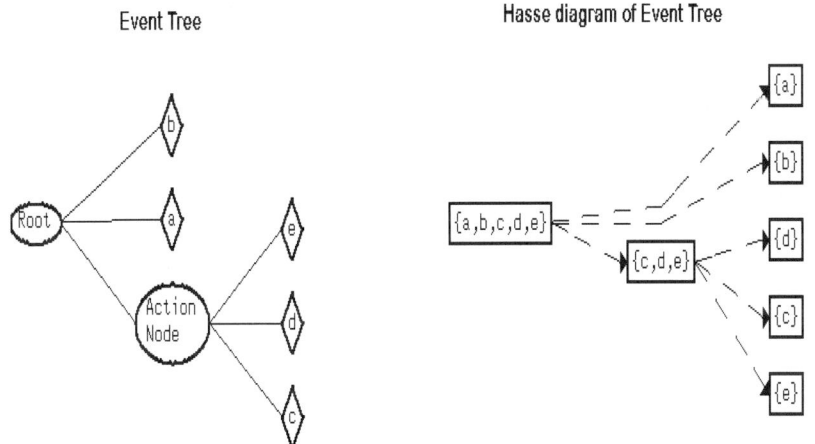

HEARSAY-III

A blackboard-based system that interprets a spoken request to retrieve information. It has a limited vocabulary of about 1000 words.

HEARSAY-II

A speech understanding system written by Lesser, Fennell, Erman, and Reddy in 1976. A series of modules composed the system that communicated through a "blackboard" (q.v.). Each of the modules represented a different knowledge source and could function asynchronously.

Hebbian learning

A form of unsupervised learning in neural networks which attempts to minimize the sum of squared distances between the input cases and a linear subspace of the data space of the training cases. It is similar to a Principal Components Analysis.

height

The parameter that sets the maximum value a radial basis function can take on is referred to as a height.
See Also: radial basis function, width.

Helmholtz machine

Probability propagation on a large, multiply-connected Bayesian network can be computationally difficult. A Helmholtz machine tackles this problem by coupling the original generative network with a second recognition network that produces a quick approximation to the desired solution. Different sets of visible variables in the network can require different recognizer networks.

Recognizer networks can be divided into factorial networks which assume a simple Naïve Bayes model, given the visible variables, and nonfactorial models which allow for a more complicated relationship among the hidden variables given the visible variables.
See Also: generalized EM, Markov Chain Monte Carlo Methods, sum-product algorithm, variational inference.

Helpmate

Helpmate is an autonomous delivery robot for hospitals and similar environments. Helpmate is capable of delivering such items as meals and medicines. It is capable of navigation around unexpected obstacles (humans or other cars). It is currently undergoing field tests in the United States.
See Also: Scrubmate.

Hepaxpert I and Hepaxpert II

Hepaxpert I and Hepaxpert II are rule-based systems that provide automatic interpretation of tests for Hepatitis A and B. They use a rule-base of over 100 rules and have seen routine use since September 1989.
See Also: http://www-uk.hpl.hp.com/people/ewc/list-main.html.

Hessian matrix

In learning algorithms that use gradient or related techniques to learn, the gradients are sometimes weighted by the inverse of the matrix of cross-products or the Hessian matrix. The Hessian matrix is the matrix of second derivatives of the error function with respect to the parameters of the learning rule.
See Also: gradient descent.

heteroassociative

Heteroassociative models are models that relate one set of variables to a different set of variables, such as a prediction or classification.

The predicting variables are different from the target variable(s).
See Also: Artificial Neural Network, autoassociative.

Heuristics

Approximation techniques or "rules of thumb" for solving problems. They are generally used when either the exact solution to a specific problem is unknown or when an exact method is known but would be too difficult or impossible to apply. They offer the tradeoff of a "pretty good" solution at a "reasonable" cost.

hidden layer

An artificial neural network may include multiple nodes that are neither the initial input nodes nor the final output nodes. These are customarily referred to as "hidden" nodes. These notes can often be arranged into layers, where each layer receives input from a "previous" layer and whose output becomes the input for the next layer. Complicated network schemes can make counting the layers difficult.
See Also: input layer, output layer.

Hidden Markov Model

A model based on a Markov chain with additional, parallel states that are completely determined by the underlying states of the Markov chain. The underlying states are usually unobserved, but the secondary state information is observed. Multiple hidden states may generate the same observable states, and a single hidden state may generate different observable states.
See Also: Markov chain.

Hierarchical Mixtures of Experts (HME)

The HME architecture is a generalization of the ideas behind decision trees and recursive partitioning algorithms. The general idea behind this architecture is to break a large (hard) problem down into set of easier problems that can be solved by "experts." In this approach, the problem is decomposed a priori into a hierarchical input space that allows overlapping clusters (i.e., "soft splits"). The "experts" (neural networks) at the bottom of the tree each produce predictions for an input vector, which then combined probabilistically as the predictions are propagated "up" the tree.
See Also: Classification And Regression Trees.

highest posterior density interval
See: credible set.

HME
See: Hierarchical Mixtures of Experts.

HMM
See: Hidden Markov Model.

hold-out sample
When fitting many data-adaptive models, the models have a tendency to over-adapt to a particular dataset and, thus, have limited generality. One means to control or measure this effect is to "hold out" some of the data and evaluate the fitted model on this "fresh" data. There are a number of schemes for doing this, such as the use of training, validation, and test sets, and methods such as jack-knifing, cross-validation, and bootstrapping. All share the characteristic of developing the model on a subset of the data and evaluating/tuning it on another.

Honda Human
In 1996, Honda Corporation demonstrated a humanoid robot, called the Honda Human, capable of bipedal walking, turning, climbing stairs, and other activities. It is the result of an ongoing program to develop human assistants and replacements for the workshop floor. *See Also:* http://www.honda.co.jp/home/hpr/e_news/robot.

Hopfield network
An additive autoassociative network where the signal functions are a bounded monotone increasing function with a symmetric synaptic matrix. These networks are globally stable and converge quickly to fixed points for all inputs. Thus, once such a network is initialized and given some input $x(0)$, it will compute $x(1)$, $x(2)$, etc., until it reaches a stable $x(\infty)$.

Horizon Effect
A term coined by Berliner to characterize the effects of partial look-ahead in game playing programs. If a program can look ahead to the end of the game, it could (theoretically) pick an optimal series of

moves. When it can only look ahead partially (e.g., five moves in a chess game), the program may choose sub-optimal moves because of its limited horizon.

Horn Clause

Logical clauses that have no more than one positive literal. There are three kinds of clauses: assertions, conditional assertions, and denials.
See Also: Logic Programming.

Horn Core

The Horn Core of a propositional formula is the weakened Horn formula implying that formula. It is also called the greatest Horn lower bound. The Horn Core does not have to be unique, as there can be many inequivalent Horn formulae implying a given formula.
See Also: Horn envelope.

Horn envelope

For a given propositional formula X, its Horn envelope is the strongest Horn formula implied by X. It is also known as the least Horn upper bound. The approximation of a formula by its Horn envelope and Horn Core can support rapid approximate reasoning.
See Also: Horn Core.

Hough Transform

The Hough Transform is an image analysis technique that allows a histogram analysis of an input feature space. Peaks in the histogram of the feature space correspond to items in the input image. For example, a point on a detected edge would contribute to all possible lines running through that point in "line space" transform of the image. A line in the input image would then translate to a high spot in the line space generated from that image.

HUGIN

HUGIN is a commercial expert-system shell and library that uses a Bayesian Belief Network. HUGIN influences diagrams to capture uncertainty in system and to provide embedded advisors in systems.
See Also: http://www.hugin.dk/.

hypergraph

A typical graph representation of a problem or solution represents a single condition at each node. When the nodes represent compound conditions, as in a complex rule, the graph is sometimes referred to as a hypergraph. Similarly, the compound nodes can be referred to as hypernodes.

hyperparameter

In knowledge representation models, the value of an uncertain attribute can be represented by a probability distribution. If the parameters of that distribution are specified by yet another distribution, the parameters of that second distribution are referred to as a hyperparameter. As an example, the uncertainty in binary events is often represented by a Bernoulli distribution or, in aggregate, by a binomial distribution. Both distributions require a parameter, p, to represent the probability that the binary event occurs. If there is uncertainty about the value of p, it can be represented by a beta distribution, which has two parameters, a and b. In this example, a and b are hyperparameters for the original event.

hyperresolution

Hyperresolution is an inference rule that can be used in automated reasoning systems. It focuses on two or more clauses, requiring one of the clauses (the nucleus) contain at least one negative literal and the remaining (the satellites) contain no negative literals. Briefly, a conclusion is yielded if a unifier (substitution of terms for variables can be found that, when applied, makes identical (except for sign) pairs of literals, one negative literal from the nucleus with one positive from a satellite. The conclusion is yielded by ignoring the paired literals, applying the unifier simultaneously to the nucleus and the satellites, and taking the union of the resulting literals. It can be considered a generalization of binary resolution, which considers exactly two clauses simultaneously.
See Also: UR-resolution.

hypothesis testing

A statistical technique for evaluation of hypotheses or conjectures about unobserved or unobservable numerical properties of a population. The statistic that measures the quantity of interest is evaluated, along with its variability, on a sample of the data from the population, and compared to the range of values consistent with one of the hypotheses. In classical frequentist hypothesis testing, if the value is rare or unusual, the hypothesis is rejected.

I

ICAI
See: Intelligent Computer-Aided Instruction.

ICD-9
See: International Classification of Diseases.

ICR
See: Optical Character Recognition.

Idiot's bayes
See: naïve bayes.

If-Then Rule
An If-Then Rule in an expert system describes a problem situation and the action an expert would take in that situation.
See Also: expert system.

iid / i.i.d.
See: independent and identically distributed.

ILA
See: Internet Learning Agent.

ILLIAD
ILLIAD is an expert system used to perform a diagnosis in internal medicine. It uses Bayesian reasoning to assign probabilities to the various diagnoses under consideration.
See Also: http://www.ami-med.com.

ILP

See: Inductive Logic Programming.

Image Analysis

The tools and techniques used to break an image into its component parts so that the program can understand or classify an image.

implicant

An implicant B of a statement A is a satisfiable conjunction of conditions which entails A. B is a prime implicant of A when no subset of B is also an implicant of A (e.g., when B is minimal).
See Also: implicate.

implicate

A sentence B is an implicate of A when B is a non-valid disjunction of conditions that is entailed by A. A is a prime implicate of B when no subset of B is an implicant of A.
See Also: implicant.

imputation

A process of "filling in" missing values in datasets. There are a wide variety of techniques, mostly covered in the statistical literature and in the literature concerning survey data.
See Also: multiple imputation.

Incidence Calculus

Incidence calculus is an uncertainty management system for expert systems. Rather than directly compute the belief in a proposition, one could randomly simulate various truth-values for the proposition that precede a target proposition and count the frequency with which the proposition is true.

incremental training

See: on-line training.

independence

In probabilistic expert systems, an attribute X is independent of another attribute Y given a set of attributes W when the probability distribution for X can be constructed without reference to the state of

Y given the state of attributes in W, X, and Y are said to be unconditionally independent when the set W is empty (i.e., there are no intervening variables). Otherwise X and Y are conditionally independent given W.

See Also: Conditional Independence, Conditional Distribution.

independent and identically distributed (iid / i.i.d.)

In Machine Learning applications, the algorithms are typically derived assuming that all the observations were selected independently and they all came from the same distribution. A counter-case would be a mixture where observations were sampled differentially from two or more subgroups, or where the selection of one observation from the population makes another observation or set of observations more likely to be chosen. The first counter-example violates the identically distributed assumption, while the second violates the independence assumption. Failure to meet this assumption can limit the generalizability of any model or knowledge derived from it.

independent variable

See: regressor.

Indicator function

A function I(A,x), which takes on values of 0 or 1 depending on whether or not x is a member of the set A.

indiscernibility relation (rough sets)

See: indiscernible.

indiscernible

In rough sets, two objects are indiscernible with respect to a set of attributes A if they have the same values for each attribute in A. A grouping of all the objects in the "universe" that are indiscernible with respect to some A is the equivalence class of A. For example, if the universe consists of the set of integers in the range of (0,100), and a single attribute for an integer is defined to be mod(i,3), the integers 1 and 4 are indiscernible with respect to mod(i,3) as they both have the same value, 1. This attribute takes on four values (0,1,2,3), thus yielding four equivalence classes.

indispensable attributes

In Rough Set Theory, indispensable attributes are in the core.

Induction

The process of inferring a general principle from data or examples.

Inductive Logic Programming (ILP)

Inductive Logic Programming (ILP) is an alternate approach to Machine Learning. Most techniques in this field are attribute-based, concentrating on learning values of attributes that best predict the outcome variables. ILP assumes the background knowledge expressed as a set of predicate definitions, a set of positive examples, and a set of negative examples. An ILP system will then attempt to extend the background knowledge so that all the positive examples can be derived while none of the negative examples can be. Although this may sound similar to the general problem of inductive learning, ILP systems require that the background knowledge and its extension be represented in predicate logic, typically Prolog.
See Also: attribute-based learning, belief net, Logic Programming, Machine Learning, Prolog.

INDUCT-RDR

INDUCT-RDR is a Machine Learning algorithm that can learn using the Ripple Down Rules technique.
See Also: Ripple Down Rules, http://www.cse.unsw.edu.au/~s2176432/rdr.html.

Inference

Refers to the processes used to draw conclusions from facts and other premises or conclusions.

Inference Engine

A term used for programs or subprograms that are specialized for the drawing of inferences. The term refers to that part of the program that performs the inference, rather that the data and premises that provides the knowledge.

influence diagram

A decision tree with additional nodes for utilities, and costs.
See also: decision tree.

information extraction

Information extraction is an area in Natural Language Parsing (NLP). It combines NLP tools such as parsing, tagging, and dictionaries with expert systems or Machine Learning tools to identify the concepts contained in a text and to structure those concepts into a coherent framework.
See Also: MetLife's Intelligent Text Analyzer.

Information Retrieval

Refers to techniques for the storage and retrieval of documents.

information table

In Rough Set Theory, a data matrix is called an information table. The rows correspond to cases and the columns to attributes. The attributes are partitioned into two types: condition attributes and decision attribute(s).
See Also: Rough Set Theory.

Inheritance Hierarchy

An organization of objects, often in a tree-shaped hierarchy, such that each object in a tree inherits the properties of an object "above" it and passes all of its properties to any objects that inherit from it.

input layer

The nodes of a neural network that can accept external input are traditionally referred to as an input layer, a reference to the typical layered network diagram of a neural network.
See Also: hidden layer, neural network, output layer.

input window

See: shift register.

in-sample testing

In-sample testing is a generic name for techniques that estimate the error rates from the same data that are used to develop the model.

This generally results in "unreasonably" low estimates of the error in the model, which are much lower than the error for independent samples.
See Also: bootstrapping, Cross-validation, out-of-sample testing.

instance

An instance of a class is an item that is a member of the class.
See Also: case, class.

instance link

In a knowledge representation scheme, an instance link is a link from a general class of objects, such as CheckingAccounts in a banking schema, to a particular instance, such as a particular person's checking account. The particular account will inherit all the slots that the general class had, such as interest rates, monthly charges, and an account number.
See Also: Semantic Network.

instance slot

An instance slot is a slot in a class that is used to describe properties of instances of that class. It does not describe the class itself.
See Also: class, own slot.

instantaneous training

See: on-line training.

instantiation

When an attribute or a relation is assigned a value, it is said to be instantiated.

INTELLECT

INTELLECT is the name of a natural language interface to database systems. It is one of the first commercial successful AI programs and is sold by Artificial Intelligence Corporation of Waltham, Massachusetts.

Intelligent Computer-Aided Instruction (ICAI)

The application of AI principles and techniques to computer-aided teaching programs. This program differs from traditional Computer-

Aided Instruction (CAI) by allowing an interaction with the student. Rather than using simple scripts to represent the subject matter, the information is stored in the form of knowledge networks, containing facts about the subject matter and rules and relationships between the facts. Traditional CAI programs are limited to the scripts devised by the author, while ICAI programs are reactive, changing their behavior in reaction to the student's response. These programs also include student models, which track which areas of the knowledge network the student seems to understand and diagnostic error rules, which attempt to diagnose the "why" of the student's errors. Finally, these programs typically have a natural language interface.

Intellipath

Intellipath is an expert system for clinical pathologists. It uses a Bayesian Network to provide diagnostic capabilities to assist in differential diagnoses. It also has the capability to explain decisions and can recommend tests and data to confirm its diagnoses.

Intension of a concept

The Intension of a concept is the set of all properties that are satisfied or shared by all members of an extension of a concept. The intension and extension can be used by Machine Learning and knowledge discovery techniques to generalize new cases and generate new concepts.
See Also: Extension of a concept, Knowledge Discovery in Databases.

interlingua

A term used in machine translation to describe artificial metalanguages. Direct translation between a set of languages would require a translator for every pair. For three languages, this would require three translation pairs, four languages would require six pairs, five languages would require 15, and so on. On the other hand, if the items are translated from a source language into a single interlingua and thence into the target language, the problem only requires maintaining translators from each language into and from the interlingua.

INTERLISP

See: LISP.

internal disjunction

An attribute level disjunction formed by taking disjunctions on the values of attributes. Manipulation of conjuctive forms that allow internal disjunctions can cause combinatorial problems.

International Classification of Diseases, 9th revision (ICD-9)

The International Classification of Diseases, 9th edition, (ICD-9) provides a classification scheme for diseases and acts as an ontology for diseases in systems such as MetLife's Intelligent Text Analyzer (MITA).
See Also: MetLife's Intelligent Text Analyzer, ontology, SNOMED.

Internet Learning Agent (ILA)

A Data Mining tool for use on the World Wide Web.

intersection

The intersection of two sets, A and B—written as A∩B—is a set containing all elements in both A and B. It is also a LISP function that takes two lists as arguments and returns a list containing the elements common to both arguments.
See Also: list, LISP, union.

INTERNIST

A program to assist in medical diagnosis, written in the mid-1970s. It later became Caduceus.
See Also: Caduceus.

interpolation net

An interpolation net is a two-layer neural network that is used to estimate a response based on input values. The first layer computes the Gaussian distance between each of the nodes and the input point, and the second layer combines each of the node's values according to the Gaussian weights.
See Also: Gaussian function.

interpreter

A computer program that reads input files and immediately translates and executes the program. Examples include LISP and BASIC interpreters, which allow you to write and evaluate code dynamically. An interpreted program is typically slower than a compiler version of the same program. However, it usually takes less time to interpret and test a program than it does to compile the complete program.

interval attribute

An interval valued attribute uses numeric values for which the relative differences are meaningful whose meaning would not be changed if the values were translated or multiplied by a positive constant. The zero in these scales is arbitrary. A familiar example would be temperature in degrees Celsius. The difference between 20 and 30 is twice as large as the difference between 20 and 25, but the 30-degree temperature is not 50 percent larger than the 20-degree temperature. The zero value in this scale is arbitrary.

This level of attribute supports the same operations as do ordinal and nominal value attributes as well as sums and differences. Scale and origin dependent operations, such as multiplication and exponentiation, do not have an intrinsic meaning for these type of attributes.
See Also: Machine Learning, nominal (attribute type), ordinal attribute, ratio attribute.

irreflexive

An irreflexive binary relationship R is one in which the relationship a ^Ra is not true. An example would be the relationship "is a parent of".
See Also: partially ordered set, reflexive.

itemset

Used in Data Mining to denote groupings of attributes. For example, the set of all 2-itemsets in a database, would be the set of all pairs of attributes. In the mining of association rules, interest is usually focused on k-itemsets where all k elements are true, and a "large" number of cases exist. The number (or proportion) of cases in an itemset is referred to as the "support" for the itemset.

J

Java

Sun Microsystems developed this object-oriented computer language in the 1990s to support programming for small devices. It has since become very popular on the World Wide Web (WWW) and is making inroads into general programming. Java is syntactically similar to C and C++ but has many semantic similarities to languages such as MODULA.
See Also: C, C++.

JavaBayes

JavaBayes is the first full implementation of a Bayesian Network in the Java programming language. In this system, a user can assign values to some of the variables in the network (sometimes called Evidence). The system will use these values to infer the optimal levels of the remaining values (also called a configuration.) It can also derive such quantities as marginal distributions for any of the unknown values, average values for univariate functions, and maximum a posteriori configurations and univariate functions. The system is freely available and runs on multiple platforms.
See Also: http://www.cs.cmu.edu/People/javabayes/index.html.

Jeremiah

Jeremiah is a commercial rule-based/fuzzy logic system that provides dentists with orthodontic treatment plans for cases suitable for treatment by general dental practitioners with a knowledge of removable orthodontic techniques.
See Also: Orthoplanner, http://www-uk.hpl.hp.com/people/ewc/list-main.html.

Jess

Jess (currently version 4.1) is a version of the CLIPS expert system that is written entirely in Java. Ernest Friedman-Hill is developed Jess at Sandia Laboratories and it is available through the World Wide Web (WWW). This system allows you to build Java applications and applets that have the ability to "reason."
See Also: CLIPS, Java, http://herzberg.ca.sandia.gov/jess.

jitter

One method to avoid over-fitting is to use jittering in training data. Noise is deliberately added to the training data. This is a sampling-based form of smoothing and works well when the model is trying to estimate a smooth relationship. This technique will, however, obscure any discontinuities that are in the underlying relationship. This is closely related to such techniques as kernel techniques, where the data points are replaced by multivariate distributions and ridge regressions, which add "prior" information to the regression function. Choosing the size of the jitter is equivalent to the statistical problem of choosing a kernel bandwidth or the size of the prior information in the ridge regression.
See Also: kernel function, kernel regression.

J-measure

The J-measure is a scoring rule for association rules. In evaluation of a rule of the form "if X occurs, then Y will occur," with a given frequency (support) and confidence, the J-measure provides a single measure that trades off rule frequency and rule confidence. The J-measure is the product of the probability of X, the IF part of the rule, with the cross-entropy of the rule.
See Also: association rules, cross entropy.

join graph

See: junction graph.

join tree

See: junction tree.

joint distribution

See: multivariate probability distribution.

junction graph

A junction graph is formed from the cliques of a graphical model. Each clique becomes a node in this graph, and any nodes that share a common variable are connected through an intersection node, labeled with the name of that common variable. Note that the junction graph is usually formed from the moral graph of the graphical model.

Figures J.1 shows a directed acyclic graph, its junction graph, and its junction tree.

See Also: clique, junction tree, Markov tree, moral graph.

Figure J.1—Directed Acyclic Graph

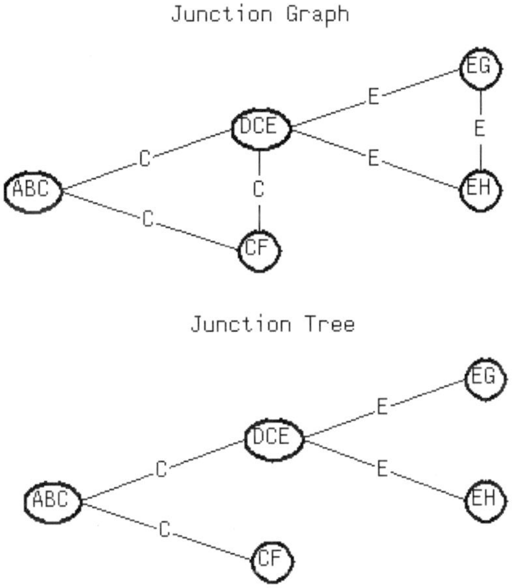

junction tree

A junction tree is a spanning Markov tree formed from a junction graph. Any two attributes in two nodes are also on the path between the two variables. A well-constructed junction tree lowers the computational costs on a graphical model. They are used to derive conditional distributions from belief nets after evidence (data) on some of the variables has been obtained.

See Also: junction graph, Markov tree.

K

KAISSA

A Russian chess playing program that won the 1974 world chess computer championship.

Kalman filter

An adaptive linear filter or controller. When the measurements and error terms meet certain distributional criteria, this filter will quickly converge to optimal behavior.

Karnaugh map

A Karnaugh map is a method for displaying multi-attribute binary relations in a single cross-classification. The attributes are combined into two groups, and, within each group, are stacked to create two compound attributes. These are used to create a cross-classification with the response as the entry. Table K.1 shows a hypothetical truth table for three attributes, and Table K.2 shows Karnaugh map of Table K.1.

Table K.1—Truth Table

A	B	C	Result
0	0	0	a
0	0	1	b
0	1	0	c
0	1	1	d
1	0	0	e
1	0	1	f
1	1	0	g
1	1	1	h

Table K.2—Karnaugh Map

{A,B}	C=0	C=1
{0,0}	a	b
{0,1}	c	d
{1,0}	e	f
{1,1}	g	h

Karnaugh maps are used to simplify logical relationships and have been generalized for use in generalized logic diagrams and decision tables.

See Also: decision table, dimension stacking, Generalized Logic Diagrams.

KDD

See: Knowledge Discovery in Databases.

KDDMS

See: Knowledge and Data Discovery Management Systems.

KDT

See: Knowledge Discovery in Text.

k-d tree

A k-d tree provides a fast method for finding the nearest neighbors of a case in a high dimensional space. The entire space of cases or examples is stored as a decision tree. The non-terminal nodes represent decisions, or tests, that are used to narrow the set of candidate points recursively. The final node points to a set of possible matches or neighbors, which can be examined individually to determine the best match. This method allows procedures to identify neighbors with a logarithmic time rather than linear time

See Also: nearest neighbor.

kernel function

Many local learning algorithms use a weighted distance function to control the influence that distant cases have on a prediction. The weighting function is referred to as a kernel function. They are typically positive functions that integrate to one and have compact support (i.e., they are only positive for "local" cases). Examples would

include a radial basis function, used in some forms of neural nets, and a simple windowing function, which is defined to be one over a small range and zero otherwise.
See Also: LOESS, radial basis function.

kernel regression

A technique that bases predictions, or classifications, on the values of other cases that is within a given distance of the target case or observation. Typically, the influence of other cases is weighted by their distance from the target.
See Also: classification, Data Mining, regression.

KIF

See: Knowledge Interchange Format.

Kinematics

The study of spatial relationships between a configuration of mechanically interconnected and constrained rigid bodies.

Kismet

Kismet is part of the COG project. It is developing a robot designed for social interactions with humans. It focuses on teaching robots to engage in meaningful social exchanges with humans. The researchers in this project have chosen to model a caretaker-infant dyad where the human acts as the caretaker. Kismet is capable of a wide range of facial expressions.
See Also: COG project, http://www.ai.mit.edu/projects/kismet.

KL-ONE

A frame-based language for Knowledge Representation. R. Brachman developed KL-ONE in 1978 at BBN. It extended the ideas of Frame Representation Language (FRL) and Knowledge Representation Language (KRL) by including the capability to have constraints involving more than one slot (referred to as a "role" in KL-ONE). For example, a persons birthday slot must be less than the value in his/her high-school graduation day slot.

KNOBS

A planning system for Air Force Tactical missions.
See Also: Planning.

KnowEXEC

KnowEXEC is an extension of CLIPS. KnowEXEC is designed to be used as a helper extension in the Netscape Navigator Browser. It allows users to download and execute CLIPS knowledge bases.
See Also: CLIPS, http://users.aimnet.com/~yilsoft/softwares/knowexec/keinfo.html.

knowledge

The values of the parameters and rules that have been learned (estimated) from data in a model represent the "knowledge" of a model.

Knowledge and Data Discovery Management Systems (KDDMS)

Knowledge and Data Discovery Management Systems (KDDMS) are used to refer to proposed "second generation" Knowledge Discovery in Databases (KDD) systems, which would include extended database support and KDD query languages.

Knowledge Base

The collection of facts available to a program. Just as a database can be thought of as an organized collection of data, a knowledge base is an organized collection of "facts" or statements of relationships between objects. The particular organization of the knowledge is dictated by the knowledge representation method chosen by the program designer.

knowledge compilation

The term knowledge compilation has been used for the process of representing a propositional formula by its optimal upper and lower Horn approximations. These approximations are also known as the Horn envelope and Horn Core of the formula.
See Also: Horn Core, Horn envelope.

Knowledge Discovery in Databases (KDD)

Knowledge Discovery in Databases is the general process of discovering knowledge in data. This process includes nine steps. First is the development of an understanding of the application domain and the goal of the process. The second step involves the creation of a data set (the "data mine"), which leads to the third and fourth steps of cleaning, preprocessing, reduction, and projection. The fifth step is choosing the Data Mining method to match the goals chosen in the first step. The sixth and seventh steps are the exploratory analysis and model/hypothesis selection, followed by the actual mining process. The final two steps involve the interpretation of the patterns and acting on the derived knowledge. In summary, KDD is an attempt to automate the entire art and practice of data analysis and database inference.

Knowledge Discovery in Text (KDT)

This sub-discipline of Knowledge Discovery in Databases (KDD) extends and adapts the techniques of KDD, which is primarily oriented toward data that can be represented numerically or structured into tables and database, into the area of textual collections, which lack the structure and numeric content of databases. An example would be a tool to analyze financial news, possibly applied to a portfolio advisor.

knowledge engineering

This term is used to refer to the techniques and tools used to build expert systems. A knowledge engineer is one who implements the process of interviewing domain experts or reviewing case histories and representing the extracted "knowledge" in an expert system or rule base.

See Also: Expert Systems.

Knowledge Interchange Format (KIF)

The Knowledge Interchange Format is a proposed standard for the specification and interchange of ontologies. It uses a first-order calculus and allows the definition of objects, functions, and relations, and the representation of Meta-Knowledge. The use of this format would allow ontologies to be exchanged between knowledge systems, as well as allow systems to import "foreign" ontologies. The

developers of this format have also released a number of ontologies as well as an ontology editor.
See Also: Knowledge Query and Manipulation Language, ontology, Ontolingua, http://www-ksl.svc.stanford.edu:5915/.

Knowledge Query and Manipulation Language (KQML)

The Knowledge Query and Manipulation Language (KQML) is both a language and protocol for exchanging information and knowledge between software agents and knowledge bases. It is extensible and specifies the operations that an agent or KnowledgeBase will allow to be performed by other agents or another Knowledge Base. It also specifies the behavior of communication facilitators, a special class of software agents. These software facilitators are designed to coordinate the behavior of other agents.
See Also: Knowledge Interchange Format, http://www.cs.umbc.edu/kqml/.

Knowledge Representation

The Knowledge Representation of a program is the means by which a program is supplied with the information from which it reasons. The collection of information available to a program is often referred to as a Knowledge Base. In building a Knowledge Base, several issues must be addressed. These include the notation to represent knowledge, the allowed operations in this notation, a method of assigning meaning to the facts in the Knowledge Base, the choice of a declarative or procedural representation, and finally a method for organizing the knowledge (e.g., frames.) The Knowledge Representation also must match the inference scheme that will be used in the program.

Knowledge Representation, Analog

Schemes for representing knowledge can be generally be divided into two types: propositional and analog. In an analog representation of a situation every element appears once, along with all of its relationships to the elements. These representations can be manipulated by procedures that are often similar to physical procedures, whereas a propositional representation is manipulated by using general rules of inference. Unlike propositional representations, which tend to be discrete, analog representations are often in a form that can be continuously modified, as in the location of a vase on a table. The structural relationships in the representation are analogous to the actual relationships among the objects being represented, rather than being represented by truth-values attached to a proposition.

Knowledge Representation Language (KRL)

A frame-based language for knowledge representation developed by Bobrow and Winograd in 1977. This scheme included the frames of Frame Representation Language (FRL) and an added pattern-based inference method as well as a number of primitives for forming instances of classes.
See Also: Frame Representation Language, Frames, Knowledge Representation.

KnowledgeSeeker

KnowledgeSeeker is an early commercial classification tree program. Unlike Classification And Regression Trees (CART), it offered multi-way splits. It also used a different set of splitting criteria.
See Also: http://www.angoss.com/.

knowledge source combination

A technique used in speech recognition and other areas where multiple sources of information ("knowledge") are combined to provide the best interpretation of the input. For example, several alternate probabilistic methods might be applied to the same input and their scores combined to determine the "most likely" meaning of the input.

Knowledge systems

See: Expert Systems.

Kohonen network

A Kohonen network is a form of unsupervised learning in neural networks and is similar to a k-means cluster analysis. Each of the hidden units acts as a cluster center and the error measure is the sum of square differences between the input data and the nearest cluster center. The clusters compete with each other for the right to respond to an input pattern. There are several types of Kohonen networks, including Vector Quantization, SOM (self-organizing maps), and Learning Vector Quantization.
See Also: ftp://ftp.sas.com/pub/neural/FAQ.html.

Kolmogorov's Axioms

The Russian mathematician Kolmogorov provided an axiomatic basis for probability. Given a space of events S, and two subsets A and B of S, a function $P()$ is a probability if

$P(A) \geq 0$
$P(S) = 1$
If $A \cap B = 0$, then $P(A \cup B) = P(A) + P(B)$.

The three conditions are also referred to as Positivity, Normalization, and Finite Additivity. A slightly different form of the axioms substitutes Countable Additivity for the latter, allowing for countable collections of sets.
See Also: probability.

Kolmogorov complexity

This is a measure of the complexity of a pattern as given by the length of a code needed to reproduce it.

KQML

See: Knowledge Query and Manipulation Language.

KRL

See: Knowledge Representation Language.

Kullback-Liebler information measure

The Kullback-Liebler information measure provides a single-number summary for comparing two distributions or models. The distance between a true distribution (or model) and some other distribution (or model) is defined to be the average difference between the log density of true and the other distribution, averaging over the true distribution.

It can be derived as an information theoretic criteria and is often used for comparing various models for data. Since the Kullback-Leibler distance requires knowledge of the true distribution, related measures, such as the Akaike Information Criteria (AIC) are often used instead.
See Also: Akaike Information Criteria, entropy.

L

L_p
   See: Ordinary Least Squares

LAD
   See: Ordinary Least Squares.

lagged variable
   See: shift register.

Lamarckian evolution
   A form of evolution in which childern are allowed to inherit aquired characteristics as well as, or instead of, simple genetic characteristics.
   See Also: genetic algorithm, evolutionary algorithm.

Lambda Calculus
   The mathematics of functions that can take other functions as arguments and returns other functions as results. It forms the foundation for procedures in LISP and later computer languages.

language model
   In speech recognition, the language model is used to compute or assign the probability of a word sequence W from an input acoustic sequence. It is typically probabilistic and depends on previously derived grammers, as well as the application domain and the speaker.

LAPART
   An ART based neural network.
   See Also: ftp://ftp.sas.com/pub/neural/FAQ2.html, http://www.wi.leidenuniv.nl/art/.

last-in first-out

Automated reasoning systems can maintain a list of retained clauses for further evaluation. A last-in first-out strategy chooses a the most recently retained clause for further evaluation, as opposed to choosing the first retained clause to drive the reasoning.
See Also: OTTER.

latent variable

An unobserved or unobservable attribute in a system that varies over units and whose variation influences recorded attributes. This can affect the results of Data Mining or other efforts based on databases that were collected for other unrelated purposes, or data collections that are formed to capture "natural" data sources (e.g., credit card transactions). If the data were not collected with a specific purpose in mind and are missing some pertinent variables, then these variables would be "latent."

lattice

A lattice is a partially ordered set which has a least upper bound and greatest lower bound for all pairs of elements in the set. One implication is that conjunction and disjunction are well defined on any finite subset of the lattice, as the subset's least upper bound and greatest lower bound, respectively. The lattice is complete if every subset has both a greatest lower bound and a least upper bound (which is always true for a finite set). A complete lattice always has a unit and a zero.
See Also: partially ordered set, sublattice.

Lauritzen-Spiegelhalter Architecture

A method for propagating data through a join tree presentation of a belief net. It is slightly less general than the Shaefer-Shenoy Architecture, in that it requires that continuers exist for the tree.

Lazy Evaluation

Evaluation of a symbol or a goal only when the results are needed.
See Also: Eager Evaluation, Greedy Evaluation.

LDA

See: Linear Discriminant Analysis.

learning

Fitting a model to data.

leaf

A node in a graph that has exactly one arc is called a leaf.
See: graph, tree.

learning rate

In neural networks and other machine learning techniques, the learning rate parameter specifies how fast the model adjusts itself to new case. A fast learning rate leads to quick adaptation, but can lead to instability, while a slow learning rate can cause the algorithm to ignore new case. These parameters are often set by hand but can also be determined by techniques such as cross-validation.

learning rate

Many learning algorithms contain a parameter, called a learning rate parameter, that is usually between 0 and 1 and controls how fast the algorithms can change, can update their internal parameters in response to new data, or can minimize their errors while learning. If the parameter is too large, the model will continually overreact to new data or errors and fail to converge; if it is too small, it will react too slowly, taking a long time to converge.

In gradient learning algorithms, the learning rate is sometimes called a step size, since it controls the size of the step from one parameter vector to another for each step (iteration) of the learning (estimation) process. It can be set by hand or algorithmically.
See Also: gradient descent.

level saturation

Level Saturation is a first-in, first-out direction strategy that can be employed in an automate reasoning system, such as otter.
See Also: direction strategies.

LSM

A form of Kohonen network. The name was derived from "Learning Subspace Method."
See Also: http://www.cis.hut.fi/nnrc/new_book.html.

Learning Vector Quatization Networks

A form of supervised form of a Kohonen network. Each class has one or more codebook vectors assigned to it; and a case is classified by assigning it to the nearest cluster, as in a nearest neighbor algorithm.
See: Vector Quantization Networks.

least absolute deviations (LAD)

See: Ordinary Least Squares.

Least General Generalization (LGG)

Least General Generalization (LGG) is a cautious generalization technique used in Inductive Logic Programming (ILP). It assumes that if two clauses are true, then their most specific generalization is also likely to be true. The LGG of two causes is computed by computing the LGG of the literal terms in their heads and bodies, substituting a variable for the parts that don't match.
See Also: Inductive Logic Programming, Logic Programming.

least mean squares

See: Ordinary Least Squares.

least upper bound

In a partially ordered set, suppose that A £ C and B £ C. If C £ D for any element that also is [3] both A and B then C is the least upper bound for elements A and B.
See Also: greatest lower bound, lattice, partially ordered set.

LGG

See: Least General Generalization.

lifer

Hendrix developed this natural language parser in 1977 at Stanford Research Institute.

lift

Lift is a measure, adapted from direct marketing techniques, to describe the gain in classification or prediction due to a classifier or other model. If $f(Y)$ is the normal success rate, and $f(Y|X)$ is the success rate given the classifier, then the lift is measured as $f(Y|X)/f(Y)$.

When the model produces a continuous response, an alternate representation, called the cumulative lift, measures the lift. This is often plotted as the cumulative success versus cumulative categories of the predictor, plotted from best to worse. The figure shows a predictor (solid line) that outperforms a "non-informative" preditor (dotted 45° line.)

Figure L..1—Cumulative Lift

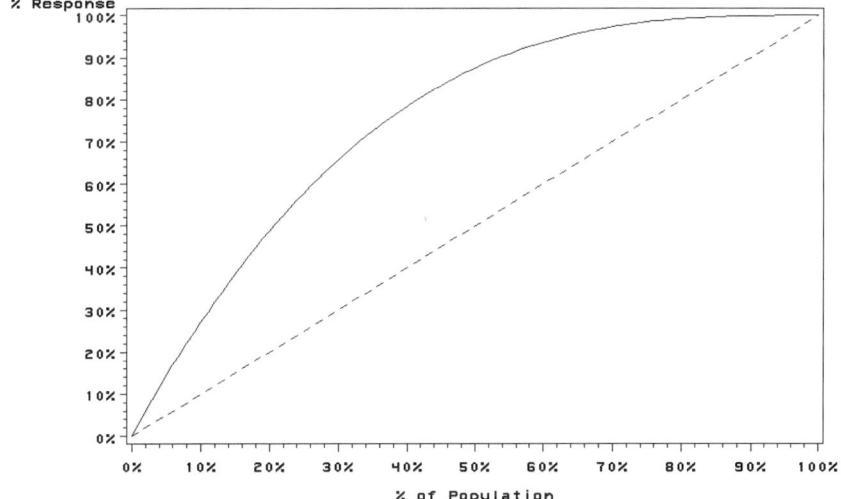

likelihood

In probabilistic and statistical methods, the likelihood is a measure of the evidence for the data when a hypothesis is assumed to be true. It is commonly used in Bayesian and Quasi-Bayesian techniques. A related measure, minimum message length, can be derived from information theoretic principles.

As an example, suppose you observe a data value X that is assumed to be Gaussian. The likelihood for that data when the assumed mean is, say, 5, and the variance is 10, is proportional to $e^{-((X-5)^2/2*10)}$, the kernel of a Gaussian distribution. A likelihood is typically calculated using the kernel, rather than the complete distribution function, which includes the normalizing constants.

See Also: Minimum Message Length.

likelihood ratio

When evaluating the likelihood of the evidence while comparing two disjoint hypotheses, H_A and H_B, the likelihood ratio is the ratio of $P(e|H_A)$ to $P(e|H_B)$. It is sometimes referred to as a Bayes factor for H_A versus H_B The posterior odds for any prior can be computed by multiplying this ratio by the prior odds ratio.
See Also: odds ratio.

Linear Discriminant Analysis (LDA)

Linear Discriminant Analysis (LDA) is a form of supervised learning, originally developed as a statistical tool, for finding an optimal linear rule to separate two classes (concept). The algorithm finds the line in a hyperspace that connects the centroids of the positive and negative examples and chooses a breakpoint along that line that best separates the class, weighting the coefficients to account for any linear correlations between the attributes. When the concept is linearly separable, LDA can completely separate the classes.

The "linear" in this term refers to the linearity of the function that combines the attributes, not to the attributes themselves. The attribute list can include powers and products of other attributes, as well as other functions such as spline functions of the "real" attribute. The rule is of the form a + b.x + c.y + d.z + ..., i.e., it is linear in the given attributes. The value of a, sometimes called the bias or the intercept, is often chosen so that any positive score on an attribute is taken to mean membership in one class, and a negative score to mean membership in the other.

It can be extended to learn multiple classes through a technique called Multiple Discriminant Analysis (MDA), which estimates k-1 linear functions to separate k classes on the basis of the attributes.
See Also: linearly separable, Machine Learning.

linear layer

Neural networks are typically arranged as layers of nodes. Each node (other than input node) usually collects its inputs and performs a transformation using an activation function. Activation functions are typically nonlinear (logistic functions or radial basis functions) but some networks such as nonlinear principle components or elliptical basis function networks include a layer of nodes that simply fit a linear model to their inputs. When the number of nodes equals the number of inputs, this is equivalent to performing an oblique rotation on

the input data; and when the number of nodes in this layer is less than the number of inputs, the layer is reducing dimensionality.
See Also: elliptical basis function network, nonlinear principal components analysis.

linear model

A linear model is an analytic model that is, in some sense, linear in the parameters of the model (rather than the attributes that are used to form the input to the model). A classic example is a linear regression, where the output is modeled as a weighted sum of the input or predictor variables. The weights are the parameters, and if they enter linearly, the model is a linear model. Models can also be considered linear if there is some invertible one-to-one transformation of the predicted variable that produces a linear model. An example of this would be the logistic model for binary data. The logistic model is a linear model for log(p/(1-p)), where p is the proportion or probability being estimated. An example of a non-linear model would be a linear regression modified to include an unknown power transformation on one of the input variables.

linear regression

A special type of linear model where the output (dependent) variable is a simple weighted sum of the input (independent) variables. When the weights are functionally independent, the model is then linear in the parameters. Classical linear regression also requires assumptions on a common error term across the domain of the predictors, as well as assumptions of independence and normality of the errors. (See Figure L.2.)
See Also: Data Mining.

linearly separable

A concept or class is said to be linearly separable in a set of (binary) attributes if the examples which are members of a class can be separated from the negative examples by a hyperplane in the attribute space. For example, for one dimension (along a line), a concept would be linearly separable if all the positive examples lay on one side of a point in the line and all of the negative examples lay on the other side. Both perceptrons and Linear Discriminant Analysis can learn concepts that are linearly separable.
See Also: Linear Discriminant Analysis, Machine Learning, perceptron.

Figure L2—Linear Regression

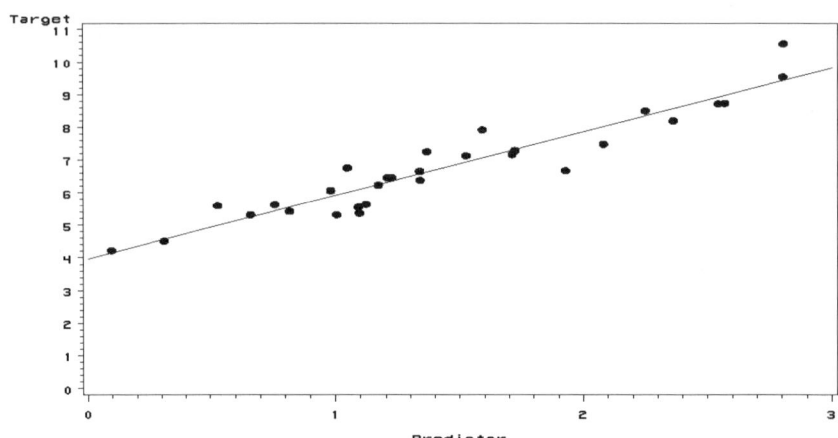

link analysis

Link analysis is a technique for exploring associations among large numbers of objects of different types. It is a relatively new area and is used in police investigations, fraud detection, epidemiology, and similar areas. Unlike many graph-based techniques, which induce a graph from a multivariate structure, link analysis begins with data that can be presented in the forms of links (e.g., telephone calls).
See Also: association rules, Bayesian Network.

linked inference rules

Linked inference rules relax the syntactic constraints of ordinary inference rules by allowing link clauses to serve as bridges between clauses that initiate inferences and clauses that complete inferences. UR-resolution, hyperresolution, and paramodulation can all be extended by allowing link clauses to link the nucleus with the satellite clauses.
See Also: hypermodulation, paramodulation, UR-resolution..

list

An ordered collection of elements, which may be other lists. In LISP, a list constructed as a cons cell, where an the left cell is an element and the right cell is pointer to other lists or to a NIL value. In PRO-

LOG, a list is a bracketed collection of objects, e.g. [a, dog, cow]
See Also: generalized list.

LISP

In 1956, John McCarthy invented LISP, the most popular language for AI work. It was designed from the beginning to be a symbolic processing language, which makes it admirably suited for AI tasks. It has been modified and extended many times since its original design. Some related or descendent languages include MacLisp, Common LISP, and Scheme.

LISP Machines

In the late 1970s and 1980s, dramatic gains in LISP processing speed were obtained by developing computers that were specialized for the LISP language. Eventually, general purpose computers became fast and cheap enough to take over the market for these specialized machines.

list

An ordered collection of items or objects. In addition to the properties it inherits from a set, It supports the notions of a previous and next item in the list and, usually, the notion of a first item ("head") and a last item ("tail").

Literate Programming

The practice of simultaneously programming and writing documentation is such a fashion that the result is designed to be read by humans while producing "real" computer code. The term was invented by D. Knuth during his development of the TeX system. Since the documentation is intermingled with the source code or pseudo-code, systems for literate programming are often referred to as WEB systems, following Knuth's nomenclature. This use of the term WEB considerably pre-dates its use in reference to the World Wide Web (WWW). It is a style that is quite suited to teaching purposes.

local

A local technique is one which only uses information from cases that are in some sense "close" to the target area. For example, classical linear regression is global because all observations contribute to the linear functions that are used to form the intercept and slope parame-

ters. LOESS regression is local because only the observations that are close to the target points are used in forming the estimate at the target point.
See Also: Radial Basis Function.

local operators
A term used in feature analysis to refer to functions that operate in a restricted neighborhood around a given item (e.g., a pixel in a picture).

local reasoning
Monotone logic had the property that if A => B, then A&C => also implies B. The logic have the attractive property of supporting local reasoning, where conclusions learned from part of the information hold for the entire set of information.
See Also: monotone logic.

local regression
Classical regression approaches assume that a particular structural relationship holds over the entire range of predictors. Local regression techniques assume that (usually) simple structures hold around each case in the data space, but that data points' "interestingness" decline the further one goes from its area. Local regressions can typically reproduce a classical regression approach when the global regularity holds and outperform it when the regularity does not hold. Smoothing splines, neural networks and regression and classification trees are all forms of local regression.
See Also: Machine Learning.

locally optimal searches (solutions)
A locally optimal search algorithm will use an algorithm that can find the best one-step or two-step result but is not guaranteed to find the globally optimum solution. Often improved results can be found by iterating the search or by adding random perturbations to a local solutions.

Loebner Prize
A prize awarded annually for the computer program that best emulates natural human behavior. The winner is determined at an annual

contest where judges sitting at computer terminals attempt to determine if the hidden respondent is a human or a machine.

LOESS

A local regression technique developed in statistics and used in Data Mining. A classic regression analysis uses all of the data to fit the regression line. Thus, all of the data will influence the prediction at every point. LOESS performs a local regression, only considering those points that are near the target point when making a prediction. "Nearness" is controlled by a window width selected by the analyst.
See Also: smoothing.

Logic

Means or methods for reasoning from a "known" or given set of facts and assumptions to other facts and conclusions. There are multiple logic systems including inductive inference, Nonmonotone logic, Predicate Logic, as well as multiple deductive logic.

Logic Databases

Also known as Declarative Logic Programming, these databases represent knowledge as logical relations and use deduction to solve problems. Logic databases are simply declarative, with no procedural element as in Logic Programming
See Also: Logic Programming.

Logic, Modal

A logic of necessity and possibility developed by C.I. Lewis (1883-1964). If a proposition is not necessarily false, then it is possible. A possible proposition may be also be true.

Logic Programming

Classical computer science deals with "how-to" knowledge, in contrast to mathematics, which deals with declarative (what is) knowledge. Logic Programming, which grew out of research in automatic theorem proving, attempts to develop mathematical relations that hold for multiple values, rather than a specific value. A logic program manipulates symbols and relations to deduce or infer new relations among the symbols.
See Also: Assumption Based Reasoning, Inductive Logic Programming, Prolog.

logical belief function

A belief function that assigns all of its mass directly to one subset of the frame is a logical belief function since it acts like an ordinary (Boolean) logic function.
See Also: belief function.

logistic autoregressive network

An autoregressive network where the probability of the current node is a linear logistic function of the ancestral nodes.
See Also: ancestral ordering.

$$P(\mathbf{x}) = \prod_i \frac{e^{\sum_{j=1}^{i-1} x_i \theta_i}}{1 + e^{\sum_{j=1}^{i-1} x_i \theta_i}}.$$

logistic function

Usually refers to the cumulative logistic function where y=1/(1+exp(-bx)). This function is commonly used as an output or signal function for neural network nodes and as a link function in statistical generalized linear models, both for its simplicity and for theoretical reasons.
See Also: signal function.

logistic regression

A specialized form of regression that can be used to generate regression functions for binary and ordinal variables. It is a generalized linear model, using a logistic function to link the expected value of the response with the linear model. Among the reasons that it is preferred for variables of this type because it correctly handles the bounded responses and the dependence between the error and the mean. (See Figure L.3.)
See Also: Data Mining, linear regression.

Figure L.3—Logistic Function

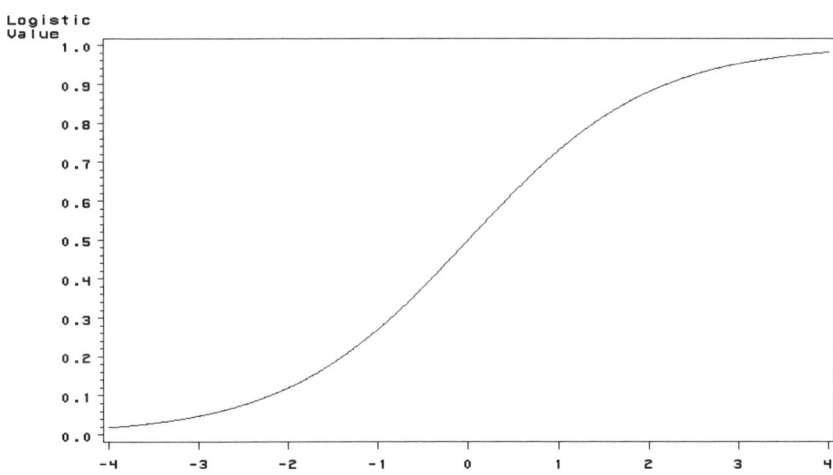

LOGO

In 1972, Seymour Papert at MIT invented LOGO, a programming language designed to teach programming to children.

long-term memory

In neural networks, the coefficients within the nodes, including their connectivity.
See Also: short-term memory.

look-ahead

Look-ahead techniques can be used to improve the results of global searches or a greedy algorithm. At each stage in a search, the program considers the results for several steps ahead of the current stage, and chooses the step that has the best result several steps ahead. At the next stage, the program repeats the search, possibly using results saved from the previous look-ahead. The number of steps that the program looks ahead is sometimes referred to as the horizon of the program. Large horizon values can lead to a combinatorial explosion

and prevent the program from reaching a solution in a reasonable time.
See Also: combinatorial explosion, greedy algorithm.

loss
See: utility.

lower approximation
In Rough Set Theory, the lower approximation of a concept X is the largest definable set contained in the concept (class) X. For example, in a medical database on heart attacks, the lower approximation of the heart attack concept would be the largest definable set of attributes among those cases with heart attacks.
A measure of uncertainty for the lower approximation is the ratio of the number of records in the lower approximation to the total number of records in the dataset. It is a relative frequency estimate, as well as a Dempster-Shafer belief function.
See Also: belief function, Rough Set Theory, upper approximation.

lower envelope
In Quasi-Bayesian representations of probability, the lower envelope of a probability is the minimum probability for a proposition over the (convex) set of probability distributions attached to those propositions. It is also directly related to the upper envelope of the probability of its complement: lower($P(X)$) = 1- upper($P(X^c)$), where X is the proposition, X^c is its complement, and lower(.) and upper(.) represent the lower and upper probability operators.
See Also: Quasi-Bayesian Theory.

lower expectation
The lower expectation of an action or a decision is the minimum expectation (average) of that action over all of the probability distributions that are feasible for that action. It has also been called a lower prevision for the action.
See Also: Quasi-Bayesian Theory.

lower prevision
Similar to the lower expectation, the lower prevision is the minimum expectation of an action over a set of probability distributions. The

term "prevision" is used in this context to emphasize the subjective nature of the probabilities involved
See Also: lower expectation.

lower/upper probability

Used in Quasi-Bayesian models for uncertainty, a lower probability is any non-negative function that satisfies the following four properties:

upper(X) = 1-lower(X^c)
lower(empty set)=0, upper(all propositions)=1
lower(x or y) >= lower(x) + lower(y) for disjoint X and Y
upper(x or y) <= upper(x) + upper(y) for disjoint X and Y

This is more general than lower/upper envelopes (e.g., all lower/upper envelopes are lower/upper probabilities, but not vice-versa).
See Also: lower envelope, Quasi-Bayesian Theory.

LTM

Used in the disccusion of ART networks to refer to long term memory.
See Also: ftp://ftp.sas.com/pub/neural/FAQ2.html, http://www.wi.leidenuniv.nl/art/.

LTM trace

The connection weights in an ART network.
See Also: ftp://ftp.sas.com/pub/neural/FAQ2.html, http://www.wi.leidenuniv.nl/art/.

LVQ

See: Kohonen networks, Learning Vector Quantization, Vector Quantization.

LVQ-SOM

A form of Kohonen network which combines features from Learning Vector Quantization network (LVQ) and Self Organizing Maps (SOM).
See Also: Kohonen network, Learning Vector Qauntization, Self Organizing Maps (SOM), http://www.cis.hut.fi/nnrc/new_book.html.

Lyapunov function

A function of a dynamic system that allows you to determine stability and equilibrium points of a system.
See Also: Robotics.

M

MACHACK 6

An early (1967) chess playing program. It used an alpha-beta algorithm with forward pruning to determine its moves. R. Greenblatt, D. Eastlake, and S. Crocker wrote MACHACK-6 at MIT.

MACE

MACE is an automated reasoning system that searches for small models of finite statements. It uses Otter langauge to specify problems and performs exhaustive searches.
See Also: OTTER.

Machine Discovery

A term for automated processes that attempt to discover patterns or knowledge in data.
See Also: Knowledge Discovery in Databases.

machine language

The binary instructions that a computer executes. Specific to a specific type of computer and (essentially) meaningless to people. It specifies simple operations in a form that can be immediately executed by a computer.
See Also: assembler, assembly language, compiler, interpreter.

Machine Learning

The capability of a program to acquire or develop new knowledge or skills. The study of Machine Learning focuses on developing computation methods for discovering new knowledge from data.

machine precision

The machine precision is the smallest number e such that $1+e \neq 1$. This number can vary with both the computer hardware and the floating

point library used to manipulate the numbers but is commonly taken to refer to the former.
See Also: condition number.

Machine Translation

The use of computers to translate automatically between two (or more) languages. This area has been a long-term problem in AI and has moved in and out of favor several times.

MacLISP

A derivative of the original LISP language that experimented with many new concepts that greatly influenced the development of Common LISP. Its successor was the New Implementation of Lisp (NIL).
See Also: Common LISP, INTERLISP, LISP.

macro

A term for a piece of computer code that expands to produce more code. This code can contain other macros and so on until their are no macros. This is used when a program is interpreted or compiled to simplify the amount of repetitive codes. Some language or interpreters only allow a single level of macros.

MACSYMA

A mathematics programming system that can be used to assist scientists and others in deriving, evaluating, and proving complex mathematics. Other programs include REDUCE, MATHEMATICA, MAPLE, and MATHCAD. The particular advantages and features of these programs change with time, but in general they greatly simplify much of the complex mathematics.

Mahalanobis distance

Mahalanobis distances are a generalization of classic Euclidean distances that allow that changes in some directions are harder or more "expensive" than changes in other directions. The relative "cost" of the differences are summarized in a weight matrix W, and the distance is calculated as the square root of $(x-y)'W(x-y)$, where x and y are the feature vectors of the two objects being compared.
See Also: Manhattan distance, metric,, Ordinary Least Squares.

mailshot response

See: database marketing.

Manhattan distance

The Manhattan distance between two cases is the function of the sum of the distances between the two objects on all of the attributes involved in the distance measure. This differs from the standard Euclidean distance, in that it does not require that a direct path between two objects be meaningful or feasible. It is named for the distance you would need to walk or drive between two points in Manhattan, as shown in the figure M.1.

Figure M.1—Manhattan distance

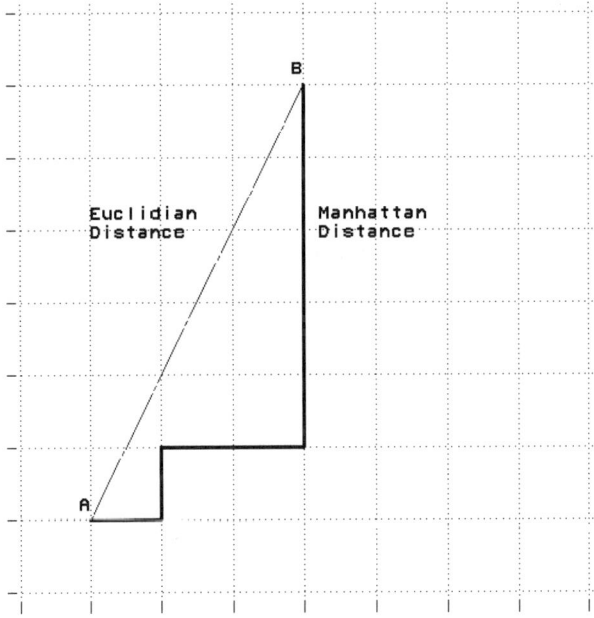

The metric can be used in both supervised and unsupervised Machine Learning algorithms.
See Also: Mahalanobis distance, metric.

Manipulator

A term used in Robotics to refer to a mechanical device that can manipulate objects.

MAP

See: Maximum A Posteriori.

Maximum A Posteriori (MAP)

In Machine Learning and statistical inference, the algorithm or person sometimes needs to choose a single hypotheses (or value) from many. If the system is based on Bayesian techniques, that choice will often be the hypothesis (or value) that has the Maximum A Posteriori (MAP) probability, i.e., the hypothesis that has the maximum probability after combining the data with prior information.
See Also: Bayesian learning.

MAPLE

See: MACSYMA.

MAPS

See: Modular Automated Parking System.

MAR

See: Missing At Random.

marginal distribution

When a multivariate probability distribution is summed along one (or more) of its attributes (dimensions), the resultant distribution is said to be a "marginal" distribution with respect to the original distribution. For example, the following multivariate distribution for the age and sex grouping of a specified population has two marginal distributions, one for age (summing over sex), with values of .2, .5, and .3 and another for sex (summing over age), values of .5 and .5. All three distributions are still regular probability distributions.

Table M.1—Marginal Distributions

Age	Female	Male	Age Marginal
young	.1	.1	.2
middle	.3	.2	.5
old	.1	.2	.3
Sex marginal	.5	.5	-NA-

marginalization

Marginalization is the process of reducing a multi-variable function to a function of (frequently) one variable, usually by adding or integrating the multi-variable function over all possible values of the variables being removed. The process is frequently used in, for example, belief nets to remove or absorb variables and constants that are not relevant to a particular question. For example, consider a model for a medical diagnosis of, say, heart disease based on a graphical model. After all available diagnostic information had been entered and propagated throughout the model, the model could be marginalized to reduce it to a "simple" probability statement about possible diagnoses for a particular patient.

Market Basket Data

A common problem in Data Mining deals with a type of data known as Market Basket Data. This is data where each record consists of a list of items that were purchased simultaneously or otherwise naturally grouped. The typical example would be purchase records from a retail store although the techniques could be applied in many other diverse problems (e.g., medical symptoms).

This label is commonly used when the purpose of the analysis is to discover association rules or dependency rules. The former are simply rules that state if item A is in the "basket," then item B is also in the basket, with two measures, the support (the percentage of cases that have both A & B) and the confidence (the percentage of cases with B among those that have A). The latter are a generalization of association rules that are covered elsewhere.

See Also: association rules, dependence rule.

Markov Chain

A model describing state transitions, where each state has a set of possible successor states and an associated probability distribution. The probability distribution depends only on the current state, and not on the history or path of states that were traversed to reach the current state. It can be represented by either its state graph, a directed graph with arcs showing permissible transitions or a transition matrix. In the example below, the transition matrix describes a three-state system. If the system is in the first state, it stays there with probability 0.5, or moves to either of the other two states with probability 0.25. If the system is in the second state, it will stay there with probability 0.3, move to the first state with the same probability, or to the third state with probability 0.4. When the system is in the third state, it stays in that state with probability 0.7 or moves to the second with probability 0.3. It will never move to state one from state three. The transition matrix forms a conditional in the probabilistic expert system sense.

Table M.2—A 3 State Transition Matrix

Starting State	Successor State		
	A	B	C
A	0.5	0.25	0.25
B	0.3	0.3	0.4
C	0.0	0.3	0.7

See Also: belief net, conditional.

Markov Chain Monte Carlo (MCMC) methods

A family of sampling-based methods for calculating the distribution of a belief net given a collection of data. Generally, the unobserved values in a belief net are randomly initialized. The algorithm then cycles through the set of unobserved values, sampling from its distribution conditional on the current settings of other values. This process is repeatedly sampled until sufficient data is gathered to generate the desired answer. It allows one to compute far more than specialized belief net architectures do, including complicated multivariate probabilities and expectations over complicated regions of the data.
See Also: belief nets, probabilistic expert system.

Markov condition

If an attribute Y is not an effect of X, then X and Y are conditionally independent given the direct causes of X.

Markov Decision Problem (MDP)

A repeated decision problem against "Nature" where the decision maker has complete information and strategic certainty, where Nature's next action depends probabilistically on its current state and the action chosen.

Markov grammar

A Markov grammar is an alternative to traditional statistical parsers. Rather than storing a series of explicit parsing rules and their associated probabilities, a Markov grammer stores transition probabilities that allow it to create rules on the fly.

Markov tree

A Markov tree representation of a graphical net is required to apply the fusion and propagation algorithm to that net. A tree is a Markov tree if its nodes are labeled with sets of variables and the tree has the property that for every subset of variables that are on the tree, the subtree constructed from nodes containing those variables is also connected.
See Also: belief net, cluster tree, junction tree.

Markov random field

A Markov random field is a general graphical model for the dependency of a set of variables represented as nodes. It has the property that the distribution of a particular node is only a function of its immediate neighbors, and the global distribution is a product of the clique potentials. For the example graph given under the factor graph entry, the global distribution can be written as

$$P(A,B,C,D) = P(A)P(B \mid A)P(C \mid A,B)P(D \mid C).$$

See Also: belief net, factor graph.

MART

A multichannel ART network.
See Also: ftp://ftp.sas.com/pub/neural/FAQ2.html, http://www.wi.leidenuniv.nl/art/.

MARS

See: Multivariate Adaptive Regression Spline.

MAS

See: Multi-Agent System.

match tracking

This term refers to an internal process in an ARTMAP network that is actrivated by a category mismatch in the F2 layer. It raises the F1 layers's vigilance parameter and causes the F1 layer to search for another category.
See Also: ART,ftp://ftp.sas.com/pub/neural/FAQ2.html, http://www.wi.leidenuniv.nl/art/.

MATHCAD

See: MACSYMA.

Mathematical Induction

Programs or routines that can derive new mathematical relationships based on a starting set of known relationships

Mathematica

A computer system for symbolic mathematics and mathematical/logical computation. It is a descendent of such programs as MACSYMA and REDUCE. Steven Wolram invented Mathematica which is available from the Mathematica Company.

maximin criteria

In a decision problem with a payoff function u(a,s), where "a" represents a member of the set of actions A, and s a member of the set of states S, the maximin value is the value of the action with the largest minimum payoff. The maximin action would be that action. It is an attractive action in decision problems where the opponent is assumed to be indifferent to the game.
See Also: minimax procedures.

maximum entropy principle

A principle for choosing a probability distribution to represent uncertainty in a system. The principle chooses the probability distribution

with the largest entropy from among the set of distributions that meets the constraints on that distribution. For example, the maximum entropy distribution for a continuous variable with a given mean and variance is the normal (Gaussian) distribution.
See Also: normal distribution

maximum likelihood

An optimization criteria used in Machine Learning, Statistics, and other models. The parameters are chosen to maximise the "likelihood" function of the responses, based on their assumed probability distributions. For example, a least squares fit is "maximum likelihood" when the response is normally distributed with a common variance given its mean. In neural networks, maximum likelihood is used for multinomial responses (i.e., multi-state responses).
See Also: likelihood.

maximum likelihood estimate

The maximum likelihood estimate is the value of the parameters in an estimate that maximize the likelihood function for the data, This determines the distribution that is most likely to have produced the data, based on the data and distribution alone. It differs from the Maximum A Posteriori (MAP) estimate, which is the maximum of the product of the likelihood (data and distribution) as well as other prior information on possible values of the estimate.
See Also: Bayesian Methods, likelihood, Maximum A Posteriori.

MCAR

See: Missing Completely At Random.

McCulloch-Pitts neurons

A neuron which produces bipolar threshold output.
See Also: bipolar.

MCMC methods

See: Monte Chain Monte Carlo methods.

MDA

See: Linear Discriminant Analysis.

MDDB
See: MultiDimensional DataBase.

MDLP
See: Minimum Description Length Principle.

MDP
See: Markov Decision Problem.

ME
See: mixture-of-experts.

Mean Square Error (MSE) criterion
The Mean Square Error (MSE) criterion can be used to provide a combined measure of the accuracy and reliability of a prediction. It is calculated as the squared difference between an estimated value or prediction and its true value. Analytically, it can be decomposed into two parts, a squared bias, which comes from the difference between the average performance of the model and the true average for that combination of attributes, and a variance effect term, due to the variability of the data.

The expected MSE is used to measure the performance of models that can be evaluated analytically, while the Predicted MSE or Predictive MSE (PMSE), which is computed on data by comparing the predicted value to the correct one, can be used as a model fitting criteria.
See Also: Cross-validation.

Means-Ends analysis
A problem-solving technique where the current state is compared to the desired end, and a new move is chosen based on what currently seems reasonable. It was first used in the CPS program, and has since been used in programs such as FDS, STRIPS, ABSTRIPS, and MPS.
See Also: ABSTRIPS, FDS, General Problem Solving, MPS, STRIPS.

member
A member of a set is an element that is in a set. The corresponding LISP function examines a list to determine if an element is a member

of that list. If it is, it returns the that element and the tail of the list; otherwise it returns a empty list.
See Also: list, LISP.

membership function

A function m(A,x), which returns the truth-value of a object or set. Typically used in fuzzy logic, where it measures an objects membership in a set. In the latter case, the membership function can range from 0, taken to mean no membership in the set A, to 1, taken to mean complete membership in A.
See Also: Indicator function.

membership query

In Machine Learning, the learner sometimes needs to query an external source to ask questions of a "teacher." When it asks a question such as "Is a robin a bird" while trying to learn the concept of bird, it is performing a membership query.
See Also: concept learning, equivalence query, Machine Learning.

Merge-Purge

A Knowledge Discovery in Databases-based (KDD-based) system developed in the mid-1990s to identify duplicate records in large databases. It has been successfully applied to the identification of duplicate welfare claims in data from the Welfare Department of the State of Washington.
See Also: Knowledge Discovery in Databases.

Merge/Purge Problem

In Knowledge Discovery in Databases (KDD) and data warehousing, a common problem involves the merging of multiple large databases from different sources, with different representations. The data has to be cleaned and joined into a single homogeneous whole before the KDD process can begin. This important process is known by several names, including the Merge/Purge problem, record linkage, instance identification, semantic integration, and data cleansing.

merit function

In many problem areas, the algorithms require a numerical method for measuring how "good" a solution, choice, or attribute is for a given purpose. The function used to assign a value to one of these is

metadata 186

referred to as a merit function. Common merit functions are least squares or, more generally, maximum likelihood, information gain or entropy, and Gini criteria.

metadata

Data about data. Used in Data Mining and data warehousing to refer to data about the meaning and range of attributes, their relationships and locations. Metadata supplies the context to understanding raw data.
See Also: data dictionary.

Meta-Knowledge

A term to signify "knowledge about knowledge," where a program not only "knows" something (i.e., has access to a database of knowledge), but "knows what it knows."

Meta-Reasoning

The capability to reason about the reasoning process rules.

meta-rule

A rule about the properties and roles of other rules.

MetLife's Intelligent Text Analyzer (MITA)

MetLife's Intelligent Text Analyzer (MITA) is a large system textual analysis of life insurance applications. It uses information extraction techniques from natural language processing to structure information from the free-form textual fields. MITA uses an ontology constructed from the SNOMED system.
See Also: ontology, SNOMED.

metric

A metric $m(\bullet,\bullet)$ is a positively valued measure that satisfies several properties:

the measure from an object to itself is zero: $m(x,x)=0$
the measure is symmetric $m(x,y) = m(y,x)$
$m(x,y) <= m(x,z)+m(z,y)$

Measures of distance can be defined for single ratio and interval attributes, as well as for pairs of objects, based on their values or on

Boolean counts of, say, equality on attributes.

Some common metrics include the classic Euclidean distance (based on the sum of squared distances along a set of attributes), the Manhattan metric, the Mahalanobis metric, and counts of differences on attributes.

See Also: Mahalanobis distance, Manhattan distance.

MGCI

See: Most General Common Instance.

MGU

See: Most General Unifier.

Micro-Planner

A subset of the PLANNER language. It was the basis for the SHRDLU language and led to the development of the several other languages including CONNIVER.

See Also: CONNIVER, SHRDLU.

MIM

MIM is a commercial package for fitting graphical and hierarchical models to continuous and categorical data. It supports both automatic and user-directed model building through a command language or a graphical interface.

See Also: Bayesian Network, graphical model.

MIMD

See: Multiple Instruction Multiple Datastream.

minimax action

In a decision problem with a payoff function u(a,s), where a represents a member of the set of actions A, and s a member of the set of states S, the minimax action is the action with the smallest maximum loss. It is the best action in a pessimistic game, where the opponent has perfect knowledge.

minimax procedures

Minimax procedures are procedures that operate to minimize the maximum loss that can result from a move or plan. It is commonly used in game theory and related problems that assume an opposing player who knows as much as you do.

Minimum Description Length Principle (MDLP)

The Minimum Description Length Principle (MDLP) states that the best theory for a given set of data is one that minimizes the sum of the length of the theory and the length of the data when using the theory as a predictor of the data. The length of both is measured in bits and the encoding scheme reflect one's a priori probabilities. The MDLP can also be viewed as a Bayesian Maximum A Posteriori (MAP) estimate.
See Also: Bayesian, posterior.

Minimum Message Length (MML)

Minimum Message Length (MML) is a technique for measuring the complexity of a rule or set of rules, that is increasing in the complexity of both the data and the rule. Selecting the MML rule is, essentially, an implementation of Ockham's Rule. In this case, the complexity of an item is measured as the negative log (base 2) of its probability. It is proportional to the likelihood function.
See Also: likelihood, Minimum Description Length Principle.

Missing At Random (MAR)

If the probability that a response attribute is missing is independent of its value and but depends on the value of the predictors, it is Missing At Random. Likelihood-based analyses can ignore the mechanism behind the missing data, but many standard supervised learning techniques can produce invalid results if the missing cases are simply ignored.
See Also: Missing Completely At Random, non-ignorably missing.

Missing Completely At Random (MCAR)

If the probability that a response attribute is missing is independent of its value and of the value of the predictors, then it is Missing Completely At Random, and can be ignored in an analysis.
See Also: Missing At Random.

missing data

Many databases have cases where not all the attribute values are known. These can be due to structural reasons (e.g., parity for males),

due to changes or variations in data collection methodology, or due to nonresponses. In the latter case, it is important to distinguish between ignorable and nonignorable nonresponse. The former must be addressed even though the latter can (usually) be treated as random.
See Also: imputation.

MITA

See: MetLife's Intelligent Text Analyzer.

mixture-of-experts (ME) models

A mixture-of-experts (ME) model is a technique that allows a model to include various submodels or "experts" within the overall model. The experts are combined by a gate function that takes the individual experts' outputs and combines them to provide a final output. These experts are a form of local model that are optimal over restricted subdomains of the total problem domain. Their combination can lead to more accurate models than a single "global" model.

An example could be a medical diagnosis program, where each of the experts is a model for a particular disease type. Each expert could then predict the likelihood that a given patient has the special disease. The gate function could then combine the individual predictions using a "softmax" function or some other voting function.

An extension of the ME model is a hierarchical ME (HME) model. In this model, the experts are arranged in a tree, so that each expert's model is a mixture of the models "below" it on the tree. In this sense, Classification And Regression Trees (CART) or a decision tree is a very primitive form of HME.
See Also: Gate Function.

MLP

See: Multiple Layer Perceptron.

MML

See: Minimum Message Length.

Mobile Robot

A free-roving robot that is able to move through space to accomplish some task. In addition to the problems facing normal robots, these robots need to be able to locate themselves in space, navigate and/or find a route to their objective as well as performing their task upon

model 190

arrival. Examples would include Dante, a robot designed for space and volcanic exploration, or robots used for nuclear repair.

model

A mathematical, logical, or physical representation of a physical item or process or a concept. A model is typically abstract, in that it represents only a subset of relevant features of the thing it is intended to represent.

model equivalence

In many Machine Learning and Data Mining environments, multiple models can yield essentially the same predictions from very different sets of variables and premises. This can be referred to as model equivalence.

model-free

A "model-free" model, such as a neural network or a fuzzy system is a model that is too complicated to write down explicitly, or in which various behaviors of the input or output are left unspecified. For example, a simple linear regression model for three inputs and one output can be written down in a single line, whereas a multi-layer feedforward neural network could take many lines to write down and is thus model-free. The linear regression model is easily susceptible to analysis, and it is possible to determine many general optimality and other properties, while the neural net is more difficult to analyze and is thus proclaimed model-free. This usage is similar to the usage of the term nonparametric in statistics.

See Also: nonparametric.

modens ponens

See: modus ponens.

modens tollens
See: modus tollens.

Modular Automated Parking System (MAPS)
The Modular Automated Parking System (MAPS) is a fuzzy logic-based system developed by Robotic Parking to park and retrieve vehicles in garages.
See Also: fuzzy logic.

modus ponens
An inference rule that says the when X is true and the rule X implies Y holds then Y is true.

modus tollens
The modus tollens is a principle of (formal) logic that holds that the negation of a consequent implies the negation of the antecendent. Symbolically it is: p->q; -q; therefore -p.

momentum
The speed at which algorithms, such as neural nets, learn can be improved in certain situations by updating the estimates in some direction other than the current gradient. One useful direction to move is often a mix of the current best direction and the last best direction. This has the effect of reducing oscillations in the updated parameter values.
See Also: gradient descent.

monotone function
A monotone increasing (decreasing) function, such as an activation function in a neural network is a function whose value always increases (decreases) when its argument(s) increase.
See Also: neural network.

monotone logic
Classical logic is mostly monotone logic which has the property that if A=>B, the (A&C) also must =>B. This prevents a system based in monotone logic from retracting a conclusion based on new or conflicting evidence (propositions).
See Also: Nonmonotone Logic.

monotonic logic

A logic that assumes that once a fact is determined it cannot be altered during the remainder of the process.
See Also: MYCIN.

monotonicity

A condition that holds when a conclusion is reached earlier, it cannot be refuted by later facts.

moral graph

One of the steps in converting a Directed Acyclic Graph (DAG) into a junction tree is the conversion of the graph to a moral graph. A moral graph of a DAG connects all immediate parents of a node and converts the resulting graph to an undirected graph. The cliques of this graph are used to construct the junction graph and junction tree. The figures below show a DAG and its moral graph, with the added edges emphasized.
See Also: clique, junction graph.

Figure M.2—A DAG and its Mora Graph

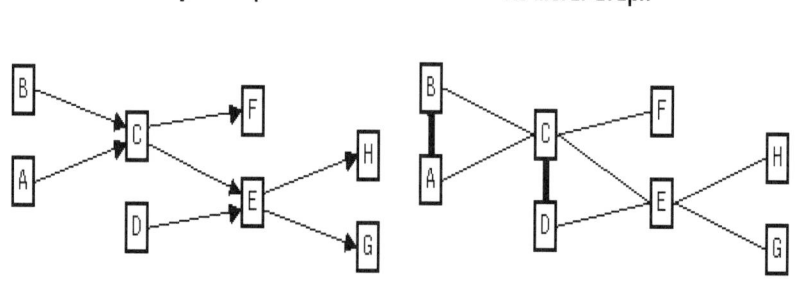

Most General Common Instance (MGCI)

The Most General Common Instance (MGCI) of two expressions A and B is an expression C that is an instance of both A and B such that any other expression D that is also an instance of A and B is also an instance of C.
See Also: Binary Resolution, Most General Unifier.

Most General Unifier (MGU)

Used in binary resolution, a Most General Unifier (MGU) is a substitution that yields the MGCI of two unifiable liters.
See Also: Binary Resolution, Most General Common Instance, Unifier.

Motion Analysis

Techniques used to reconstruct the three-dimensional motion of an object based on a series of perspective views.

MPS

A program designed to solve certain difficult puzzle problems, such as Rubik's cube. Similar to Means-Ends analysis, it tracks the current state and applies a series of operations designed to bring the current state closed to the final state. The operations were defined in such a way that any components that are at their final state are not changed by the movement of another, less important one.
See Also: Means-Ends analysis.

Ms. Malaprop

A natural language understanding system developed in the 1970s by E. Charniak at the University of Geneva.

MSBN

MSBN is a belief network manipulation and inference tool developed by the Decision Theory and Adaptive Systems Group at Microsoft. It provides a graphical interface to create and modify belief networks and can provide assessment of probabilities.
See Also: http://www.research.microsoft.com/research/dtg/msbn.

MSE criterion

See: Mean Square Error criterion.

Multi-Agent System (MAS)

See: Distributed Artificial Intelligence.

multi-class

Many classification systems are developed for binary data. Multi-class variables are those with more than two categories. This form of

variable is also known as multinomial.
See Also: ADABOOST.MH, binomial distribution, multi-label.

multi-label

Most class variables belong to a single class. Target variables that can belong to more than one class have been called multi-label. An example would be classifications on textual objects that can belong to multiple categories.
See Also: ADABOOST.MH, multi-class.

MultiDimensional DataBase (MDDB)

MDDB is a Case Based Reasoning system that is used to diagnosis dysmorphic syndromes, an area with poor medical knowledge by rich information. The system is based on records of over 3000 patients.

MDDB is commonly used in OnLine Analytical Processing (OLAP) and related systems. Rather than treat a database of multi-attribute records as a two-dimensional table with rows as records and the attributes (variables) as columns, the data is organized as a k-dimensional rectangle, with one dimension for each attribute. The dimension corresponding to the **i**-th attribute has **n**$_i$ levels, each corresponding to one of the values that the **i**-th attribute can assume in this representation. A cell at the intersection of specified values for each of the **k** attributes contains summary data on all the records that are classified as belonging to that cell. Typically, the marginal cells (cells where one or more dimensions have been suppressed) contain information on *all* of the cells in the missing dimension(s).
See Also: OnLine Analytic Processing, http://www.med.uni-rostock.de/HTML/english/research/gs52.index.html.

multinomial coefficient

The multinomial coefficient counts the number of ways that n items can be partitioned into K groups, each of size k_i, where each k_i ρ0, and $\Sigma\ k_i = n$.
See Also: binomial distribution, binomial coefficient.

multinomial distribution

See: binomial distribution.

Multiple Discriminant Analysis (MDA)

See: Linear Discriminant Analysis.

multiple imputation

A technique for "filling in" missing values in datasets. A rule for missingness is induced or assumed, and multiple imputed datasets are generated. Each is analyzed in a routine fashion, and the results adjusted and combined for the imputation.

Multiple Instruction Multiple Datastream (MIMD)

Multiple Instruction Multiple Datastream (MIMD) computer architectures. Where there are multiple processors, each performs a different set of computations on their own data.
See Also: Single Instruction Multiple Datastream.

Multiple Layer Perceptron (MLP)

The Multiple Layer Perceptron (MLP) is a neural network that has one or more hidden layers of nodes. Each of the nodes uses an activation function on the inner product of the inputs and the weights (i.e., a generalized linear model) and a "bias" setting.
See Also: activation function, Radial Basis Function.

multivalent

A logic or system that can take on multiple values. The values may be discrete, such as Lukasiewicz's trivalent logic [0, 1/2, 1], or continuous, such as probabilities or fuzzy membership scores, both of which are defined over the range 0-1. Typically, a value of zero implies absolute falsehood or impossibility while a value of one (1) implies absolute truth or necessity. Mutlivalent logics allow one to capture degrees of certainty, and support non-monotone logics.
See Also: fuzzy logic, non-monotone logic, probability.

Multivariate Adaptive Regression Spline (MARS)

MARS is an acronym for Multivariate Adaptive Regression Spline, a statistical technique for adaptively estimating a multi-attribute function. Like CART and other techniques, this method recursively fits a function to the data. It adaptively adjusts for regions with poor fits by adding spline functions to the model for that region.
See Also: Classification And Regression Trees, recursive partitioning, spline.

multivariate probability distribution

A probability distribution whose states are indexed by multiple variables. An example would be a bivariate distribution on Age and Gender, where Age had been categorized into three states of young, middle-aged, and old and Gender has two states of female and male. A multivariate distribution on Age and Gender would have six states (young female, young male, middle-aged female, etc.), each with an associated probability. The total of the six probabilities would be one.

mutation

In evolutionary programming, some mechanism for generating "new" behaviors needs is introduced, taking its name from biologic mutation. In biologic mutation, random errors can be introduced into offspring. In a similar vein, machine models will introduce variability into their offspring, in the hopes of improving their fitness.
See Also: Evolutionary Programming.

Mutual Subroutines

See: Coroutines.

MYCIN

A medical diagnosis system that was designed to be a consultant on difficult cases of meningitis or bacterial disease. It also included "certainty" factors in its diagnosis to indicate the strength of belief about a hypothesis.
See Also: Caduceus, EMYCIN, INTERNIST.

N

naïve Bayes

A naïve Bayes classifier, like a Bayes classifier, classifies on the basis of the predicted probabilities of the classes given the inputs. However, a naïve Bayes classifier treats the inputs as independent given the class, and estimates the distribution by simple counting, so that it is actually a frequentist approach. Its general form is

$$\Pr(Class_i \mid \mathbf{X}) \propto \Pr(Class_i) \prod_j \Pr(x_j \mid Class_i).$$

It is also known as "simple Bayes" or, more derisively, "idiot's Bayes." Its performance can be improved by techniques such as boosting or augmented naïve Bayes classifiers. Due to its simplicity, it is often used as reference point when comparing classifiers.

As an example, suppose you have a d-category classification problem, with three binary predictors X_1, X_2, and X_3, and you have a case with values 0, 1, and 1, respectively. Then the naïve Bayes algorithm would score the d-th category as:

$P(d|0,1,1) \propto P(d)P(X_1=0|d)P(X_2=1|d)P(X_3=1|d),$

where $P(\bullet|d)$ is the observed probability for the X value given the category.

See Also: Bayes rule, boosting, TAN Bayes.

Natural Language Generation

The complement of natural language understanding, Natural Language Generation is concerned with computer generation of text in order to explain items, ask questions, or provide direction.

See Also: Proteus, ERMA.

Natural Language Interface

A vague term, this phrase is often used to describe program front ends that appear to understand questions or directives provided by a user.

Natural Language Understanding

The capability of a program or system to understand (usually restricted) questions or directives from persons. A wide variety of techniques can be employed, such as pattern matching, syntactic parsing, Semantic Grammar, word experts, connectionism, etc.

NAVEX

A real-time expert system that uses radar data to monitor the position and velocity of the space shuttle. The program is rule based and uses frames.

NAVLAB project

The NAVLAB project is an ongoing program that is developing self-navigating robot vehicles. They have outfitted a series of vehicles (including cars, vans, and buses) with computer and sensor equipment with the purpose of developing vehicles that are capable of self-navigation, both on regular roads and as off-road vehicles.

Some of their projects include:

- NAVLAB 1
  NAVLAB 1 was built on a Chevy van and carried its own power supplies, computers, and computer operators. It was capable or reaching a speed of 20 miles per hour.

- NAVLAB 2
  NAVLAB 2 was built on a HMMWV and used the ALVINN navigation system. It was able to navigate at speeds up to 60 miles per hour. It has since been converted to use as an off-road robot.

- NAVLAB 5
  NAVLAB 5 is a modified Pontiac, augmented with computers, sensors, and actuators is designed to navigate on regular highways and streets. In a recent "No Hands Across America", NAVLAB 5 was able to navigate over 98 percent of the distance by itself. Assistants controlled the throttle and brake. It was controlled by the RALPH computer program.

See Also: ALVINN, RALPH, http://www.cs.cmu.edu.

NDS

A rule-based expert system developed by Smart Systems Technology and Shell Development Corporation to discover faults in the COMNET national communications network.

nearest neighbor

A term for techniques that predict or classify an observations based on the values of previous observations that are "near" to the target value in some sense. Typical distance measures can be based on a Manhattan metric or a function of the Euclidean distance. The reference set can either be the k nearest neighbors or all of the neighbors within a given distance. In the latter case, the technique can also be referred to as a kernel classifier or predictor.
See Also: Manhattan distance, Data Mining, classification, regression.

necessary and sufficient conditions

In developing descriptions for an object or for a rule to hold, attributes can have necessary conditions (values, ranges, etc.) that must hold for the rule to hold and sufficient conditions, meaning that if the condition on the attribute holds then the rule must hold. A necessary and sufficient set of conditions on a set of attributes is a collection of conditions that such that the rule is always true when the condition(s) hold and always are met whenever the rule is true.

Negation Normal Form (NNF)

In mathematical logic, both the Conjunctive Normal Form (CNF) and the Disjunctive Normal Form (DNF) are special cases of a negation normal form (NNF). A proposition is in Negation Normal Form when it is either a literal (i.e., an atom in the language), a disjunction of NNFs or a conjunction of NNFs.

negative evidence

Evidence that can be used to predict the non-occurrence of several conditions.

negative paramodulation

Negative paramodulation is an inference rule that can be used in automated reasoning systems. It reasons from negated equalities rather

than equalities. The rule is sound if the functions involved satisfy certain cancellation-like properties. For example, from AB and AC=D, we can derive BCD by negative paramodulation provided that a right cancellation holds for a product.
See Also: hyperresolution, paramodulation.

negmax

A technique for searching trees that is equivalent to the minimax procedure.
See Also: Minimax principle.

Nelder-Mead Simplex Algorithm

The Nelder-Mead Simplex Algorithm is simple method for searching for maxima or minima over smooth functions. For a k-dimensional problem, the algorithm starts with k+1 (often randomly chosen) starting values, and evaluates the function at each point. It looks to see which point has the highest value. If the difference between that value and the other is sufficiently large, it moves in that direction, and evaluates another set of points. When the difference between the points is not large it contracts the simplex around the center of the existing points and reevaluates the functions. When the difference is sufficiently small, it finishes.

Neo-Classic

An implementation of the ATT Classic system in C++.
See Also: Classic, C-Classic.

NeoGanesh

NeoGanesh is a knowledge-based system for ventilator management in Intensive Care Units. It interprets data in real time and can control the mechanical assistance to the patient.
See Also: http://www-uk.hpl.hp.com/people/ewc/list-main.html.

NEOMYCIN

A rule-based system derived from MYCIN. It is rule based and uses forward chaining.
See Also: MYCIN.

Netica

Netica is a commercial system for building, manipulating, and implementing expert systems based on the Belief Network and influence diagrams. The networks can be complied into a form suitable for fast reasoning, and can accept data in a wide variety of formats. These networks can be used to find optimal decisions, and can be used to construct conditional plans.
See Also: http://www.norsys.com/.

NETL

A language for the frame-based representation of semantic networks. It was developed at MIT and implemented in MacLISP.

NETtalk

NETtalk, created in 1978, is a classic example of a training multi-layer perceptron network that was used to study the conversion of text to spoken words. The network converted the text input into a series of feature vectors, which were then mapped into a sequence of phonemes and stress markers. When the system was trained on 1024 words extracted from a child's speech, it was 95 percent accurate in producing the correct phoneme, and achieved a 78 percent accuracy on a second set of about 450 words that were not in the training set. The network was fairly robust to variations in the node weights and required a much smaller storage space than comparable dictionary lookup programs.
See Also: perceptron, neural network.

Neural net programs

There are a large number of freeware, shareware, and commercial neural net packages available. Many of can be downloaded over the Internet. A large listing is maintained in the Sarle97 reference.

neural network

See: artificial neural network.

NEUREX

A rule-based expert system for the diagnosis of diseases of the nervous system. It uses both forward chaining and backward chaining, as well as MYCIN like certainty factors to assist in location and classification of the damage.

neuron

In biology, a neuron is a specialized form of cell that transmits electrical impulses. Generally it contains a central body or soma, input tendrils, called axons, and output tendrils, called dendrites. When a neuron receives a sufficiently large signal along its axons from other neurons or sensory nerves it generates an electrical impulse which travels to the dendrites. At the end of the dendrites there are synaptic junctions with other neurons or other outputs, such as muscles. The signal causes the synaptic junction to release chemicals that (may) cause the target to fire.

In neural networks, a neuron is a single processing unit that receives inputs from other processing units, sums or otherwise collects the inputs and generates an output signal as a (usually non-linear) function of the collected inputs.

n-gram

This is the general term for a related family of Markov techniques for modeling natural language. A *bigram* would model the natural language as a series of word pairs, and would model the language as a series of probabilistic transitions between pairs of words. Similarly, a *trigram*-based model would model the transition to the next word on the basis of the last two words. In general, an n-gram-based model would model the language based on the last n-1 words or units.

A popular "toy" based on n-grams is the variation of the so-called "travesty" program, where the input is a chunk of text, and the output is a bigram-based or trigram-based random walk down the transition tree. This is often used as an example of natural language generation. As the order of the approximation increases, the output begins to sound more and more like input.

Although presented above as a technique operating at the word level, it can also be applied at a "higher" level to various syntactic units (e.g., treating *the red haired boy* as a single "unit" rather than four separate words) or a class-based model, where the probability of a transition estimated from the class of the words comprises the vocabulary. An example of the latter approach would be to combine all cases of the pair *(fruit name) ripens* to estimate the probability that the word *apple* is followed by the word *ripens*.

NIL

A LISP symbol that represents an empty list.

NLPCA

See: NonLinear Principal Components Analysis.

n-monotone

See: Choquet Capability.

NNF

See: Negation Normal Form.

NOAH

Earl Sacerdoti developed this hierarchical planner in the mid-1970s at SRI International.

node

In a network or graph, a node is a point on the graph which can be connected to other points through arcs. Typically, a node represents some object or concept, and the arcs show connections between the objects or concepts.

node coloring

Node coloring is a technique for examining or selecting important nodes in a graph-based model. Each node in the target graph is evaluated with respect to some importance measure, and assigned a "color" to match the importance. A plot of the graph can then be examined to evaluate the important nodes. This is used, for example, in the examination of belief nets.
See Also: graphical model, belief net.

noise

In general, extraneous information or signals that masks or confuses the target problem.

noisy channel model

The noisy channel model is used in empirical natural language processing as a basic model for the statistical analysis of language. The model assumes that language is generated "clearly" and then passed through a noisy channel before being "received." The goal becomes to recover the original "clear" communication from the noisy input.

noisy data

Data which contain errors due to the way in which they are collected and measured are usually referred to as being noisy. Continuous measurements are often mixed with Gaussian noise, unless they are near the upper or lower bounds of the measurement system, in which case the noise tends to be skewed towards the center of the scale. Many statistical methods make the a priori assumption that the data is noisy.
See Also: Knowledge Discovery in Databases, Data Mining, Machine Learning.

nominal attribute (type)

A classical taxonomy for numerically valued attributes breaks them into nominal, ordinal, interval, and ratio types. An attribute is nominal if the meaning of the value doesn't change if you reorder the attributes or shuffle the values assigned to each meaning. An example would be a variable such as sex, which could be encoded as 0=male and 1=female just as meaningfully as using 1=male and 0=female.

Since the numeric values of these attributes are arbitrary, any operation beyond counting and manipulations appropriate to proportions are meaningless.
See Also: interval attribute, Machine Learning, ordinal attribute ratio attribute.

nonfactorial recognition network

See: Helmholtz machine, naïve Bayes.

non-ignorably missing

When response attribute can be missing due to another unobserved attribute of a case that is related to the response attribute, the data is non-ignorably missing. This can happen when, for example, a loan officer selects applicants based on an unmeasured attribute, such as a general impression. In order to construct a valid model for the response, the mechanism that causes the missing data must also be modeled.

See Also: imputation, Missing At Random, Missing Completely At Random.

NONLIN

A planning systems for turbine overhaul and naval re-supply missions (1984).
See Also: Planning.

non-linear model

A prediction or classification model that is not linear in its parameters. This does not usually include models that can be transformed or re-expressed as a linear model. For example, the model $y = \alpha + \beta x^\delta$ is non-linear in α, β, and δ, while $y = \beta x^\delta$ is not intrinsically non-linear as it can be rewritten as $\log(y) = \log(\beta) + \delta \log(x)$.
See Also: Data Mining, linear model, regression.

NonLinear Principal Components Analysis (NLPCA)

NLPCA is a nonlinear extension of a principal components analysis and can be used for data reduction/compression, and auto-associative model development. It is usually implemented as a multilayer feed-forward auto-associative neural network with five layers. As illustrated in Figure N.1 on page 206, the network has input and output layers, two "dense" inner layers with sigmoidal activation functions and a sparse linear layer in the middle.

The first sigmoidal layer models any complex associations in the input, the linear layer acts as a bottleneck to reduce this complex association into a small number of linear components, while the second sigmoidal layer expands the linear components into a model for the output data which, in this case, is the input data.
See Also: Principal Curves, Principal Components Analysis.

Non-linearity

A descriptor applied to functions or systems where the output or response is not proportional to the input or impulse driving the system over the (entire) range of system inputs. In a range where the system produces a relatively small response to large changes in the input, the system can be thought of as "damping" the input. Conversely, if the system produces a relatively large change in response to small changes in the input, the system is amplifying the input. An example of a linear system would be the relationship $y = b*x$. In this case the change in the output is proportional to the change in the input. A simple nonlinear system would be y=x*x. When x is in the range [-1,1], the change in y for small changes in x is smaller than the change in x (i.e., damped), while otherwise the change is larger (i.e., amplified). *See Also:* Robotics.

Figure N.1—Non-Linear Principal Components Network

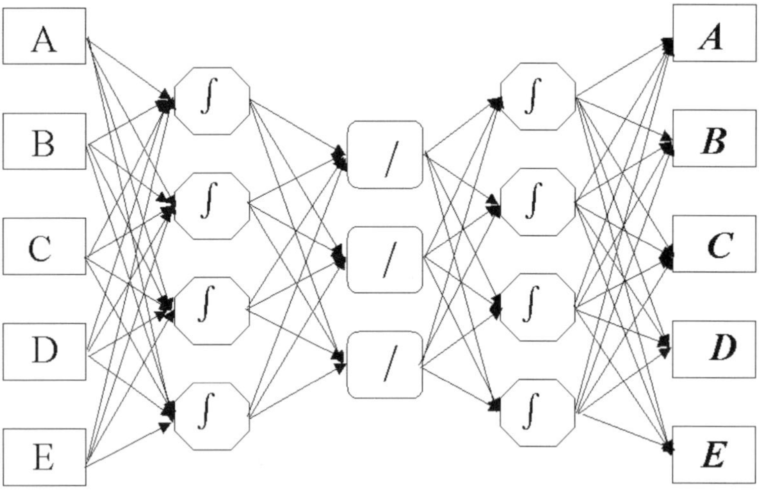

Nonmonotone Logic

Systems with default reasoning capability can draw conclusions that use assumed premises to compensate for partial information. These reasoning methods often have a nonmonotone property such that the addition of further information to the system can cause it to revise or abandon conclusions that were held prior to the addition of that data. This is contrary to standard logic where the conclusion based on a set of premises still holds when additional premises are added. For example, in mathematics, if a conclusion is known to hold when a given set of assumptions hold, then further assumptions (that agree with the earlier ones) can only strengthen the relationship or allow you to derive more restrictive conclusions. However, the original conclusions still hold. By contrast, a Nonmonotone Logic (e.g., a probabilistic one) might drop the conclusion with the addition of further information. For example, in reasoning about a series of games, such as a baseball or football season, one might conclude early in the season that a certain team was best. As the season progressed, this conclusion might be abandoned or refuted by the results of later games.

non-monotonic reasoning

Reasoning techniques that allow conclusions to be retracted as additional evidence is acquired.

nonparametric

A procedure is nonparametric if it does not rely upon "simple" parametric forms in the data, such as a Gaussian, Poisson, or binomial distributions. Typically, a nonparametric distribution relies upon the data to form the distribution, and derives its properties from the way the data was sampled (selected) and the way in which it is manipulated (e.g., randomization tests, classification trees). This makes the procedure more robust, but less efficient when a parametric distribution is reasonable. For example, a tree-based classifier can outperform a logistic regression when the data are not linear, but will be less effective when the data do meet the linearity assumptions of a logistic regression.

Note that nonparametric procedures essentially treat the data as the distribution, so that the base distribution involved is the observed data distribution, which is a form of a tabular distribution.

These procedures are sometimes called "distribution free," again meaning "doesn't use a simple parametric form," rather than "doesn't have any distribution."

See Also: parametric distribution.

non-terminal symbol

A symbol in a grammar that can be rewritten into further symbols when processing a statement.

See Also: production, terminal symbol.

Non-Von

A family of massively parallel computer architectures developed at Columbia University in the mid-1980s. The systems are characterized by a special form of "active memory", consisting of many elements each with a small amount of local memory, a specialized CPU, and I/O switches that permit the machine to be dynamically reconfigured.

normal distribution

The most well-known continuous probability distribution, the so-called "bell-shaped curve." The probability density function for this parametric distribution is:

$$\frac{1}{s\sqrt{2\pi}} \exp\left(-\left(\frac{x-m}{s}\right)^2\right)$$

where the parameters m and s are the mean and the standard deviation, respectively. Figure N.2 depicts a "standard" normal distribution, when the mean is 0 and the standard deviation is one (1).
See Also: probability distribution.

Figure N.2—Standard Normal Distribution

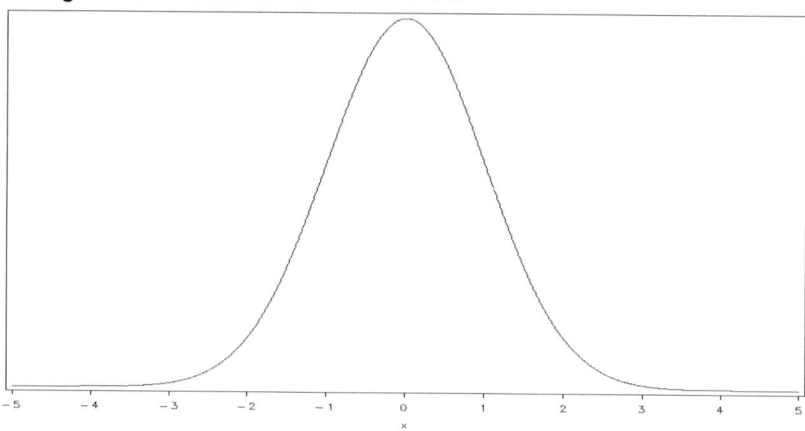

normalization

Usually refers to the process of dividing a data set by the square root of its sum of squares, so that the data set has a length of one. In reference to probability scores, normalization usually refers to the process of dividing the scores by their sum, so that the total of the scores becomes one. In the context of neural networks, normalization refers to the process of rescaling a vector to the (0,1) range.

normalized mutual information

Normalized mutual information is a variant of the entropy measure, used in creating classification trees. Entropy is known to favor multi-

way splits, and normalized mutual information penalizes multi-way splits by dividing the gain from a split by the logarithm of the number of leaves in the split.
See Also: C4.5, entropy.

normalized radial basis function (NRBF)

Normalized mutual information is a variant of the entropy measure, used in creating classification trees. Entropy is known to favor multi-way splits, and normalized mutual information penalizes multi-way splits by dividing the gain from a split by the logarithm of the number of leaves in the split.

not applicable data

Some attributes are not meaningful for all members of a universe and are termed non-applicable. An example would be the parity of person. It is only meaningful for adult females. Attributes that are only applicable for subsets of the data can cause considerable difficulty for Machine Learning and Data Mining algorithms that are not specialized to handle them.
See Also: Knowledge Discovery in Databases, Machine Learning.

NPC

An expert system developed by Digital Equipment Corporation (DEC) for troubleshooting DECnet-based computer networks.

NPPC

See: Nuclear Power Plant Consultant.

NRBF

See: normalized radial basis function.

NRBFEH

A normalized radial basis function (NRBF) with unequal widths but equal heights on each node.
See Also: height, radial basis function, width, ftp://ftp.sas.com/pub/neural/FAQ2.html.

NRBFEQ

A normalized radial basis function (NRBF) with equal widths and heights on each node. The NRBFEQ architecture is a smoothed

variant of the learning vector quantization (LVQ) and counterpropagation architectures.
See Also: height, radial basis function, width, ftp://ftp.sas.com/pub/neural/FAQ2.html.

NRBFEV

A normalized radial basis function (NRBF) with equal volumes on each node.
See Also: height, radial basis function, width, ftp://ftp.sas.com/pub/neural/FAQ2.html.

NRBFEW

A normalized radial basis function (NRBF) with equal widths but unequal heights on each node.
See Also: height, radial basis function, width, ftp://ftp.sas.com/pub/neural/FAQ2.html.

NRBFUN

A normalized radial basis function (NRBF) with unequal widths and heights on each node.
See Also: height, radial basis function, width, ftp://ftp.sas.com/pub/neural/FAQ2.html.

Nuclear Power Plant Consultant (NPPC)

The Nuclear Power Plant Consultant (NPPC) is an expert system to assist nuclear plant operators in determining the causes of abnormal events.

NUDGE

A frame-based front end for planning and scheduling algorithms. It takes incomplete and possibly contradictory scheduling requests and attempts to complete and reconcile them.

null

Generally, a null is a symbol representing an empty set or a zero (i.e., a symbol for "nothing"). In LISP a null is an S-expression that is both an atom and a list (e.g., "()";).
See Also: atom, list, LISP, S-expression.

Object Oriented Language

A computer language that treats data and data structures as objects, and which can send and receive messages or commands, and act upon those. This differs from traditional procedural languages, where the results are obtained through a series of procedures that is applied to the data.

Object Oriented Programming

See: object oriented languages.

Occam Algorithm

An Occam Algorithm is a general structure for applying Probably Approximately Correct (PAC) models. It has two basic steps. First, draw a random sample from the target distribution, and then return all the rules that are consistent with the concepts. The size of the sample should be large with respect to the number of attribute and the set of possible rules.

OCEAN

An expert system developed by Teknowledge for internal use by NCR. Similar to XCON, it checks system configurations.

OCEAN SURVEILLANCE

A rule-based expert system developed for the United States Navy to track and identify remotely sensed naval vessels.

OCR

See: Optical Character Recognition

OCSS

An expert system to assist chemists in synthesizing complex organic molecules.

odds ratio

The odds ratio is defined as the ratio of probability for a proposition to the probability against the proposition (P(A)/(1-P(A)).) A value less than one indicates the complement is more probable, while large values indicate a probability greater than one. When evaluating probabilistic data, the odds ratio for a proposition is commonly used.

off-line training

Iterative learning techniques that process the entire learning set as a batch and use the combined error to adjust the estimates of the model for the next iteration of the training process.
See Also: on-line training.

OLAP

See: OnLine Analytical Processing.

OLS

See: Ordinary Least Squares.

OML

See: Ontology Markup Language.

OnLine Analytical Processing (OLAP)

An approach to the analysis of data warehouses. OLAP tools primarily focus on supporting multidimensional analysis and in supporting and simplifying the data analytic process by persons. This is in contrast to a Knowledge Discovery in Databases (KDD) approach, which attempts to automate as much of the process as is possible.
See Also: Data Mining, Knowledge Discovery in Databases.

on-line training

Machine Learning techniques which continuously update their estimates with each new observation are using on-line training. Usually,

the learning algorithm can be re-expressed as a series of difference equations, so that calculations are quick and simple.
See Also: off-line training.

ONOCIN

A rule-based expert system to advise physicians about treatment protocols for lymphoma and Hodgkin's disease. Written in INTERLISP at Stanford University, the program uses both backward chaining and forward chaining.

Ontolingua

Ontolingua is a set of computer tools built around the Knowledge Interchange Format (KIF) that simplify the construction, analysis, and translation of computer ontologies.
See Also: Knowledge Interchange Format, ontology.

ontology

An ontology is a particular theory or model about the nature of a domain of objects and the relationships among them. Any knowledge model has an explicit or implicit ontology. A formal ontology includes a set of terms and their definitions and axioms (a priori rules) to relate the terms. The terms are typically organized into some form of a taxonomy. Axioms represent the relationships between the terms and can specify constraints on values and uses of terms. See the specific projects mentioned below for examples.
See Also: Cyc, Generalized Upper Model, Knowledge Interchange Format, PLINUS, Toronto Virtual Enterprise, Unified Medical Language System, Wordnet.

Ontology Markup Language (OML)

OML is an eXtended Markup Language (XML) application that extends the SHOE effort to add knowledge representation to the World Wide Web (WWW) into a full XML DTD. It also differs from the SHOE objects in that the OML files are intended to be separate from the HyperText Markup Language (HTML) pages to which they refer. OML also forms a subset of Conceptual Knowledge Markup Language (CKML), which allows richer knowledge representation capabilities.

See Also: Conceptual Knowledge Markup Language, Knowledge Interchange Format, SHOE, http://asimov.eecs.wsu.edu/WAVE/Ontologies/OML/.

operating system

A program that manages a computer's hardware and software components. This program schedules the operation of other programs and provides a uniform interface to the hardware. Examples include UNIX, DOS, and Windows NT.

operational definition

A definition of an idea or method that provides precise instructions on how to measure, observe, or implement the idea. For example, although probability is formally defined as a measure on a set that maps the set onto [0,1], an operational definition might specify probability as a function of the odds that would make a specific bet fair.

operationalization

The process of converting an abstract specification of a process into a set of specific, concrete steps to execute the process.

operator

A procedure or function to transform a problem or program state into another, usually simpler problem or program state.

OPM

A blackboard-based planning system. It attempts to plan sequences of tasks that satisfy conflicting goals and constraints. Given a list of tasks, their dependencies, priorities and constraints, it attempts to find feasible solutions to the problem.

opportunistic search

A search method used by systems that do not have a fixed approach to solving a problem. At various stages throughout the problem solving process, these systems can reevaluate their strategy for solving a problem.

OPS83

A derivative of OPS5, this is a compiled language for use in production expert system. It also allows procedural programming in the form of a PASCAL-like language. It was developed at Carnegie-Mellon University and runs on a variety of computers.

OPS5

A language for building expert systems. It keeps knowledge in the form of if-then rules and supports a wide variety of control structures, and an efficient forward chaining interpreter.

optical character recognition (ICR)

The process of converting the image of an item containing text into the character-based representation of the image. A distinct is often made between optical character recognition (OCR) and image character recognition(ICR). In this sense, optical character recognition indicates a real-time process, with the recognition engine directly receiving input from an optical sensor, while image character recognition indicates that the recognition engine is working from a stored image and is not necessarily operating in real-time.

optical flow

The pattern of movement of image features. A technique used in Motion Analysis and image understanding.
See Also: Motion Analysis.

Optimal Factoring Problem

Probabilistic Networks offer a very flexible way to represent uncertainty and its propagation through attributes. However, it can be very "expensive" to compute marginal and joint probabilities from large and complicated nets. One solution is to find an optimal factoring of the network for a given set of target nodes in the network that minimizes the cost of computing the target probabilities.
See Also: Bayesian Network.

optimal solution

A solution that is known to be best according to some criteria, e.g. an optimal cost solution would be one that is cheapest, while an optimal time solution is one that is fastest, but not necessarily cheapest.

ORBF

An acronym for "Ordinary Radial Basis Function."
See Also: radial basis function, ftp://ftp.sas.com/pub/neural/FAQ2.html.

ORBFEQ

An ordinary radial basis function with equal widths on each node.
See Also: radial basis function, width, ftp://ftp.sas.com/pub/neural/FAQ2.html.

ORBFUN

An ordinary radial basis function with unequal widths on each node.
See Also: radial basis function, width, ftp://ftp.sas.com/pub/neural/FAQ2.html.

ordinal attribute

An ordinal attribute is one that takes on values whose order has external meaning but whose particular values or differences between values do not have meaning. An example is an unanchored rating by a person on a nine-point scale. Assigning one object a value of three and another a value of six does not imply that the second object has twice the value of the first. It only implies that it has more. By extension, you could also infer that the latter also has more than any other objects that are rated as 1, 2, 4, or 5 by the same person, and less than objects that are rated as 7, 8, or 9.

The results of operations other than proportion level operations and order-specific counting (e.g., the number of cases with a score less than three) are dependent on the scaling, which is arbitrary. Using techniques designed for continuous measures on ordinal variables often leads to misleading or silly results.
See Also: interval attribute, Machine Learning, logistic regression, nominal attribute (type), ratio attribute.

Ordinary Least Squares (OLS)

An ordinary least squares (OLS) function uses the sum of the squared deviations between the observed and fitted values as its minimization criteria. This is equivalent to minimizing the Euclidian distance between the pbserved and fitted values. Variants include weighted least squares, which weights the individual squared differences according to a set of weights, Least Absolute Deviations (LAD) which minimize the absolute differences, and general L_p criteria, where the p-th power of the absolute difference is minimized. OLS and LAD are L_2 and L_1, respectively.

OLS is known in the neural network literature as "least mean squares." The same acronym has been used in the neural network literature as Orthogonal Least Squares a technique for forward stepwise selection in Radial Basis function (RBF) networks. The latter technique starts with a large set of candidate points and selects a subset that is useful for predictions.
See Also: Radial Basis Function.

orthographic projection

A method to represent a three-dimensional object in a two-dimensional space (i.e., on a paper or screen). A point (x,y.z) in three-dimensional space is represented by a (scaled) point (x,y) in two-dimensional space, rather than being foreshortened by a perspective transformation. This preserves distances.

Orthoplanner

Orthoplanner is a knowledge-based system to provide dentists with orthodontic treatment plans for cases where fixed orthodontic appliance techniques must be employed. It uses a number of techniques including rulebase reading, forward chaining, backward chaining, and fuzzy logic-based representations of orthodontic knowledge.
See Also: Jeremiah, http://www-uk.hpl.hp.com/people/ewc/list-main.html.

OTTER

OTTER is an automated deduction system designed to prove theorems stated in first-order logic with equality. Otter's inference rules are based on resolution and paramodulation, and it includes facilities for term rewriting, term orderings, Knuth-Bendix completion, weighting, and strategies for directing and restricting searches for proofs. Otter can also be used as a symbolic calculator and has an embedded equational programming system. Otter is a fourth-generation Argonne National Laboratory deduction system whose ancestors (dating from the early 1960s) include the TP series, NIUTP, AURA, and ITP. Currently, the main application of Otter is research in abstract algebra and formal logic.

Otter is a freely available system, coded in C, and is available through the WWW.
See Also: http://www.mcs.anl.gov/AR/otter/, restriction strategy, set of support strategy.

outlier

Refers to a record or observation that has data value(s) that is(are) outside the normal or expected range for the values. A simple form occurs when a single attribute is "out of range," but other forms can occur when combinations of values are individually valid but jointly unusual. The implication of calling a record an outlier is that the values are correct, but they do not fit the current model for the data. A major task in data cleaning is the identification of unusual attribute values and distinguishing between those that are simply in error and those that are correct but unusual.
See Also: data cleaning, Data Mining, data warehousing.

out-of-sample testing

Out-of-sample testing is a general name for split-sample and related technologies for giving "honest" estimates of the errors produced by a induction/learning technique. Two samples are drawn from the data. The (usually) larger of the two is designated the "training" set, and the other the "validation" set. Models developed on the training set are then applied to the validation set to estimate the error of the models.
See Also: bootstrapping, Cross-validation, in-sample testing.

output flipping

See: output smearing.

output layer

In neural networks, the nodes that produce external output are commonly called the output layer.
See Also: input layer, hidden layer, neural network.

output smearing

Recent research has focused on methods for combining predictors such as neural networks or classification trees. Typically, multiple training sets are generated and a predictor developed on each set. The predictions can then be combined using techniques such as Bootstrap AGGregation (bagging) or arcing-boosting (ADABOOST). Output smearing and output flipping offer an alternate to generating multiple

training sets by maintaining the same feature vectors but perturbing the output. When the output is continuous or has been encoded in a set of binary vectors, new training sets are generated by adding small amounts of Gaussian noise to the response. Output flipping is a similar technique for categorical responses, where the labels are randomly flipped or exchange so as to maintain the same relative proportion of the classes.
See Also: ADABOOST, arcing, Bootstrap AGGregation.

overfitting

A term used in neural networks, recursive partitioning, and other automated modeling areas. If the training data is considered to consist both signal and noise (i.e., noisy data), a modeling technique has begun to overfit when it begins capturing the "noise" instead of the "signal." This usually occurs when a model is allowed to increase its number of "parameters" such as regression coefficients, splits in recursive partitioning schemes, or hidden units in neural networks.

The effect of overfitting is to reduce the applicability of the model to other data sets, (i.e., to limit its generalizability). In the extreme, the model can only "predict" its input. The most straightforward way to eliminate this effect is to require a very large number of observations per parameter in the model.

overlap

In fuzzy logic, the overlap of a fuzzy set A is the fuzzy union of set A with its complement B. In classical set theory, this union would define the universe. In fuzzy logic it is simply the fuzzy set defined by the element-wise maximums of the membership function $m(A,x)$ and $(1-m(A,x))$.
See Also: fuzzy logic, membership function, underlap.

OWL

A knowledge-engineering language for frame-based representations. It uses a semantic net taxonomy and was implemented in LISP at MIT.

own slot

An own slot is a slot in a class that is used to describe properties that are specific to the class itself, rather than to any particular instance of the class.
See Also: class, instance slot.

P

PAC learning model
See: Probably Approximately Correct learning model.

PAGE1
An expert system developed at Honeywell to troubleshoot their Page Printing System. It is implemented in LISP and LOOPS.

PALLADIO
An expert system to support the design and testing of VLSI circuits. It was developed at Stanford University and implemented in LOOPS.

PAM
A goal-based story understanding system written in 1978.

pan
To move an image in the horizontal plane.

Pandemonium
One of the earliest attempts (1959) at Machine Learning, using an approach similar to a neural network. Lower-order demons learned to simplify features in the input data which were passed up to higher-order demons, etc.
See Also: Machine Learning, Artificial neural networks.

paradigm
A point of view or means of approaching problems. Particular tools can be good for one paradigm but not for another.

paradox

1. A contradiction in conclusions indicating a fallacy in the assumption or logic.
2. A commercial expert system for the management of relational databases.

parallel coordinate visualization

A visualization technique used in Data Mining, clustering, and related fields. A database with multiple attributes is represented as a two-dimensional figure with multiple parallel axes along one dimension. Any point in the database is represented as a line connecting its coordinates. Groups of similar points show up as bands of lines. Figure P.1 shows a scatterplot and a parallel coordinates plot of the same data.

Figure P.1—Parallel Coordinates Plot

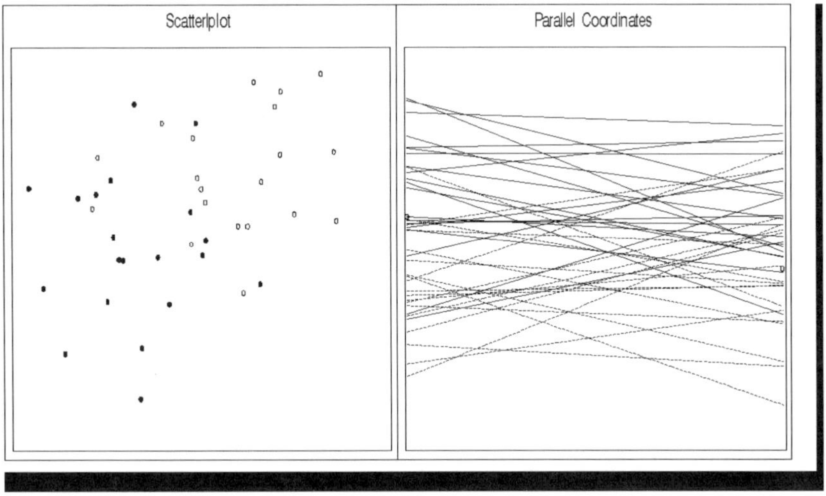

parallel processing

A computer architecture that includes (or emulates) multiple CPUs. This allows either multiple programs to run simultaneously and/or multiple programs to attack the same problems simultaneously.

parallel search

A simultaneous search along multiple paths.

parameter learning

A learning method used when a fixed functional form of the solution is assumed, and only requires the specific of the value of a parameter B, possibly vector-valued. The parameter B is estimated from a set W of training cases and chosen to minimize some criteria, such as mean squared error.

parametric Bayesian networks

Many uses of Bayesian networks, particularly for binary and multinomial data, use the observed conditional distributions to propagate probability through the network. A parametric Bayesian network replaces these observed distributions with some parametric form (e.g., a logistic function).
See Also: variational techniques.

parametric distribution

A probability function that is completely specified by a mathematical function and a "few" numbers (parameters). Common examples include the normal, Poisson, and binomial distributions. The normal distribution requires a mean and a variance parameter, the Poisson requires a mean parameter, and the binomial requires both a size and probability parameter.
See Also: algorithmic distribution, tabular distribution.

paramodulation

Paramodulation is an inference rule that can be used in automated reasoning systems. Paramodulation always focuses on two clauses, requiring that one of the clauses contain at least one literal asserting the equality of two expressions.
See Also: hyperresoltion.

paraphrase

To represent the meaning of a sentence in some other form.

PARRY

A program that emulates a paranoid personality. Similar to Eliza, it is based on a small word set and simple rules but appears to reply like an intelligent person.
See Also: Eliza.

parse tree

A (graphical) tree depicting the results of parsing a sentence.

PARSIFAL

A natural language parsing system.

parsing

The act of breaking down a sentence and identifying its components. The set of acceptable sentences is defined by the grammar of the language that the parser is designed to accept.

Parsing, expectation-driven

A top-down form of parsing which looks for concepts rather that grammatical elements.

Partial Least Squares (PLS)

Partial Least Squares is a technique used in Machine Learning when linear or multiple regression techniques are inappropriate. Multiple Linear Regression (MLR) techniques work well when there are a (relatively) small number of independent (orthogonal) attributes and the focus is on understanding the relationship between the attributes and the target variable. However, in many Machine Learning situations, the attributes are highly collinear and the goal is predicting rather than understanding the implications of individual coefficients. In this case, MLR methods may not be efficient or appropriate.

PLS offers an alternate means to handle this situation. The predictor attributes and the target variable(s) are projected into a lower dimensional space, where the regression is solved. The projections are chosen so that the target dimensions and the attribute dimensions have high pairwise associations. The results are projected back into the original attribute measurement space.

partially ordered set

A partially ordered set is a set with a partial ordering on it. A partial ordering is formed by a binary relation r between the elements that is transitive ($a\ r\ b$ and $b\ r\ c$ implies $a\ r\ c$), reflexive ($a\ r\ a$ is true for all elements in the set) and asymmetric ($a\ r\ b$ and $b\ r\ a$ implies $a=b$). A *zero* of partially ordered set is an element that is less than or equal to all other elements in the set; and a *unit* of a partially ordered set is an element which is greater than or equal to all other elements in the set. A partially ordered set can have at most one unit and one zero.

When either $a\ r\ b$ or $b\ r\ a$ holds, a and b are said to be *ordered*; otherwise they are *unordered*. When $a\ r\ b$, a is an *ancestor* of b, and b is called a *descendent* of a. If a and b have no common descendent, they are *divergent*.

An example of a partially ordered set would be the set of actions A = "make supper," B = "eat supper," C = "clean dishes," D = "walk dog." The partial orderings ($A\ r\ B$, $B\ r\ C$, and $B\ r\ D$) would indicate that I made supper before I ate it, I ate supper before I walked the dog and before I cleaned the dishes, but that I haven't said whether I washed the dishes or walked the dog first after eating supper. A graph of this set is shown in Figure P.2. The zero of this partially ordered set is "make supper."

See Also: quasi ordering.

Figure P.2—A Graph of a Partially Ordered Set

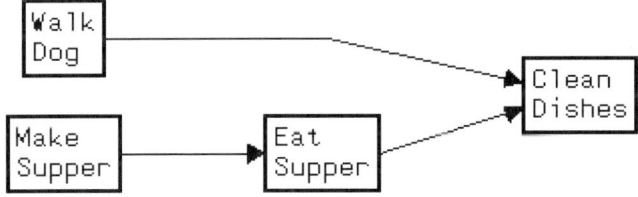

partition

A collection of subsets forms a partition of a universe if the subsets are disjoint and cover all elements (objects) in the universe.

Part-Of-Speech (POS) tagging

One of the early successes in empirical natural language processing, this process is used to assign the lexical syntactic class (e.g., noun, verb, adjective) to the words in a sentence. A number of techniques are available to perform this task and have accuracy rates approaching that of a human. It is often used in as a preprocessing technique prior to other tasks in language processing.

path

A path on a graph is an ordered sequence of nodes that have links between adjacent pairs of nodes in the sequence. The path is cyclic if the path begins and ends on the same node.

PATHFINDER

A frame-based expert system that assist physician in the diagnosis of lymph node samples. The program is able to provide a justification for the questions it poses or the conclusions that it reaches.

path matrix

A path matrix can be used to determine the shortest path between two nodes in a graph. The path matrix has a zero in the i,j-th cell if the shortest (cheapest) path between node i and node j is a direct arc, an integer specifying some other node k if the shortest path passes through k, and some inadmissible value if there is no path between i and j (i.e., the graph is not connected).
See Also: adjacency matrix.

Pathology Expert Interpretative Reporting System (PIERS)

PIERS is an expert system that adds interpretative comments to automatically generated pathology reports. It uses Ripple Down Rules to allow pathologists to update the rule base and has been in service since 1991.
See Also: Ripple Down Rules, http://www.cse.unsw.edu.au/~s2176432/About.html.

PATHREC

A frame-based and rules-based expert system for the management of patient records. It was developed at Ohio State University and implemented in LISP.

pathway
A series of links in a network.

pattern
An outline, or template, of an object.

Pattern Directed Invocation
A modification used in a Procedural Representation of a Knowledge Base. Rather than explicitly writing the query, it is given as a goal, and a variety of procedures can be used to satisfy it using a method such as backtracking. This adds some of the flexibility available in a declarative Knowledge Base, at the expense of the control available in a pure Procedural Representation.
See Also: Declarative Representation, Knowledge Base, Knowledge Representation, Procedural Representation.

pattern matching
The process of comparing an input set to a series of patterns to identify the input item. The input set may be broken done into pieces or otherwise manipulated to facilitate the pattern matching process.

pattern recognition
Automatic identification of image components by classification into categories.

payoff
See: utility.

payoff uncertainty
A decision-making agent requires a set of valid actions, a set of observable environmental and state variables, and a reward function which specifies the reward or cost of making a decision (choosing an action) under various conditions. If the reward function is unknown or uncertain, the agent faces payoff uncertainty.
See Also: strategic uncertainty.

PCA
See: Principal Components Analysis.

PCFG

See: Probabilistic Context Free Grammar.

peeling

Peeling is a marginalization technique used in a graphical model. It successively eliminates variables not in the target set, propagating their associated belief and probability values to the remaining variables in the model. It is limited in that it can only produce one set of marginals at a time. An alternate approach is the fusion and propagation algorithm.
See Also: fusion and propagation, graphical model, marginalization.

perceptron

A simple pattern recognition device that was the precursor of modern neural nets. The original perceptron took a weighted sum of a set of inputs, added a constant "bias" or "offset" and returned a zero or one, depending on whether or not the sum was above or below a threshold. Perceptron-type circuits underlie modern neural nets.

perceptron algorithm

An algorithm for determining the weights vector in a perceptron model.

perfect decision tree

A decision tree which correctly classifies all observations.
See Also: decision tree.

PERFEX

PERFEX is a rule-based expert system that assists in the interpretation of cardiac SPECT data. It infers the extent and severity of Coronary Artery Disease (CAD) from perfusion distributions and can provide an automatic report in English with a justification. It currently has over 250 rules.
See Also: http://www.cc.gatech.edu/gvu/visualization/perfex/.

Performance Mentor

An Expert System designed to aid managers in evaluating the performance of subordinates.

performance standards

A set of standards against which actual instances are measured or compared. An external performance standard is often used in teaching and evaluating expert systems and learning systems.

PESKI

See: Probabilities Expert Systems Knowledge and Inference.

Phenomenology

A philosophy of intentionality and meaning; it has been applied to AI in debates on the role of intentionality and cognition. Many of the debates between the schools of Husserl and Heidegger over the nature of intentionality have been carried over into AI discussions.

Phonemes

The basic units of human speech. Words are composed of sequences of phonemes.

PIERS

See: Pathology Expert Interpretative Reporting System.

pixel

A pixel is the smallest unit in a computer representation of an image, or the smallest addressable unit in on computer screen. For example, a 640x480 image is 640 pixels wide by 480 pixels high.
See Also: voxel.

PLANDoc

A system developed by BellCore that generates English text from the output of a computer program that determines upgrades to the wiring service of a phone company.
See Also: generation, Natural Language Understanding.

Planning

The (automated) generation of a sequence of specific steps for a program, robot, or organization taken in order to reach a specified goal. This depends on a complete specification of the current state and the set of permissible actions.
See Also: Blocks World.

plausibilities

See: Assumption Based Reasoning.

plausibility

The plausibility of proposition in the Dempster-Shafer theory is the upper probability of the proposition. It represents the upper bound on the probability that a proposition is true.
See Also: belief function, lower/upper probability.

Plausible Reasoning

Reasoning systems that allow inference based on what is plausible rather than the more rigorous requirements of standard first-order logic. There are a variety of logic systems that support this type of reasoning.

PLINUS

The PLINUS project is developing an ontology that is focused on ceramic materials science. Its ontology is organized around the chemical composition of materials. The project is developing ontologies for materials, processes, and properties. Rather than use a traditional hierarchical taxonomy, the project has started with a set of core concepts, such as element names, and states of matter, and has built further concepts such as the compositions of these concepts.
See Also: ontology.

PLS

See: Partial Least Squares.

plus strategy

The plus strategy is a method that can be used in evolutionary algorithms. At each generation, the surviving parents generate offspring and the parents and the offspring compete in the next generation.
See Also: comma strategy.

PMML

See: Predictive Model Markup Language.

PMSE

See: Mean Square Error criterion.

PNN
See: Probabilistic Neural Network.

POEMS
See: PostOperative Expert Medical System.

Poisson distribution
The Poisson distribution models the distribution of the number of events in an interval when the process that generates the events is a Poisson process. The probability of k events in an interval of length L when the event rate is a is $P(k)=e^{-aL}(aL)^k/k!$.
See Also: Poisson process.

Poisson process
A Poisson process is a basic model for the number of events that can occur in an interval (usually of time or space). It assumes that the rate at which the events occur is constant over the interval, that the probability of having two events occur simultaneously is negligible, and that the occurrence of events are independent (so that the occurrence of one event neither "blocks" or "promotes" other events anywhere in the interval). It differs from a Bernoulli process, which assumes that there is a sequence of discrete observed events. The distribution of the number of events in a fixed interval is Poisson.
See Also: Bernoulli process.

Polya tree
A Polya tree is a nonparametric Bayesian device used to specify and estimate a distribution. Parametric Bayesian models specify a family of distributions by selecting a parametric form, such as a Gaussian distribution, and place prior distributions or hierarchical priors on the parameters. A Polya tree divides the range of variables into a large number of small bins and places a tree structure, such as a binary tree, on top of the bins. In addition to the split information at each of the tree nodes, the nodes also contain a prior distribution, such as a beta distribution for a binary tree, on the splits. When the distribution is to be updated, a new observation is dropped down the tree, and the split information is updated using Bayes theorem at each node. When a random sample needs to be selected, a similar process is performed, dropping down the tree and randomly choosing a split at each node

until the terminal node is reached, where a value is generated from the distribution assigned to that bin.

As an example, consider an attribute that has the range (0,1). Divide the range into eight ($8=2^3$) bins, and place a three-level binary tree on top of the bins. The top-level node would split the range into (0,.5] and (.5,1]. The second level nodes would subdivide each large bin into two smaller bins (e.g., (0,.5] $\Rightarrow$ (0,.25] and (.25,.5]), and the third level would further subdivide each of the second level nodes into two further bins. The final node would contain a uniform distribution over its range.

See Also: Bayesian Network, binary tree, k-d tree, nonparametric.

POP-2

A European based programming language, with an Algol-like syntax, that is similar to LISP. It was developed at the University of Edinburgh in the early 1970s and has evolved into the POP-11 and POPProlog programming systems.

Positive Definite

Used in the analysis of control functions. A matrix M, perhaps describing the transition function of a system, is positive definite if and only if the matrix product y'My > 0 for all vectors y not equal to zero.

See Also: Robotics.

positive predictive value

The positive predictive value of a classification rule (with respect to a specific outcome) is an estimate of the probability that a case that is predicted to be in a specific category actually belongs in that category. It is a function of three quantities: the sensitivity and specificity of the classification rule with respect to that outcome and the proportion of positives in the cases being evaluated with the rule (e.g., the incidence of positives in the target population).

As an example, suppose you have developed a credit classification rule that catches all the bad credit risks (i.e., is 100 percent sensitive) but only misclassifies 10 percent of the good credit risks (i.e., is 90 percent specific). If you apply it to a customer set that only has 10 percent bad credit risks, the positive predictive value is only 52 percent. To see this, note that 10 percent of the target population that is a bad credit risk will be correctly identified, but that an additional

10 percent of the remaining good 90 percent will also be classified as being bad. So, of the total classified as being bad, only 53 percent (10%/(10% + 10%*90%)) are actually bad.

POS tagging
See: Part-Of-Speech tagging.

posterior distribution
The probability distribution that is assigned to values of an attribute X after observing some data C. This distribution is also a conditional distribution for the attribute X conditional on the data C.
See Also: Bayesian probability, probabilistic expert systems, probability.

PostOperative Expert Medical System (POEMS)
POEMS is a decision support system for postoperative medical care. It can also learn from the cases presented to it when its recommendations are confirmed or denied by medical experts.
See Also: http://www-uk.hpl.hp.com/people/ewc/list-main.html.

PPN
See: projection pursuit network.

PPR
See: projection pursuit regression.

Preclass
Preclass is a commercial program for constructing classification trees from data. It uses Cross-validation and can accommodate user-specified priors and misclassification costs.
See Also: http://www.prevision.com/, classification tree.

predicate expression of arity n
In a predicate calculus, a predicate expression of arity n is a predicate formula with n distinguishable variables $x_1, \ldots, x_n$.

Predicate Logic
An inferential logic that reasons from sentences that are composed of terms (e.g., nouns) and predicates (verbs). It is the modern descen-

dent of classical Aristotelian logic. A first-order predicate logic allows the things represented by the terms to be variable; a second-order predicate logic also allows the predicates to range over classes of predicates.

Predicted Mean Square Error

See: Mean Square Error criterion.

Predictive Mean Square Error

See: Mean Square Error criterion.

predictive model

Models designed to predict the value of an attribute or set of attributes based on other the values of other attributes. Prediction is often distinguished from classification, where the objective is to categorize an observation. In this context, prediction implies the generation of values or ranges for an attribute or group of related attributes. In a general sense, however, classification is just a (possibly constrained) form of multivariate prediction.
See Also: classification, Data Mining, regression.

Predictive Model Markup Language (PMML)

PMML is an eXtended Markup Language (XML) application designed to allow "automatic" interpretation of predictive models via the Internet, supporting distributed mining and prediction.

predictive value

See: positive predictive value.

PredictPLUS

PredictPLUS is a commercially available hybrid regression and neural network system aimed at the online quality control industry. The system uses a genetic variable selection algorithm and a mixture of Partial Least Squares (PLS) regression, neural networks and Fuzzy PLS systems to develop optimal models.
See Also: Artificial Neural Network, Partial Least Squares.

prime implicant

See: implicant.

prime implicate

See: implicate.

priming

The F2 layer of an ART network can be activated internal before an input pattern is presented. This primes the F1 layer to be sensitive to certain input patterns.
See Also: ART,ftp://ftp.sas.com/pub/neural/FAQ2.html, http://www.wi.leidenuniv.nl/art/.

primitive

Denotes a basic, indivisible, symbol, concept, or utterance in a language or logic system. For example, the basic unit of English speech is the phoneme. In a computer language, a "+" sign, indicating an addition operation, is a basic symbol. In a logic, primitives would include such connectives as AND, OR, NOT, and IMPLIES.

Principal Components Analysis (PCA)

Principal Components Analysis is a feature extraction and data reduction technique. It extracts the best linear functions of an attribute matrix, where "best" is measured in terms of the total accounted variation. Each successive component is orthogonal to all the previously extracted components. In the scatterplot in Figure P.3, the first principal component falls along the primary data axis, and the second component is orthogonal to it. It should be apparent that a simple PCA is a simple scaling and rotation of the original data axes.

Figure P.3—Scatterplots: Simple Principal Components Analysis

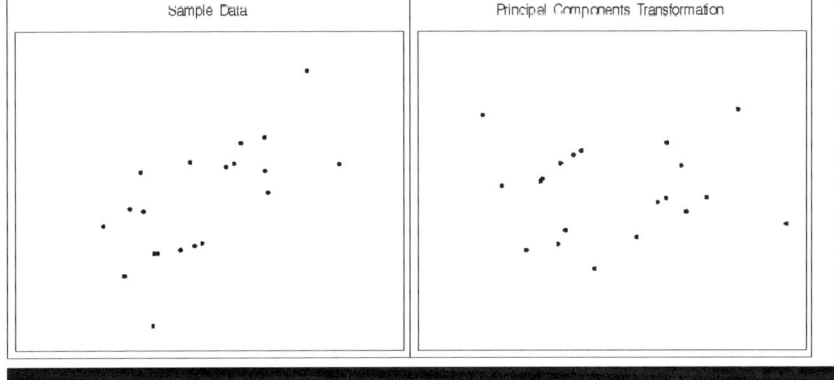

See Also: NonLinear Principal Components Analysis, Principal Curves.

principal components regression

Some Machine Learning algorithms simplify the problem of a very large number of predictors by performing a Principal Components Analysis on the predictors and using the larger components in the analysis. This has the further computational advantage of having independent components which can simplify and stabilize the computation.

See Also: Principal Components Analysis.

Principal Curves and Surfaces

Principal Curves and Surfaces are a non-linear extension of a Principal Component Analysis. For Principal Components, the technique extracts the "best" linear combinations of a data matrix. A Principal Curve analysis will extract a series of orthogonal smooth curves that best summarizes, or models, the input matrix. A Principal Surface analysis is an extension to higher order structures and directly extracts a flexible surface from the data; on the other hand, a Principal Curve analysis extracts an implicit surface, since the prediction surface is the sum of all the orthogonal principal curves. A related technique, called NonLinear Principal Components Analysis (NLPCA) has been implemented using neural networks. All three of these techniques will reproduce the principal components when the data is truly from a linear space.

See Also: Nonlinear Principal Components Analysis, Principal Components Analysis.

PRISM

A credit card fraud monitoring system. It was developed in part from the application of Knowledge Discovery in Databases (KDD) techniques

See Also: Knowledge Discovery in Databases.

Probabilistic Context Free Grammar (PCFG)

These are grammars that are developed from large databases of text. The grammars attach probabilities to the various productions in the grammar. If the grammars are developed using supervised learning (i.e., a tagged text corpus), the probabilities can be directly estimated by counting the various productions and perhaps smoothing or otherwise post-processing the results. For an unsupervised corpus, some form of estimation and maximization strategy needs to be employed.

probabilistic inference

Probabilistic inference is the process of inferring the probabilities of interest in a (Bayesian) model conditional on the values (configuration) of other attributes in the model. For simpler models, such as a regression tree or decision tree model, this can be a fairly straightforward problem. For more complex models, such as a Bayesian network, exact inference can be quite difficult, and may require either approximations or sampling based approaches, such as Markov Chain Monte Carlo (MCMC) methods.
See Also: Gibbs sampling, Simulated Annealing.

probabilistic model

A probabilistic model is a model that allows you to compute the probability of every well-formed proposition that can be formed from the elementary propositions in the model.

Probabilistic Neural Network (PNN)

A neural network, suggested by Donald Specht, that uses the training cases as hidden units. Input cases are then compared to each hidden unit and the unit fires (returns a one) if the input is "close enough." The distance between the normalized input and each case is typically measure using a Radial Basis Function (RBF), such as a Gaussian distribution. The distance is measured with respect to a bandwidth or smoothing parameter, usually univariate. The technique is equivalent to the statistical technique of kernel discriminant analysis.

Probabilities Expert Systems Knowledge and Inference (PESKI)

PESKI is a new generic expert systems shell. It is freely available as an inference engine, Knowledge Base acquisition, verification and validation, and Data Mining tools. The objective is to merge probability theory and expert systems.
See Also: http://www.afit.af.mil/Schools/EN/ENG/LABS/AI/Research/peski3.html.

probability

Probability is a method for representing uncertainty about propositions or events. It represents the uncertainty about a proposition on a scale from 0 to 1, with a 0 representing complete certainty that the proposition is false or an event will not occur and a value of one will represent the opposite. Formally, a probability measure is one that follows Kolmogorov's Axioms. There are two main schools of thought on the meaning of probability. Frequentists take a narrow interpretation of probability allowing only hypothetically repeatable events or experiments as being quantifiable by probability, while Bayesians take a broader interpretation that allows reasoning about "one-shot" events and propositions based on the current knowledge about nature. The Bayesian interpretation is most commonly used in artificial intelligence, while the Frequentist interpretation is most commonly taught in statistics courses.

The label "Bayesian" arises from the central role that the Bayes Theorem plays in this use of probability. It allows one to reason from effects to causes and encourages the use of probability measures to describe supposedly fixed events or propositions which Frequentists disallow. The probability for these events reflects one's state of knowledge about the event, rather than being an assertion that the unknown event can vary. For example, a Bayesian would have no qualms about making statements about the probability that a given die, rolled and hidden from his sight is, for example, a six. A Frequentist would be unable to make such a statement, preferring to talk about his confidence in the method when applied to a hypothetically large number of repeated experiments. In the end, they would act in similar ways. When the long run data are available, Bayesians and Frequentists end up with the same estimates.

See Also: Bayes Theorem, Kolmogorov's Axioms.

probability assessment

The process of obtaining probabilities to represent a degree of uncertainty or of belief is referred to as probability assessment. If there are physical models or data, they can be used to estimate the values in a models. Often, however, the probabilities need to be specified by an individual or group. There are a wide variety of techniques for evoking these probabilities, using some form of imagination of possible data, analogous reasoning, or estimation of "fair" betting odds. These

can lead to sets of distributions for the probabilities and, hence, to Quasi-Bayesian models
See Also: Bayesian Network, Quasi-Bayesian Theory.

probability density function

For continuous variables, the probability distribution is defined over intervals or sets. The most common definition is via the cumulative probability distribution, or its derivative, the probability density function.
See Also: cumulative probability distribution.

probability distribution

A table or algorithm for associating a probability value with a state of a system. By convention, the values are all greater than or equal to zero, and their total for the entire system is one. For example, a probability distribution for a fair six-sided die would assign a value of 1/6 to each side. An arbitrary probability distribution would assign any set of six nonnegative numbers to the die, such that their total was one. When the states are indexed by a single variable or key, the distribution is usually referred to as a univariate distribution. When the states are indexed by multiple variables, it is referred to as a multivariate distribution. Probability distributions are also characterized as being continuous, discrete, or mixed, depending on whether the variables that are associated with them are continuous, discrete, or mixed. Examples would be age, gender, and age crossed with gender. Note that age in years, months, weeks, or even days is truly discrete even though they are usually treated as being continuous.
See Also: multivariate probability distribution, probability, probability density function.

Probability theory

See: probability.

probability tree

A probability tree is a tree of events or actions with probabilities attached to the arcs. It provides a convenient way to represent and compute the probabilities associated with complex events or states.

Probably Approximately Correct (PAC) learning model

A Probably Approximately Correct (PAC) learning model is a Machine-Learning model that attempts to bound the error rate of the model so that with probability P the error in the final rule for a concept is less than some specified value e. The model assumes it can learn from some external source that will present random samples from the attribute space, chosen according to some unknown distribution over the attribute space. The random sampling and the unknown distribution are required in order to calculate the value P. It is usually assumed that the distribution is stationary over time. PAC models can efficiently learn concepts that can be represented by conjunctions of binary attributes.
See Also: Machine Learning.

PROBART

A probabalistic ARTMAP network that can learn from noisy data.
See Also: ftp://ftp.sas.com/pub/neural/FAQ2.html, http://www.wi.leidenuniv.nl/art/.

problem reduction

Problem reduction is a generic term for the technique of decomposing a difficult problem into smaller, simpler problems. This can be recursive, until a problem solving system has generated a chain of simple solutions to the overall problem. An example is a mathematical system such as Mathematica, which can solve a seemingly complex mathematical problem by reducing the initial problem (e.g., an integral) to a simpler problem by applying a series of rules and identities.

procedural language

A computer language, such as C++ or FORTRAN, that requires the programmer give a step-by-step of the procedures used to solve a problem.
See Also: declarative language.

Procedural Representation

A Knowledge Base that uses a Procedural Representation (as opposed to a declarative representation) represents knowledge as a series of procedures and associated data structures. An example would be a Knowledge Base that contains a "person" procedure. This

procedure would contain a list of persons, such as Socrates, Aristotle, Archie Bunker, and Plato. When executed with an argument of "Descartes," the person procedure would search its list of persons and return "False." A further procedure called "mortal" could build on this with a list of mortal things, including the persons() function. Then, the call mortal("Plato") would eventually invoke the person("Plato") and return "True." This form of representation has the advantage that it explicitly directs the method and order of query evaluation, but it can be very difficult to change when a new fact is added. Hybrid methods, such as pattern-directed invocation have been developed to overcome the limits of this form of representation.
See Also: Declarative Representation, Knowledge Base, Knowledge Representation.

production

A rule that processes input and produces a sequence of terminal and non-terminal symbols, which can also be passed to further productions. The rules that a compiler or an expert system uses are often called productions.
See Also: non-terminal symbol, terminal symbol.

Production System

A method of Knowledge Representation in which knowledge is represented as collections of rules and consequences or represented as actions that can be taken when the rule is true. This form of representation is commonly used in expert systems.
See Also: Knowledge Representation, memory.

Production Systems

See: Expert System.

product set

The product set of two sets, denoted A and B, is a new set where each element in the new set is a pair, with one term each from A and B. Every possible pair of elements from A and B is included in the product set.

Programming Assistant

A programming system that provides support and/or advice to a programmer in the non-clerical aspects of programming.

projection pursuit networks

A neural network form of a projection pursuit regression, where subnetworks are used to estimate the nonlinear transformations.
See Also: ftp://ftp.sas.com/pub/neural/FAQ2.html.

projection pursuit regression

Projection pursuit is a form of supervised learning. It is a statistics and Machine Learning technique that iteratively searches for smooth linear combinations of attributes to predict a response. It generalizes the additive model, which looks for linear combinations of smoothed attributes. It has recently been shown that, in a certain technical sense, it evades the "curse of dimensionality."
See Also: additive models, Multivariate Adaptive Regression Spline.

Prolog

The Prolog language is for logic programming and was used in the Japanese fifth-generation computer project. A. Colmerauer developed Prolog in 1970 at the University of Marseille.
See Also: Logic Programming.

proportional attribute

See: ratio attribute.

propositional Calculus

See: Propositional Logic.

Propositional Logic

A means for making inferences from propositions. Given a sequence of propositions, Propositional Logic attempts to infer further prepositions based on the propositions and the rules of propositional inference. If differs from Predicate Logic in that it does not attempt to make inferences about individuals or classes.

prospective data analysis

A modeling process that is designed to predict future events based on past performance or attributes.
See Also: Data Mining, Data modeling, retrospective data analysis.

Prospector

An Expert System that interpreted mineral data and could be used to help find ore deposits based on geologic data. Duda Hart and others wrote Prospector in the late 1970s at SRI International.
See Also: Expert System.

Proteus

An early (1974) program that produced excellent texts analyzing Tic-Tac-Toe games.
See Also: Natural Language Generation.

Protheses

In this context, a computer-assisted mechanical device that replaces or extends some natural human function. An example would be a voice-directed wheelchair, or an implanted chip to direct muscle movement in an artificial limb.

prototype vectors

The category prototypes in ART networks, which are represented as vectors.
See Also: ART, ftp://ftp.sas.com/pub/neural/FAQ2.html, http://www.wi.leidenuniv.nl/art/.

Proximity Sensor

A device to sense environmental conditions near to a robot. These could allow a robot to navigate in a disorderly or an unknown environment or to "sense" environmentally hostile conditions (e.g., fire, cold, a ledge).

pruning

Techniques used to reduce the size of search spaces or classification and regression trees are called pruning techniques. Typically, they involve monitoring some criteria that should decrease or stopping a search or removing branches when they begin to increase.
See Also: Classification And Regression Trees, Alpha-Beta pruning.

PUFF

PUFF is a program to diagnose pulmonary test results. It has been in production since the late 1970s. Its Knowledge Base was later incorporated into the commercial "Pulmonary Consult" product.

Pulcinella

Pulcinella is system for building, modifying, and evaluating uncertainty models using a wide variety of uncertainty systems. It included modules for propositional calculus, probability theory, Dempster-Shafer belief theory and possibility theory, and can be extended to use other systems. Pulcinella separates the structural knowledge (i.e., the relationships between concepts and attributes) from the quantitative representation of uncertainty, thus, allowing the same model to be evaluated using multiple uncertainty systems.
See Also: belief net, ftp://iridia.ulb.ac.be/pub/saffiotti.

Q

quadratic scoring rule

See: Brier scoring rule.

Quasi-Bayesian Theory

Bayesian methods for representing uncertainty in decision and inference problems assume that the uncertainty can be represented by a single probability distribution. However, in practice, it is often difficult to specify a single distribution for states of an attributes. This may be due to incomplete knowledge about the attributes or to an inability or lack of desire to specify a single distribution. Quasi-Bayesian Theory offers a generalization of classical Bayesian theory to encompass these situations, by allowing operations on a set of distributions. In particular, since it is concerned with linear operations on these distributions (e.g., average gains or losses), it works with convex sets of distributions.
See Also: lower expectation.

quasi ordering

If a binary relationship on some members of a set is transitive and reflexive, but not necessarily asymmetric, it is called a quasi ordering. A quasi ordering can be converted into a partial ordering by grouping together elements that are symmetric (i.e., both A^rB and B^rA are true).
See Also: partially ordered set.

quasi support function

See: support function.

quasi-supports

See: Assumption Based Reasoning.

Question Answering

The study or capability for a program, such as an Expert System to answer questions about its conclusions, requests, or knowledge. It requires the ability to understand natural language questions and to generate natural language text.

queue

A set of objects ordered so that the first object entered into the queue is also the first object removed. This property is also referred to as First-In, First-Out (FIFO).

R

RAD

See: Rapid Application Development.

Radial Basis Function (RBF)

An alternative to the common linear functions underlying many modeling techniques such as (generalized) regression models and neural networks. In these models, the (preliminary) response is computed at each node as is the sum of the products between the weight vector and the input vectors. In a RBF model, the response is a (weighted) sum of the distance between the input points and the weights, which now represent "ideal" or "kernel" points. This can be applied in regression models using thin plate splines, neural networks, and recursive partitioning models. The distance function varies across models, but two common classes are decay models (thin plate splines and Gaussian distance functions) and interval models (CART) where the function returns a 0/1 response. The distance function is sometimes scaled by a parameter called the "width", which is somewhat analogous to the bias used in perceptrons.

See Also: CART, normalized radial basis function (NRBF).

Rainbow

Rainbow is a Machine Learning program that performs document classification. It uses a "bag of words representation" to analyze the data and a Bayes classifier to classify the target documents.

See Also: bag of words representation, http://www.cs.cmu.edu/afs/cs.cmu.edu/project/theo-11/www/naive-bayes.html.

RALPH

See: Rapidly Adapting Lateral Position Handler.

Rapid Application Development (RAD)

Rather than spend a long time analyzing a problem and then developing a solution, a RAD system emphasizes quick incremental improvements from an "acceptable" prototype. The tools involved are usually Graphical User Interface-based (GUI-based) and allow quick incremental compilers to test the current status of the project. RAD is important in many Data Mining or OnLine Analytical Processing (OLAP) systems where the target of the analysis is changing quickly and intensive effort on optimizing a particular structure or query would lead to answering old questions.
See Also: Data Mining, data warehousing, OnLine Analytical Processing.

Rapidly Adapting Lateral Position Handler (RALPH)

RALPH is a neural net-based system for autonomous vehicle navigation. It is designed to handle a wide variety of road conditions and can quickly learn from human drivers. It recently completed over 98 percent of a drive across America. In that test, its human handlers were primarily needed to intervene to prevent it from taking off-ramps and passing slower vehicles.
See Also: NAVLAB project, http://www.cs.cmu.edu.

random sub-sampling

Random sub-sampling is a general name for techniques such as cross-validation. Like out-of-sample techniques, models are tested on data that was not used in the learning phase to estimate a "true" error. However, random sub-sampling techniques repeat this process multiple times in order to get an improved estimate of the process, and, in procedures such as Cross-validation, estimate "hyper-parameters."
See Also: bootstrapping, Cross-validation.

random world model

A model for reasoning that assumes all basic events are equally likely. Also known as the "principle of insufficient reasoning." The underlying assumption behind Rough Set Theory.
See Also: Rough Set Theory.

RankBoost

RankBoost is an extension of the basic ADABoost methodology that has been modified to handle training data that contains partial orderings. An example would be movie or book ratings where each respondent orders (ranks) a small subset of the available movies/books. The RankBoost algorithm derives a combined ordering that attempts to preserve the original orderings.

RaPID

RaPiD is a knowledge-based assistant for designing Removable Partial Dentures (RPDs). It uses techniques from logic databases, declarative graphics, and critiquing, together with expert design knowledge, to provide a Computer-Aided Design-style (CAD-style) graphical interface for both instructional and professional use.
See Also: http://www-uk.hpl.hp.com/people/ewc/list-main.html.

ratio attribute

A ratio-valued attribute takes on values for which the absolute value is meaningful, and has a true zero, such as a weight or count. Ratios of these numbers refer to ratios of physical quantities. Translation or scaling of these numbers would change their meaning. A ratio attribute can be either continuous valued or discrete valued (e.g., a count).
See Also: interval attribute, Machine Learning, nominal attribute (type), ordinal attribute.

Rational Monotonicity

Rational Monotonicity is a variant of monotone logic that allows one to retain the existing conclusions whenever new information cannot be negated by existing conclusions.
See Also: monotone logic.

RBF

See: Radial Basis Function.

RDR

See: Ripple Down Rules.

Real Time Data System (RTDS)

See: Real Time Operation System.

Real Time Operation System (RTOS)

A Real Time Operation System is designed to respond to data at (approximately) the same speed at which it arrives. This requires that the system emphasize speed rather than completeness or flexibility of, say, a workstation. The latter may need computational speed but typically does not need to respond immediately and continuously to a series of input events. A Real Time Operation System is always designed to respond to an input within a given (short) time frame while a workstation is not.

Reasoning

This term can have multiple meanings. It can refer to the ability to draw conclusions from a set of facts or assumptions, the ability to analyze or organize information, the ability to solve problems, and the ability to persuade. In one form or another, it is the basis for most AI programs with the notable exception of the last meaning.

Reasoning, Causal

Reasoning about the behavior of systems for the purpose of explaining the causes of past events or from a current state to future events.

Reasoning, Default

A generic term for the ability of a Reasoning System to reach conclusions that are not strict consequences of the current state. A default reasoning ability allows a system to continue to operate on partial data. The implementation varies with the system designer as there is no hard definition of default reasoning. It usually takes the form of some local generalizations or presumptions that attempt to bridge any gaps in the knowledge. Some logic systems that can apply here include monotone logic and Nonmonotone logic, and Bayesian, fuzzy or similar logic based on measures of certainty or uncertainty. Such systems can also use belief selection systems to choose among alternate belief systems, and corresponding methods to revise those beliefs as additional information becomes available.

Reasoning, Precise and Imprecise

Reasoning systems can be described by the amount of precision they use in making any reasoning steps. At the most precise end are reasoning systems that are only concerned with logically valid relationships known with certainty. An obvious example would be classical Aristotelian systems, mathematics, and other classical logic systems. In these cases, the conclusions are true if the premises are true. At the other end are systems such a probabilistic or fuzzy systems that reason about things that are either ill-defined and/or not known with certainty. In these systems, additional information about the truth, certainty, or precision of the premises are included in the computation and evaluation of any conclusions. The imprecise systems are used in many expert systems and embedded systems controllers.

Reasoning System

A term for a computer system or subsystem that can perform reasoning tasks. Such a system usually includes a Knowledge Representation scheme, a set of reasoning rules, and an inference engine to do the actual reasoning. Examples include an Expert System such as a medical diagnosis system or a theorem prover. The representation can vary with the subject matter and type of reasoning being performed. For example, a reasoning system that allows imprecision will also need methods to store and reason about the imprecision as well as to represent the propositions and symbols about which the system is reasoning. The knowledge representation scheme will depend on the particular form of logic used. For example, a reasoning system that allows uncertainty or imprecision will need to track a measure of uncertainty in addition to the propositions, symbols, and goals that a precise system would track.

recall

See: sensitivity.

recognition network

See: Helmholtz machine

recursive data structure

A structure, such as a tree or a list, that can be defined from recursive operations on its elements. For example, a tree can be constructed by combining two (or more) trees as sub-trees of an existing element.

recursive partitioning

Recursive partitioning is an algorithm for generating classification and decision trees. Starting from a root node representing all of the test data, the data is split into two or more child nodes that form a complete partition of the data in the parent node. The process is separately repeated on the data in each of the child nodes, and so on, until some termination criteria is reached.

This technique has proven very effective at devising accurate classifiers and predictors, and widely available implementations include Automatic Interaction Detection (AID), CHAID, Classification And Regression Trees (CART), C4.5, and KnowledgeSeeker, as well as other Machine Learning programs. These implementations also form the basis for boosting and other arcing techniques.

See Also: ADABOOST, arcing, C4.5, Classification And Regression Trees.

Recursive Transition Network (RTN)

A means to represent the rules of a language in a form that can be efficiently used in a computer. The network consists of states (nodes) and (allowable) transitions to other states. The states indicate which parts of the sentence or phrase have been recognized, and the transitions indicate which new substructures are allowed. The transitions also dictate the new state to which the system will move when a particular substructure is recognized.

Reduce

See: MACSYMA.

reduct

Among other things, Rough Set Theory is concerned with reducing the number of attributes in an information table (database) by finding redundant attributes. A set of attributes X that define the same indiscernability relations (equivalence classes) as a larger set of attributes Y is a reduct of the original set.

When the reduct is the smallest possible reduct for a set of attributes, it is called a minimal reduct. Note that neither the reduct nor the minimal reduct of Y is unique. An attribute that is in all reducts is in the core.

See Also: core, indiscernable, Rough Set Theory.

redundant attributes

In Rough Set Theory, redundant attributes are those not in any reduct.

Redzone Robotics, Inc.

Redzone Robotics, Inc. is a robotics company that produces robots that can enter hazardous and inaccessible locations for inspection and repair purposes. Their products include:

- Fury

    An inspection robot designed to enter fuel tanks and similar structures and perform inspections. Fury is constructed of segmented sections, like a snake or insect, so that it can enter tanks through openings as small as four inches in diameter. It uses magnetic traction, allowing it to move up the sides and around the interior of a tank.

- Houdini

    Houdini is a collapsible robot designed to enter nuclear areas and perform various cleanup and inspection tasks. It can collapse into a smaller size as it maneuvers through tight areas and then expand into a large robot, capable of bulldozing sludge and other hazardous materials.

- Pioneer

    Currently in development, Pioneer is a "hardened" inspection and work robot designed to enter contaminated nuclear environments, such as the Chernobyl and Three Mile Island sites. These sites can quickly degrade normal robots, particularly their wiring, sensors, and wheels.

references

An object is a reference when its only function is to point to another object or its contents. This capability allows a program to manipulate and store collections of objects by reference easily, rather than manipulating their contents. It also allows for collections of "anonymous" items, whose number and contents are only known at run-time.

References, Free & Bound

A term used in programming. A bound reference to a variable occurs when the variable is mentioned in a context in which it has a value. A free reference occurs when a variable is mentioned in a context

where its value is unknown (e.g., an external reference in a function).
See Also: LISP.

reflectance pattern

A reflectance pattern is an observation whose attributes have been normalized so that their values add up to one.
See Also: ANN, normalization.

reflexive

A binary relationship R is reflexive if the relationship a^Ra is true. An example would be the relationship "is equal to." A counter-example would be the relationship "is less than." This relationship is termed "irreflexive."
See Also: irreflexive.

regression

Regression commonly refers to the process of developing an empirical (data-driven) model to predict and/or explain one or more attributes in a database or set of data. It is most frequently associated with the simple linear model ($y=mx+b$) taught in most introductory statistics courses; the same ideas have been extended in many directions, including classification problems. When the emphasis is on hypothesis testing and simple models, the regression output is typically a few parameters that provide a direct linkage from the input variables to the predicted variables (or classification). In other situations the emphasis is on explaining as much of the variability in the output variables as is "reasonable" from the input variables. In this case, there are a number of "advanced" techniques, such as smoothing splines, decision trees, neural nets, and so forth, for which there are many "free" parameters. The meaning of any one of these parameters can be obscure. Many Data Mining techniques are, at their core, variations on well-known regression techniques.
See Also: classification, Clustering, decision trees, neural nets.

Regression Methods

Regression methods are used to generate functions that relate a set of input variables, often called independent variables, to some output variables, often called dependent variables. The function is typically referred to as a "regression function." These techniques underlie many Knowledge Discovery in Databases (KDD) and Machine

Learning processes. Many persons are familiar with regression in its elementary form, also known as "simple linear regression." In this form, a real valued variable Y is predicted by a value X through an equation of the form Y=a+bX, where a and b are constants. However, regression has been extended far beyond the original concept. There are forms of regression for classification, for decision trees, and for general non-linear regression, among others. Examples of these would be multivariate logistic regression, classification and regression trees and their many generalizations, and feed-forward neural networks.
See Also: Data Mining, Knowledge Discovery in Databases, Neural Networks.

regressor

A regressor is an attribute or variable that is used to predict the value of another variable. Its usage is taken from regression analysis, where the regressors are used to predict the target (dependent) attribute, often via a linear model.

Relational Graphs

See: Constraint Satisfaction, Semantic Nets.

Relational OnLine Analytic Processing (ROLAP)

Relational OnLine Analytic Processing is the use of standard relational database structures for OnLine Analytic Processing (OLAP) and Data Mining. This can sacrifice the performance of an MDDB for limited development costs.
See Also: Data Mining, OnLine Analytic Processing.

relative entropy

See: Kullback-Liebler information measure.

relative least general generalization

In Inductive Logic Programming, the relative least general generalization of two clauses is the least general clause that is more general than each of the clauses relative to the background knowledge of the system.
See Also: Inductive Logic Programming, Logic Programming.

relaxation procedures

A relaxation procedure is one that uses relaxation formulae to compute the values of a network of nodes iteratively. Each node is initialized to an arbitrary value, and the value of the nodes are slowly relaxed from this values by recomputing a new value based on a weighted combination of its current value and a projected value computed from its neighboring nodes. When a new value is introduced into a node or set of nodes, the same procedure is applied until the network stabilizes. Constraints can be added by creating specific relationships between the nodes and by adding fixed nodes.
See Also: constraint propagation.

relevance diagram

A relevance diagram is a special form an influence diagram that includes only probabilistic information, without the utilities and other information in the influence diagram. It is a form of a Bayes net.
See Also: Bayesian Network, influence diagram.

representation

A representation is a set of conventions about how to describe a class of things. Representation will generally consist of four parts:

1. a lexicon that determines which symbols are in it vocabulary;
2. a structural part that describes the constraints on the symbols;
3. a collection of methods or procedures that allow the symbols to be manipulated and queried; and
4. a semantics that specifies the meaning of the symbols and their relationships.

re-ranking

In handwriting and text recognition systems, the task of re-ranking allows the candidate interpretations developed by the recognizer to be ranked or scored according to the language model.
See Also: Word n-gram re-ranking, Word-Tag Model.

rescaling

Strictly speaking, rescaling is multiplying or dividing a variable by some constant. Often used in the sense of standardizing.
See Also: standardizing.

reset wave

The reset wave in an ART network is a non-specific signal to the F2 layer, which disables any active F2 for the duration of the presentation of the current input pattern. It is generated by an insufficient match between a category prototype and the current input pattern.
See Also: ART, ftp://ftp.sas.com/pub/neural/FAQ2.html, http://www.wi.leidenuniv.nl/art/.

resolution

Resolution is a rule used in logical inference. It states that if there is an axiom of the form (A OR B) and another of the form (Not(B) OR C), then (A or C) logically follows.
See Also: modus ponens, modus tollens.

resonance

When an ART network matches a case to a profile, it is said to resonate.
See Also: ftp://ftp.sas.com/pub/neural/FAQ2.html, http://www.wi.leidenuniv.nl/art/.

resonance restriction

Resonance restriction strategies restrict an automated reasoning program by discarding conclusions that do not match (ignoring variables) one of the patterns, called resonators—chosen by the researcher.
See Also: OTTER.

restriction strategy

Restriction strategies are used in automated reasoning systems to limit the space of conclusions that can be considered. This stops the space of conclusions from growing wildly.
See Also: OTTER.

resubstitution error

The resubstitution error of a model is its error measured on the data used to train the model. Since the model is optimized for that particular set of data, its error is usually much lower than the error in an independent sample from the same target group, and can thus be quite

misleading. A better measure of a model's error is obtained from a hold-out sample.
See Also: accuracy, hold-out sample, Split-sample validation.

Rete Algorithm

The Rete match algorithm is a fast pattern matching algorithm for comparing a set of patterns to a set of objects. It is used in expert and other rule-based systems to search a set of rules to select which ones match the current set of data. In a typical rule-based system, the IF clauses do not change quickly, and the Rete method exploits this by "remembering" the set of matches and partial matches from the last pass through the rule base. It also exploits the common patterns in these cases by compiling the rules in order to eliminate common sub-patterns to the rules, so that it can operate on entire sets of rules at once.

retrospective data analysis

A modeling process that is designed to understand past trends or events. A common problem in data analysis or Data Mining is that the objective is to predict future events based on past events, but that data are all based on past events. A common solution is to cross-validate the analysis by using sampling, "hold one out" or bootstrap analyses. Each of these techniques attempts to provide "new" data by only using part of the database by only using part of the data to form the data and then using the remainder to validate the model.
See Also: Cross-validation, bootstrapping.

reward

See: utility.

Ripple Down Rules (RDR)

Ripple Down Rules (RDR) provide a means that allows a domain expert to build a rule-based system without training in knowledge engineering. The Knowledge Base contains rules if the form IF [condition] THEN [conclusion] BECAUSE [] EXCEPT [exceptions]. If the rule fires falsely, the user can add an exception to the exception list. If it fails to fire, an else condition can be added to the rule.

Ripple Down Rules form the basis of the Pathology Expert Interpretative Reporting System (PIERS) Expert System for

pathology reports and has been implemented in the INDUCT-RDR Machine Learning algorithm.
See Also: INDUCT-RDR, Pathology Expert Interpretative Reporting System, http://www.cse.unsw.edu.au/~s2176432/About.html.

R-MINI

An algorithm for the generation of minimal classification rules. It is an adaptation of the MINI algorithm for minimizing two-level logic and switching functions used in VLSI design.

Robot

A robot is a general-purpose system that can perform multiple tasks under conditions that might not be known a priori. Robots can include such things as sensors and other input devices, a computer-based controller, and some form of an actuator, such as a mechanical hand or drill that it can use upon its environment. The Japanese have classified industrial robots into five categories: slave manipulators operated by humans, limited sequence manipulators, "teach-replay" robots, computer-controlled robots, and "intelligent" robots. The United States Robotic Industries Association defines a robot as "a reprogrammable, multifunctional manipulator (or device) designed to move material, parts, tools, or specialized devices through variable programmed motions for the performance of a variety of tasks."

Robotics

The study of robots, their construction, and control.

Rocchio Algorithm

The Rocchio Algorithm is a Knowledge Discovery in Text (KDT) algorithm for textual classification. A document to be classified is represented by a "feature vector" of indexing terms, with the frequency of the each term replaced by a weighted score, which sums to one across all of the indexing terms. The target categories are also represented by "prototype" feature vectors, and a document will be classified as being within a category if its feature vector is "close" to the prototype vector.
See Also: Knowledge Discovery in Text.

ROLAP

See: Relational OnLine Analytic Processing.

Rosetta

Rosetta is a toolkit for analyzing tables of categorical attributes within the framework of Rough Set Theory. It supports browsing and pre-processing of the data, reduct generation and rule generation, and validation and extraction of rules. The Graphical User Interface (GUI) version runs under Windows 95 and Windows NT. A free non-commercial version is available at the Uniform Resource Locator (URL) below.
See Also: http://www.idi.ntnu.no/~aleks/rosetta/.

ROSIE

A software tool designed the early 1980s at the Rand Corporation to assist the building of an expert system. It is a rule-based procedure-oriented system that can become an expert system with the addition of Knowledge Base.
See Also: Expert Systems.

Rough Set Data Analysis (RSDA)

A method of analysis that uses Rough Set theory to reduce the predictor set and form upper and lower approximations to the decision attributes.
See Also: Rough Set Theory.

Rough Set Theory

Rough Set Theory provides a sample-based approach to dealing with vagueness and uncertainty. Unlike probabilistic and fuzzy approaches which require probability distributions, belief functions, or membership functions to operate, a rough set model only uses upper and lower approximations to the observed data. In a certain sense, it is a "Frequentist" version of a Bayesian system.

The starting point of a rough set is a table of observations called an information table, with attributes partitioned into "condition attributes," which are descriptive and "decision attributes." These are sometimes simply referred to as attributes and decisions. The rough set analysis attempts to reduce the data in this table into a series of equivalence classes called "indiscernability relations."
See Also: lower approximation, upper approximation.

RSDA

See: Rough Set Data Analysis.

RSES

RSES is a commercial Data Mining and analysis program that uses the Rough Set Theory to extract rules from datasets. It includes multiple search algorithms and can partition continuous attributes.
See Also: Rough Set Theory.

RTDS

See: Real Time Data System.

RTN

See: Recursive Transition Network.

RTOS

See: Real Time Operation System.

rule base

A database of IF-Then Rules used in an expert system.
See Also: expert system, If-Then Rules.

rule induction

A form of data analysis aimed at developing rules or relationships between attributes through the analysis of relevant databases, rather than from theoretical models. Rule induction usually refers to if-then clauses although other predictive models can provide "rules" to summarize the data.
See Also: data analysis, Data Mining, regression.

ruleset

An alternative form of output for tree classifier programs is a simplified set of classification rules referred to as a ruleset. These are usually in a form that can be imported into other programs (e.g., C code) or can be formatted for reading.
See Also: classification tree.

run-time typing
The ability of a program to allow a variables type to be determined at run-time implying that it can change from run to run. Most languages support compile time typing, where the type of a variable is set when the program is compiled.

S

saddle point

In game theory, a situation in which the minimum of the maximum losses for one player is the same as the maximum of the minimum losses for another player.

SahmAlert

SahmAlert is a C Language Integrated Production System-based (CLIPS-based) Expert System that is used to identify micro-organisms that have unusual patterns of antibiotic resistance.
See Also: C Language Integrated Production System, http://www-uk.hpl.hp.com/people/ewc/list-main.html.

schema

A schema is a complete description of the attributes and allowable values of the attributes in a model. It can also include dependencies and relationships between the attributes. In genetic algorithms a schema is a template (such as a bit pattern with wildcards) that matches some genomes.
See Also: Machine Learning.

Schema theorem

A theorem showing that a genetic algorithm gives an exponentially increasing number of reproductive trials to above average schema. Since each chromosome contains a great many schema, the rate of schema processing in the population is very high.
See Also: Machine Learning.

Scheme

Developed in the 1970s, Scheme is an important dialect of LISP and has since become one of the major LISP dialects.

Schwartz Information Criteria

The Schwartz Information Criteria, also known as the Bayesian Information Criteria (BIC), is an adaptation of the Akaike Information Criteria (AIC) that addresses a defect of that measure, where larger datasets from the same data source tend to increase their complexity quickly (i.e., the number of parameters in the model). The AIC is defined as the sum of -2*log-likelihood of the data plus twice the number of parameters in the model. Schwartz derived a related criteria that uses log(N) times the number of parameters instead of twice that number. Since the penalty term increases with the sample size, it greatly slows the growth of model complexity.
See Also: Akaike Information Criteria.

scoring rule

A scoring rule is a generic term for a method that assigns a numerical result to a result of some algorithm, allowing multiple answers to be compared according to some overall "goodness" measure. One example might be a similarity score in a Case Based Reasoning (CBR) system that evaluates how close previous cases are to the current problem. A second would be a squared (or absolute) difference to measure the difference between a model's prediction and the actual result. In the first case, a high score would indicate that the item was close to the particular case, and in the second case, a high score would indicate the prediction was far from the target.

Scrubmate

Scrubmate is an autonomous cleaning robot for institutions. It is capable of tasks such as washing floors and cleaning restrooms.
See Also: Helpmate, MOBile robOT.

segmentation

Segmentation refers to the process of identifying homogeneous subgroups within a data table. It is often used in a marketing context to describe subgroups of consumers that behave similarly and can be treated as a (somewhat) homogeneous subgroup.
See Also: Clustering.

selection bias

A systematic difference between a target population and the sample of data. For example, Data Mining on customer complaint databases has a selection bias in that the data only capture customers who were motivated and able to contact the manufacturer about their complaint and does not capture complaints or customers who were not motivated nor able.

Self Organizing Map (SOM)

A self organizing map is a form of Kohonen network that arranges its clusters in a (usually) two-dimensional grid so that the codebook vectors (the cluster centers) that are close to each other on the grid are also close in the k-dimensional feature space. The converse is not necessarily true, as codebook vectors that are close in feature-space might not be close on the grid. The map is similar in concept to the maps produced by descriptive techniques such as multi-dimensional scaling (MDS)

self-stabilization

A property of neural networks (e.g., ART models). As a network trains itself on a finite number of cases, the various weights should gradually stabilize.
See Also: ART, ftp://ftp.sas.com/pub/neural/FAQ2.html, http://www.wi.leidenuniv.nl/art/.

SEM

See: Structural Equation Model.

semantic analysis

Semantic analysis is used in natural language processing to determine the meaning of the text being analyzed, as opposed to syntactic analysis which is focused on determining the use of a word (e.g., verb, noun).
See Also: word sense disambiguation.

Semantic Grammar

A grammar in which the categories refer to both semantic and syntactic concepts.

Semantic Memory

A term introduced into AI by Quillian as a part of his memory models. Information is stored in a network, where each node represents a word sense and the arcs connect associated words. This is also referred to as a semantic network or an associative memory. Quillian proposed these models as a means of explaining the associative aspect of human memory, where the thought of "Sue's Brother" leads to other things that are known about him if he exists.
See Also: Production System.

Semantic Networks

See: Semantic Memory.

Semantics

The semantics of a language or knowledge representation scheme is the meaning associated with the symbols or facts of the language or knowledge representation.

sensitivity

The sensitivity of classification rule is a measure of its ability to correctly classify observations into a particular category. It is defined to be the ratio of the number of true positives to the number of positives in a test set. This value is usually inversely related to the specificity of the test for a given set of data and a particular classification rule. Note that this measure is different from the positive predictive value of a rule, which is a measure of the probability that a positive is a true positive. If multiple classification categories exist, each category will have its own sensitivity, specificity, and positive predictive value.
See Also: positive predictive value, specificity.

sensitivity analysis

Sensitivity analysis is a general term used to refer to the process of varying key parameters or relationships in a model to determine how sensitive the conclusions are to the (assumed or estimated) values of the parameters or input.

sentenial logic

See: Propositional Logic.

separable support function

See: support function.

sequence-based analysis

Similar to, and often synonymous with, time series analysis, sequence analysis looks at an ordered progression of objects and attempts to predict the values of further items in a series. The term is sometimes used in Data Mining to refer to analysis of a linked series of purchases but can also be used in medical and biological contexts.
See Also: Data Mining, time series analysis.

sequence mining

Sequence mining is an extension of Data Mining to time-based data. In this context, association rules would be of the form "if A occurs then B occurs within time T."

set

A basic collection of objects. In a classic "crisp" set, an object is either a member of the set or not. Objects (and sets) can be added to or subtracted from a set, and the number of objects in a (finite) set can be counted.
See Also: Array, fuzzy set, Graph, list, probability tree.

Seth

Seth is an Expert System designed to provide advice on the treatment and monitoring of drug poisoning cases.
See Also: http://www-uk.hpl.hp.com/people/ewc/list-main.html, http://www.chu-rouen.fr/dsii/publi/seth.html.

set of support strategies

In automated reasoning systems, a set of support strategy can be used to limit the paths the program might take. The researcher provides an initial set of clauses in a support list, and restricts the program from performing inference when all of the current clauses are complements of the list. New clauses can be added to the set of support clauses as the reasoning proceeds.
See Also: OTTER.

Set Point Control

In Robotics or Control Theory, Set Point Control or regulation involves the problems associated with bringing a system to a certain set point and keeping it there.
See Also: Robotics.

S-expression

In LISP, an S-expression (Symbolic expression) is an atom, a list, or a collection of S-expressions surrounded by parenthesis.
See Also: atom, list, LISP.

Shafer-Shenoy Architecture

A method for propagating data through a join tree representation of a belief net that computes all the resulting marginals simultaneously.

shift register

Used in neural network literature to indicate attribute values that are the previous value of another value. For example, in a stock market application, previous day's prices might be kept in a shift register.
See Also: Artificial Neural Network.

SHOE

See: Simple HTML Ontology Extension.

Shopbot

An Internet-based Data Mining tool that learns to extract product information from World Wide Web (WWW) vendors.

short-term memory

In a neural network, the current state of a system.
See Also: long-term memory.

SIC

See: Schwartz Information Criteria.

siftware

See: KDD software, http://www.kdnuggets.com

signal function

A bounded monotone non-decreasing function. The output function from nodes in neural network functions are signal functions. The bounded condition says the function will always be in a certain range and the monotone non-decreasing condition says that larger inputs will always produce an output at least as large as a smaller input. Common examples include logistic functions, threshold functions, and threshold linear functions.

signal state space

A term used in the discussion of neural networks, a signal state space is the space defined by all possible outputs of model. If the model had one continuous bounded output, its state space would be that bounded interval. With two such outputs, the state space can form a rectangle with three a hyper-rectangle or cube, and so on.

SIMD

See: Single Instruction Multiple Datastream.

Simple HTML Ontology Extension (SHOE)

SHOE is a simple Hypertext Markup Language-based (HTML-based) knowledge representation language. Its purpose is to provide a means for authors to add knowledge representation capabilities to World Wide Web (WWW) pages, with the aim of increasing the usefulness of the Web. Unlike Knowledge Interchange Format (KIF), it has limited semantics to enable it to be easily parsed. SHOE contains two categories of tags: one for constructing simple ontologies, and a second for using the ontologies on the page. As an example of the former, the ontology might declare that there are "beings" of a type "dog" and that a "dog" can have a property called a "name;" the latter might declare that the WWW document is about a "dog" named "Lassie."

See Also: Knowledge Interchange Format, Knowledge Query and Manipulation Language, Ontology Markup Language, http://www.cs.umd.edu/projects/plus/SHOE/.

simple support function

See: support function.

Simpson's paradox

Simpson's paradox occurs when a dataset seems to support an association between two items at one level of analysis but disappears upon further sub-analysis of the same data. It usually occurs in observational and "found" data collected for other purposes.

An example would be a strong association between the sex of a shopper and the purchase of, say, coffee. If the data were further studied, it might be found that purchase of coffee was associated with the number of items purchased, and that men and women simply had different size baskets but each bought coffee with equal frequency, given the number of items begin purchased. The appearance of the association at one level (sex of shopper) is an example of Simpson's paradox and is caused in this case by the hidden associations with the true causal factor, the number of items bought in one trip.

Simulated Annealing

A Monte Carlo based maximization/minimization technique used for complex problems with many parameters and constraints. It mimics the process of annealing, which starts with a high temperature mix of metal and slowly cools the mix, allowing optimal structures to form as the material cools. The Simulated Annealing procedure randomly generates a large number of possible solutions, keeping both good and bad solutions. These are randomly perturbed and can replace the existing solutions, even when the are worse. As the simulation progresses, the requirements for replacing an existing solution or staying in the pool becomes stricter and stricter, mimicking the slow cooling of metallic annealing. Eventually, the process yields a small set of optimal solutions.

See Also: Gibbs sampling, Markov Chain Monte Carlo methods.

Single Instruction Multiple Datastream (SIMD)

Single Instruction Multiple Datastream (SIMD) is a computer architecture, where there are multiple processors each performing the same set of computations on their own data.

See Also: Multiple Instruction Multiple Datastream.

singly connected

Some network propagation schemes require that the network be singly connected, meaning that there is only one path between any

two nodes. This would be satisfied, for example, in a model that could be represented by a tree.
See Also: Bayesian Network.

singular diagram

Suppose X is a finite set with a partial ordering R between its elements. A graph G is a singular diagram of elements in X if some or all of the elements of X form the nodes of the graph G. If an arc between a pair of distinct nodes a and b exist in the graph then $a^R b$ in the partial ordering. The graph G represents the relation R on X if G has all the elements for the set X has its nodes, and is a complete singular diagram if all the relationships in the partially ordered set are represented by arcs in the graph. A special form of incomplete singular graph is referred to as a Hasse diagram.

Two common examples of singular diagrams are graphs of event trees or decision trees and a graph representing a set of logical implications.
See Also: Directed Acyclic Graph, Hasse diagram, event tree, partially ordered set.

SIPE

A planning system for aircraft carrier deck operations (1984).

SKICAT

An application used by astronomers to perform knowledge discovery on sky survey images. The system uses image analysis techniques to catalog and classify sky objects. In an early application (1996), using a multi-terabyte image database collected during the Second Palomar observatory Sky Study, it was able to outperform both humans and traditional programs in classifying faint sky objects.
See Also: Knowledge Discovery in Databases.

Skolem function

In formal inference, resolution proofs require that existential quantifiers be eliminated. A Skolem function allows a system to replace an existentially qualified phrase such as *exists(y)[A(x,y)&B(y)]* with the phrase *A(x,C(x))&B(C(x))*, where *C(x)* is understood to stand for a function of x that returns a value of y satisfying the first clause.
See Also: resolution.

slab

An alternate name for a layer in a neural network.
See Also: input layer, hidden layer, output layer.

slice

In a probabilistic expert systems, any one of the tables in a conditional is termed a slice. The term is analogously used in Data Mining to indicate a subset of the variables.
See Also: conditional, Data Mining.

slice sampling

A method for drawing samples from an arbitrary bounded continuous distribution. An initial value is drawn from a uniform distribution and the density at that value $f(z_0)$ is determined. Any value z_i with $f(z_i) \geq f(z_0)$ is now a feasible value. The sampling is repeated. If $f(z_i) \leq f(z_0)$, the boundary of the sampling interval is contracted. If $f(z_i) \geq f(z_0)$, the current value of z is accepted.
See Also: Gibbs sampling, Markov Chain Monte Carlo Methods.

slots

In frame-based systems, slots designate the positions of possible values or links to other objects. In a database table, the slots for items in the table would correspond to possible attributes and would be filled in an item by slot values. In an employee model, there could be slots for employee name, employee number, employee type and so on.
See Also: Frames.

SMART

A hierarchial ART network capable of learning self-consistent cluster hierarchies.
See Also: ftp://ftp.sas.com/pub/neural/FAQ2.html, http://www.wi.leidenuniv.nl/art/.

Smet's rule

Smet's rule provides a method for producing joint belief functions from conditional belief functions. It provides a method for constructing joint belief functions from a set of Bayesian conditional belief functions. It is also known as Smet's rule of conditional embedding.
See Also: belief function.

smoothing

Smoothing is a nonparametric process for estimating functions and probabilities. The basic assumption is that estimates for values that are "close" to each other should also have "similar" values. A classical type of smoothing would replace the estimate of a probability with the (weighted) average of the "raw" probabilities at all the nearby points. The technique is particularly useful in "empirical" learning algorithms where due to time or size limitations, you are only able to observe a limited training set. Smoothing the results allows you to shift some of the "learning" onto unobserved combinations.

In a regression or function estimation context, an empirical estimate would estimate the value of a function at a point by the mean of the data at that point, while a smoothed estimate would use the mean of all "nearby" points.

See Also: nonparametric.

SMP

See: MACSYMA.

SNOB

SNOB is a program for unsupervised classification, clustering, or modeling of multivariate data. SNOB used a minimum description length algorithm to automatically determine the number of classes and their predictors. Rather than using all of the attributes, like some earlier statistical techniques, this algorithm determines which attributes are useful for a particular class or subset of classes. SNOB is written in FORTRAN 77 and is freely available.

See Also: AutoClass, Machine Learning, Minimum Description Length Principle, http://www.cs.monash.edu.au/software/snob/.

SNOMED

SNOMED is a systematized nomenclature of human and veterinary medicine is a manually constructed classification scheme that provides a hierarchical structure for information about medicine. It has been used as the basis for ontologies in systems such as Metropolitan Life's Intelligent Text Analyzer (MITA).

See Also: Metropolitan Life's Intelligent Text Analyzer.

Soar

Soar is an AI programming language and architectural system that implements a theory of cognition. It provides an architecture for knowledge-based problem solving and learning. It can interact with external environments. It represents "permanent" knowledge through production rules and temporary knowledge as objects with attributes and values. Its sole learning mechanism is called chunking.

Its primary purpose has been the construction of intelligent agents and as a means for modeling thinking. It has been used for production scheduling, robotics control, and natural language instruction.

See Also: chunking, Software Agent, http://www.nottingham.ac.uk/pub/soar/.

softmax

A type of activation function that is used in neural networks when a group of nodes must meet a common constraint, such as adding up to one. For a group of (output) nodes that must add up to one (e.g., a classification probability) you would add a new output layer that takes the raw output layer (assumed to be positive) and normalizes each of the outputs by the sum of the outputs. This approach can be generalized to other constraints on the output. An example, for three inputs A, B, and C, would give a classification probability of the class associated with A as

$$C(A) = \frac{A}{A+B+C}.$$

See Also: Activation functions.

soft selection

Selection by proportion reduction according to fitness level in a genetic algorithm
See Also: hard selection.

soft split

In classical tree models, the split at a node is complete; that is, a single case can only follow a single node down a tree. A "soft split" generalizes that idea and allows a single case to be propagated down multiple nodes with different weights. A single observation is thus

split into multiple "pieces," with associated weights. The final prediction or classification would then be a weighted combination of the predictions of the final pieces.
See Also: Classification And Regression Trees, Hierarchical Mixtures of Experts.

Software Agent

The term "Software Agent" was coined to describe a software robot, an entity that "lives" in a computer or a network of computers. An agent would have some intelligence or understanding of a particular area and be able to follow instructions autonomously and interact with both humans and other agents or systems. Typically, an agent would be expected to demonstrate some intelligence in understanding a user's statement of a problem or goal and exercise some degree of adaptive reasoning in finding a solution.

software, belief network

A extensive commented list of software for constructing and manipulating a belief network, Bayesian Network, influence diagram, or probabilistic graphical model is maintained at http://bayes.stat.washington.edu/almond/belief.htm. This includes hyperlinks as well as pricing information
See Also: belief net, Bayesian Network, graphical model, influence diagram.

software, Knowledge Discovery in Databases (KDD)

An extensive list of public domain, research, and commercial systems for Data Mining and Knowledge Discovery is maintained at http://www.kdnuggets.com/siftware.html
See Also: Data Mining, Knowledge Discovery in Databases.

Sojourner

Sojourner is a micro-robot made famous by the 1997 Mars Pathfinder mission. It was able to perform autonomous navigation, hazard avoidance, and numerous experiments on the Martian surface.
See Also: http://mars.sgi.com/rover/.

SOM

See: self-organizing map.

sorties paradox

A classic paradox occasionally used in defense of fuzzy logic methods. An example is Zeno's pile of sand. If you remove a single grain, it is still a pile. Repeat the process and, eventually, no pile of sand exists. When does the pile lose its "pileness" since the earlier operation showed that removing a grain of sand does not change the pileness? As with many paradoxes, it relies on loose definitions and/or a specific viewpoint.

sparse data problem

A common problem for statistical and other empirical learning techniques is the sparse data problem. If the learning is limited to simple frequency counts of "events" in the training sets, the model will always behave poorly on new input that introduces related but "new" events. The more detailed the original model becomes, the more data required to learn (estimate) the various parts of the model; therefore, the amount of data supporting any one part becomes increasingly sparser. Practically speaking, this simply means that the input data can rarely cover all possible cases. One approach for dealing with this problem is use of theoretical knowledge to add structure to the empirical model or the use of smoothing techniques to "fill in" the missing data.

specificity

The specificity of a classification rule is a measure of the rule's ability to classify "negative" cases correctly. It is the ratio of the number of true negatives in a test set divided by the total number of negatives in that set. Note that this is not the probability that a negative classification is actually a negative case. The latter depends on the proportion of positive and negative cases in the target set.
See Also: positive predictive value, sensitivity.

spectral analysis

A form of time series analysis that treats the observed sequence of events or measurements as being analogous to a radio or similar signal. The signal is assumed to be a mix of "pure" signals at various frequencies and the model estimates the power (amplitude) at the various frequencies. Typically the signals are represented by a Fourier Series, a mixture of sine and cosine functions. Other basis functions

can also be used, such as Hadamard functions (which take on values of 1 and -1) or wavelets.
See Also: time series analysis, Box-Jenkins Analysis.

speech recognition

This area is also referred to as Automatic Speech Recognition (ASR), and concerns the process of breaking continuous speech into a discrete series of recognized words. It is complicated by the wide variety of pronunciations of words by different speakers and by the same speaker under different circumstances. Other problems include homonyms (*dear* versus *deer*) and related forms of ambiguity (*youth in Asia* and *euthanasia*) as well as slurring and other forms of contraction (*howareya* and *how are you*).

spline

A spline is a mathematical function defined over a compact region of a (continuous) variables range. It is generally continuous and is often represented by a low order polynomial function (or its integral). The knots of a spline are its points of inflection. Its degree is a measure of the number of continuous derivatives.

These functions underlie many Data Mining and nonparametric or semi-parametric regression functions. Since they are only defined over a region of the full attribute range, they allow the function to adapt well to data in their region of support without strongly influencing the results in regions outside that region.

Techniques such as Classification And Regression Trees (CART) and C4.5 that recursively partition the attribute space can be thought of as recursive spline functions with zero-order splines (constant values) fit in each region. The attributes in each sub-region so defined can then be searched for further places to partition that region adaptively for improved prediction.

See Also: C4.5, Classification And Regression Trees, Multivariate Adaptive Regression Spline, nonparametric.

Split-sample validation

A method for estimating the error in automated modeling techniques such as neural networks, recursive partitioning, and Data Mining. The data are split into two parts, a larger part for estimation and a small hold out sample used to estimate the true error. The technique is best used when there is a very large amount of data available as it reduces the size of the training data.

spurious correlation

In Data Mining and other forms of Machine Learning, the analysis can produce a number of nonsensical or meaningless associations. These can be referred to as "spurious correlations." They can occur as a artifact of the data source (e.g., people with good credit) or as the result of a hidden association with variable (e.g., good credit with ownership of certain items when both are results of a high income) or simply due to chance.

Some common strategies to reduce the likelihood of their occurrence would be sub-stratification of the data on "meaningful" attributes, or split-sample techniques and Cross-validation. Another approach would be to raise the acceptance criteria to filter out more of the noisy associations.

See Also: Simpson's paradox.

stability-plasticity dilemma

A phrase referring to the tradeoff between having a machine learning algorithm that is stable in the presence of noisy inputs (stability) and being sensitive to novel inputs (plasticity).

stack

A set of objects ordered such that the last (most-recent) object added to the set is the next to be removed. This ordering is also referred to as Last In Last Out or LIFO.

See Also: list, queue.

standardizing

A numeric variable can be standardized by subtracting a "mean" or some other center and then dividing by its range or standard deviation. Dividing by the range yields a new variable in the [0,1] range, and dividing by the standard deviation yields a variable with a unit variance. Standardization allows one to use techniques that require variables to be in a [0,1] range such as certain activation functions in neural networks and spline basis decompositions. It also can improve the numeric stability of a technique.

state space

A generic term that refers to mathematical space defined by the collection of all possible states of an aspect of a system. For example, a system with four binary input sensors would have $2^4 = 16$ states in its input "state space."

state-space representation

A state-space representation is a method to represent both the current state of a system and the space of possible actions or transitions to new states. They are often represented, respectively, as nodes, and arcs in a graph. The nodes maintain a complete description of the current state of the system and the arcs define possible actions. In a Means-Ends analysis, the objective is to move the system from an initial state to some defined goal state.
See Also: Means-Ends analysis.

Statistical Inference

Reasoning based on the mathematics of probability and statistics, which can be used to weigh hypotheses about some condition.

statistical query

In the study of Machine Learning algorithms on noisy data, a statistical query is a pair consisting of a query and an error tolerance. The query has the form of a bounded region of the attribute space (Tweety is yellow and has a beak) and a class (Tweety is a bird.) The query can be passed to a statistics oracle, which returns the probability that the query is true within the given tolerance.
See Also: statistics oracle.

statistics oracle

A statistics oracle is a function that returns an approximation to the correct probability that a specified statistical query is true. The approximation is within a specified tolerance ε of the true probability. The statistics oracle needs to be defined for a concept class and a distribution over the instance space. The oracle may be operating samples from a large database or on a noisy source of data.
See Also: statistical query.

STM

An acronym used in the discussion of ART networks to refer to short term memeory.
See Also: ftp://ftp.sas.com/pub/neural/FAQ2.html, http://www.wi.leidenuniv.nl/art/.

strategic uncertainty

When an agent does not know how its actions will affect its environment or the environment changes unpredictably, it faces strategic uncertainty.
See Also: payoff uncertainty.

Strategist

A commercially available graphical program to build and analyze models based Bayesian Belief Networks and Hierarchical Influence Diagrams. It supports arbitrary joint, marginal, and conditional queries.
See Also: http://www.prevision.com/strategist.html.

STRIPS

A program to solve problems a robot might encounter. It uses Propositional Logic to represent the current and goal states and a Means-End analysis to derive a solution.
See Also: Means-Ends analysis, Propositional Logic.

structural equation model

A structural equation model is a modeling technique, commonly used in social and behavioral sciences to represent relationships among sets of latent variables. The models suppose the existence of underlying variables, called either latent variables or factors, that influence the observable variables; these variables are classified as being either "exogenous" (independent) or "endogenous" (dependent.) These models predate more modern methods such as independence models and fuzzy cognitive maps.

structure, data

A composite data type composed of other data types, which may be either simple or composite.
See Also: data type.

sublattice

A sublattice L_0 of a lattice L is a subset of the lattice L such that the elements x ∨ y and x ∧ y are in L_0 whenever x and y are in L_0.
See Also: lattice.

Subsethood

In fuzzy logic, the subsethood S(A,B) is a measure of the degree to which a fuzzy set A is a subset of another fuzzy set B. It is the ratio of the fuzzy count of the intersection of A and B to the fuzzy count of A. Note that the B can be a proper (crisp) subset of A, yet still have a well-defined value for S(A,B). It is similar to the concept of conditional probability P(B|A).
See Also: fuzzy count, fuzzy logic.

Subsumption Architecture

R. Brooks, at MIT, developed Subsumption Architecture as a novel approach to robotics control. Rather than have a central control controlling each action in detail, this architecture takes a bottom-up approach, building very small control units that have a defined reflex cycle, and combines these together in a layered hierarchy. Each behavior is modeled by a finite-state matchine with only a few states. This approach has been successful at developing robots that exhibit insect level intelligence.

subsumption strategies

Subsumption is a redundancy control strategy in automated reasoning systems. Subsumption enables the program to discard the specific statement in the presence of the more general statement. A variation of subsumption, back subsumption, enables the program to discard retained information when newly deduced information is logically more general.
See Also: OTTER.

subtautolgy

A subtautolgy in a clause is a proper subterm of the clause that is true. Eliminating subtautologis is restriction strategy that can be used in automated reasoning systems.
See Also: OTTER.

sum-product algorithm

The sum-product algorithm is a method for probability propagation in singly-connected Bayesian networks. Rather than a using a full multivariate representation, a factored model is used, which decomposes the multivariate probability into combinations of products and sums.

See Also: generalized EM, generalized forward-backward algorithm, factor graph, Markov random fields.

superimposition fraud

Fraud detection is a very active area in Data Mining. Superimposition frauds are methods to commit fraud by "piggy-backing" on a legitimate account. One example would be the practice of "shoulder surfing" to learn PIN numbers or credit card numbers. Once this information has been obtained, the thief will attempt to exploit it quickly and obtain goods or money. A fraud detection system needs to detect changes quickly from normal behavior. Data Mining is used to discover these patterns.

supervised learning

The goal of supervised learning is for a computer to process a set of data whose attributes have been divided into two groups and derive a relationship between the values of one and the values of the other. These two groups are sometimes called predictor and targets, respectively. In statistical terminology, they are called independent and dependent variables, respectively. The learning is "supervised" because the distinction between the predictors and the target variables is chosen by the investigator or some other outside agency (e.g., a data mining process.)

Some examples include various forms of regression analysis (logistic and linear), where the investigator also specifies the functional form of the relationship that is to be learned, classification, and decision trees, that attempt to partition the space of target variables into subsets that are homogeneous with respect to the target variables. Feed-forward neural networks are another example.

See Also: unsupervised learning.

Supervised SOM

A form of Kohonen network.
See Also: Kohonen network, SOM, http://www.cis.hut.fi/nnrc/new_book.html.

support function

Dempster-Shafer theory contains a hierarchy of support functions as special cases of belief functions. A simple support function corresponds "to a body of evidence whose precise and full effect is to support a subset A to the degree s." A separable support function is one that can be obtained by combining simple support functions; a general support function is one that can be generated from a separable support function by "coarsening" its frame of discernment. Support functions can be generalized to quasi support functions by considering a sequence of support functions that has contradictory weight that grow to infinity as the sequence goes to infinity. The limit of this sequence is a quasi support function.
See Also: belief function, Dempster-Shafer theory, frame of discernment.

supports

See: Assumption Based Reasoning.

support threshold

A lower bound on the proportion of cases in a database (or other population) for which both sides of an association rule holds. An association rule that holds for ten percent of the rows in a database would also meet the criteria of having at least five percent support. A binary attribute set is said to be covering with respect to a database and a support threshold s if all members of the set are true in at least a proportion s of the population.
See Also: association rules, confidence threshold, covering.

Symbol (LISP)

In LISP, a symbol is an object that contains additional information beyond the identifier/location pair of a variable. In addition to the location, which is referred to as the value cell, it can have other properties associated with it, such as methods and functions.

synaptic matrix

In neural networks, a rectangular table showing the connections between two sets of neurons. Each row would represent a single neuron in the first set, while each column would represent a neuron in the second set. Thus the element in the i-th row and j-th column would describe the connection between the i-th neuron in the first group and the j-th neuron in the second set.

syntactic ambiguity

If an input phase or sentence can be represented by several different parse trees, the input is said to exhibit syntactic ambiguity. This generally complicates the processing of the input and can lead to quite different meanings from the same input data.

syntactic parsing

A Natural Language Parsing technique that assigns the syntactic role markers to input text. The syntactic role of a word or word phrase can be later used in determining the meaning of the input. The parsed text is often represented as a parse tree, where the input sentence is broken down into increasingly finer parts.
See Also: part-of-speech tagging.

T

tabula rasa method

An algorithm for Machine Learning which starts with no prior knowledge of the subject matter other than the basic mechanisms for learning from input. Although the addition of prior knowledge can speed up and otherwise improve the learning capability of an algorithm, tabula rasa methods have been quite successful and are generally easy to implement and test.
See Also: Machine Learning.

tabular distribution

A probability distribution is tabular when it is specified by a table listing the probability value for each configuration of the attribute(s) it is associated with. It is usually distinguished from an algorithmic distribution which is evaluated from an algorithm.
See Also: algorithmic distribution, parametric distribution.

tail

A LISP function that returns all elements of a list except the first.
See Also: head, list, LISP.

tail strategies

One strategy an automated reasoning system can use to choose clauses for further evaluation is to prefer clauses which are short. In systems such as OTTER, a tail strategy is used to choose two term clauses whose second term (the tail) are short.
See Also: OTTER.

TAN Bayes

A Tree Augmented Naïve Bayes classifier. Naïve Bayes classifiers assume that the prediction variables are independent given the class. A TAN Bayes model allows a limited form of dependency, such that any prediction variable can depend on a single other prediction variable (with no cycles in the graph, given the class. In Figure T.1, the solid lines represent the Naïve Bayes model, while the broken lines represent a possible TAN Bayes augmentation.

Figure T.1—Tree Augmented Bayes Model

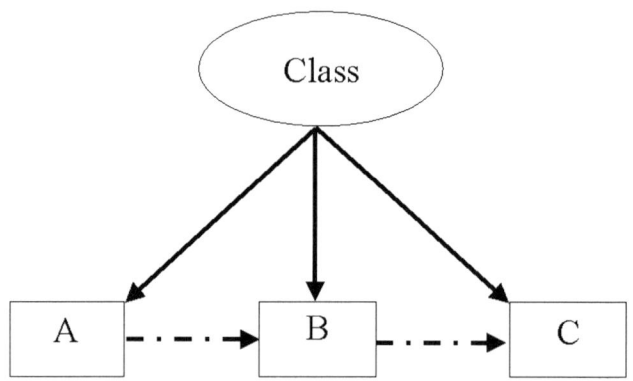

TASA

See: Telecommunication Alarm-Sequence Analyzer.

taxonomy

A taxonomy is a hierarchical organization of the members of an attribute domain. It is usually presented in a tree. The classifications are exhaustive and disjoint.

Telecommunication Alarm-Sequence Analyzer (TASA)

A Telecommunications Alarm-Sequence Analyzer was built in the mid-1990s as a joint venture between a manufacturer of telecommunications equipment and three telephone-network companies. The program uses Knowledge Discovery to Databases (KDD) to analyze alarm streams to locate common alarm episodes and provides identification rules for them. The large numbers of rules generated in this fashion are then further analyzed using grouping, pruning and ordering tools to refine and structure these rules.
See Also: Knowledge Discovery in Databases.

template, association

See: association rule templates.

Template matching

A image analysis technique that compares input images to a stored set of templates. The best match is the recognized item. It is limited in its sensitivity to noise and, for character recognition, style changes.

templates, inclusive

See: association rule templates.

templates, restrictive

See: association rule templates.

Temporal Reasoning

A term for logic that develops a general theory of time. This system requires a means of describing what is true and false over time as well as describing the meaning of a real change.

terminal symbol

A terminal symbol is a symbol in a grammar that has no further production rules associated with it.
See Also: non-terminal symbol, production.

test set

When training a neural network, Classification And Regression Trees (CART) and other models, the data that are used to evaluate the completed model are referred to as the test set. Ideally, this should be separate from the training set, which is used to fit the model, and from any validation set that is used to tune overall model structure or complexity.

TETRAD II

A multi-module program that uses path models and a Bayesian Network to construct and explore causal relationships in data. The program is based on an axiomatic connection between causal structure and statistical independence.
See Also: http://hss.cmu.edu/HTML/departments/philosophy/TETRAD/tetrad.html.

THAID

A later version of the Automatic Interaction Detection (AID) program.
See Also: Automatic Interaction Detection, Classification And Regression Trees.

Theorem Proving System (TPS)

A Theorem Proving System an automated first-order logic systems. It can run in automatic, interactive, and a mixed mode. It can translate expansion proofs into natural deduction proofs, and, in certain cases, translate deduction proofs into expansion proofs. It can also solve unification problems in higher-order logic.

A simplified version, called the Educational Theorem Proving System (ETPS), provides interactive construction of natural deduction proofs.

theory patching

Theory patching is a form of theory revision which allows revisions to individual components of a given domain theory to classify all training examples correctly. It differs from standard (Machine Learning) learning problems in that the theory is treated as being only partially revisable rather than replaceable.
See Also: http://www.jair.com/.

threshold function

A signal function that produces a signal whenever the input is above a certain threshold. A plot of a threshold output against its input would resemble a step; so, it is also sometimes referred to as a step function. It is used in neural networks and as an input variable transform in other models.
See Also: Indicator function, signal function.

threshold(ed) linear function

A signal function that is composed of a bounded linear function. Whenever the input exceeds a certain level, the output is bounded to the maximum and, similarly, when the output drops below a particular value. It is used as an output function in a neural network.
See Also: signal function.

Time Invariant Systems

In Robotics, a system that can be described in terms of its current state, which can include velocity information, without regard to its past history or, more specifically, the time origin. When a system has memory (e.g., momentum or velocity), that system can be made time invariant by including measures of the memory as part of the state variable describing the system.
See Also: Robotics.

time series analysis

A special form of data analysis where the observations are sequences in time. The objective of such an analysis to derive rules to predict future observation in a series. This is often distinguished from regular data analysis because of the time ordering of the events and the (assumed) correlation of events with their past.
See Also: Data Mining.

time series data

Data taken from ordered sequences of events or measurements. Since the values are often correlated, the data usually require special analytic techniques
See Also: Machine Learning, time series analysis.

top-down

Top-down searches are similar to backward chaining or goal driven searches, in that the method starts with the final goal and the current state. Top-down attempts to work backward from the goal to the current state in order to find a path that allows one to move from the current state. In a top-down analysis, one starts with the goal and examines all rules or steps that could have lead directly to it. For each rule that qualifies as a possible predecessor, the algorithm then searches for its predecessor, and so on, until either the current state is reached or all possibilities are exhausted.
See Also: backward chaining, Bottom-Up, data-driven, Forward Chaining, goal-driven.

Top-down pathways

The weighted connections from the F2 layer of an ART network to the F1 layer.

See Also: ftp://ftp.sas.com/pub/neural/FAQ2.html, http://www.wi.leidenuniv.nl/art/.

Toronto Virtual Enterprise (TOVE)

The TOVE project is a domain-specific ontology designed to model enterprises. The project has several interlinked ontologies for various parts of an enterprise that are interlinked by axioms and relations. Some of the ontologies include activities, time, products, and organizations.

See Also: ontology.

TOVE

See: Toronto Virtual Enterprise.

TPS

See: Theorem Proving System.

training set

When developing a neural network, Classification And Regression Trees (CART), or other self-teaching method, the data are usually divided into two or three subsets. The largest of these, the training set, is used to actually fit the model. The other one or two are used in model validation and evaluation.

transduction

Some Machine Learning and statistical algorithms allow the system to maintain multiple simultaneous hypotheses (models) about the state of their worlds, each hypothesis being weighted by a probability or related measures. In this situation, the system can make predictions about some decision or future data through transduction. To make the prediction about some future data, the system makes the prediction for each applicable hypothesis and then forms a weighted average of the predictions, where the weights are proportional to the probabilities of the individual models.

This is in contrast to techniques that require the choice of a single hypothesis at some stage in the learning/modeling process. Here the model is usually chosen according to some optimality criterion, such as Maximum A Posteriori (MAP), MINIMAX, Minimum Description Length Principle (MDLP), or Mean Square Error (MSE) criterion.

See Also: Maximum A Posteriori, Mean Square Error criterion, Minimum Description Length Principle, minmax procedures, mixture-of-experts models.

transfer function

See: Activation functions.

Transformational Grammar

A theory for human languages that holds that any sentence in that language can be generated by a series of transformations on a basic set of sentences.

transformational tagging

A second-order technique for Natural Language Parsing. Once a sentence of text has been initially tagged, a transformational tagger would begin applying transformation rules to the initial tags to improve the parsing of the data.

transition matrix

See: Markov chain.

traveling salesman problem

A classic problem in optimization and planning. A "traveling salesman" has to visit a number of "cities" at specified locations. The problem is to select a route that minimizes the total distance traveled, including a return to the starting point.

travesty

See: n-gram.

tree

A partially ordered set where each object is either a parent or child of other objects, and no object is a parent to any of its ancestors. The parent/child/ancestors terms are metaphors for a simple ordering relationship. If object A precedes object B then object A is the "parent" of B and B is "a child of" B. A is an ancestor of B as is any ancestor of A.

Figure T.2—An Example of a Tree

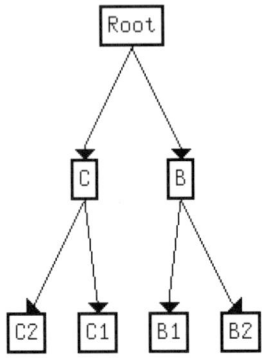

tree recursion

Tree recursion is a special form of recursion where each level of evaluation makes multiple recursive calls to the same function or procedure. It is used, for example, in developing a classification tree.
See Also: classification tree, combinatorial explosion.

triangulated graphs

A graph is triangulated if every cycle of length 4 or more in the graph has a chord. Triangulation is required for calculation of many properties of a graphical model. Figure T.3 shows a 4-cyle (ABCD) that has been triangulated by the addition of a BD arc, indicated by the dotted line.
See Also: graphical model.

Figure T.3—A Triangulated Graph

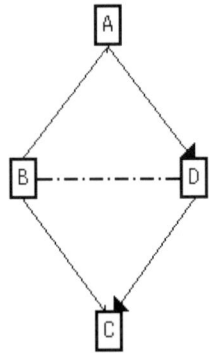

trigger procedures
See: demon procedures.

trigram
See: n-gram.

true negative rate
See: sensitivity.

true positive rate
See: sensitivity.

truth-value
The truth-value of a proposition is a measure of the truth of a proposition. Classical binary logic allows values of True (1) or False (0). Other multi-valued or continuous logic, such as Lukasiewicz' multi-valued logic, probability logic, or fuzzy logic allow intermediate values in the (0,1) interval. Truth values are important in propagating and calculating uncertainty values.

TSP
See: traveling salesman problem.

tuple
A tuple is a collection of attributes or attribute values.
See Also: feature vector.

twoing
Twoing is a multi-class splitting criteria introduced in the Classification And Regression Trees (CART) program. Recall that CART produces only binary splits. The twoing criteria find a binary superclass of the available classes in each node that maximizes the twoing criteria.
The twoing criteria itself is a weighted squared sum over the classes in the nodes of the absolute difference between the probability of each class being in the left node and the probability of being in the right node.
See Also: Classification And Regression Trees, Gini Index.

two-monotone (2-monotone)
See: Choquet Capability.

2/3 rule
A rule for calculating the output of each node in the F1 layer of an ART network. At least two of the three inputs (input pattern, G1 gain control, top-down prototype) have to be active for the node to become active.
See Also: ART, ftp://ftp.sas.com/pub/neural/FAQ2.html, http://www.wi.leidenuniv.nl/art/.

U

UMLS

See: Unified Medical Language System.

unbound variable or symbol

See: bound variable or symbol.

uncertainty propagation

Uncertainty propagation refers to the process of updating or revising the uncertainty measures of a set of propositions or attributes due to changes in assumption or information about related propositions or attributes. In some contexts, propagation is separated from revision, where the latter term is used to refer to the mutual change in uncertainty for a set of propositions when new knowledge is introduced into the system.

uncertainty sampling

A method for selecting cases to train classifiers that produce probabilistic output. After the initial training of a classifier, a series of observations are run through the program, and ranked according to the uncertainty of the predictions. The most uncertain ones are selected, properly classified, and used to train the classifier further. This can be repeated until the classifier performs satisfactorily.

unconditional independence

Two attributes are unconditionally independent if their joint probabilities are the product of their independent probabilities over the domain of interest. Independence implies lack of correlation. The converse is not true.
See Also: Bayesian Network, belief net.

underlap

Underlap is the fuzzy size of the set M (A È not(A)), an extension of the crisp set notion of cardinality. This measure is used in defining the fuzzy entropy of the set.

undirected graph

An undirected graph is a graph that contains a finite number of nodes as well as undirected links between some of those nodes. Figure U.1 shows an example of an undirected graph. Note that it contains two directed arcs (AD, DC).

Figure U.1—An Undirected Graph

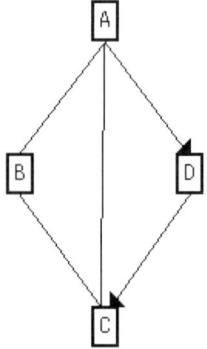

unidirectional network

An interconnected one-layer neural network. When the synaptic matrix is symmetric, the network forms a Bi-directional Associative Memory (BAM).
See Also: Bidirectional Associative Memory.

Unified Medical Language System (UMLS)

The UMLS ontology is a medical ontology system designed to assist in the retrieval and integration of multiple medical information systems. It has a concept hierarchy of 135 medical concepts as well as a semantic network that represents additional relationships between the categories.
See Also: ontology, Semantic Network, http://wwwkss.nlm.nih.gov/Docs/umls.fact.html.

Unifier

When representing information in clause-form, a substitution for the literals A and B, yielding C and D, respectively, is said to be a unifier if C=D. The substitution is said to "unify" the literals A and B, and the literals are said to be unifiable. If there exists a substitution such that all other unifying substitutions a special cases of this unifier, then the unifier is called the Most General Unifier (MGU).
See Also: Binary Resolution, Most General Common Instance.

union

The union of two sets, A and B (written as $A \cup B$). The set contains all of a single copy of any elements—either A or B. It is also a LISP function that takes two lists as arguments and returns a list containing the elements that are in either of the original lists, with no duplicates.
See Also: list, LISP, intersection.

unique name assumption

A simplifying assumption used in knowledge and database that assumes that each item has a unique name, so that items with different names can be assumed to represent different things.

unit

See: partially ordered set.

universal quantifier

The "universal quantifier" in logic is the quantifier implying "for all" on a proposition. It states that a relationship holds for all instances of the proposition. It is often represented by an upside down capital A.
See Also: existential quantifier.

universe

The set of all cases in a particular application domain.
See Also: Machine Learning.

unsupervised learning

The goal of unsupervised learning is for a computer to process a set of data and extract a structure which is relevant to the problem at hand. This can take different forms. In cluster analysis and some

forms of density estimation, the goal is to find a small number "groups" of observations which have a simple structure. Graphical and other forms of dependency models reduce the interrelations between the variables to a smaller number. In neural networks, unsupervised learning is a form of cluster analysis or density estimation, where the network is being trained to reproduce the input. It is also referred to as auto-association. Prominent techniques include Kohonen networks and Hebbian learning.
See Also: supervised learning.

upper approximation

In Rough Set Theory, the upper approximation to a concept X is the smallest definable set containing the concept X. For example, if we were examining a database on credit risks, the upper approximation to the class (concept) of bad credit risks, would be the smallest set of attributes that contained all the cases labeled bad credit risks.

A measure of this set is the quality of the upper approximation. It is equivalent to a Dempster-Shafer plausibility function and is computed as the ratio of the number of cases in the upper approximation to the total number of cases in the database.
See Also: lower approximation, plausibility, Rough Set Theory.

upper envelope

The upper envelope for a proposition is the maximum of the (convex) set of probabilities attached to the proposition.
See Also: lower envelope, Quasi-Bayesian Theory.

upper expectation

The maximum expectation over a (convex) set of probabilities.
See Also: lower expectation.

upper prevision

See: upper expectation.

upward closure

A collection of sets is upwardly closed with respect to a property if, when a set P has a property, all sets containing P have that property. An example would be a dependency in a market basket analysis.

Once a set of items are known to be dependent, any larger set containing those items is also known to be dependent.
See Also: dependence rule, downward closure.

UR-Resolution

UR-resolution is an inference rule that can be used in automated reasoning systems. It focuses on two or more clauses, requiring that one of the clauses (the nucleus) contain at least two literals and the remaining (the satellites) contain exactly one literal. Briefly, a conclusion is yielded if a unifier (substitution of terms) for variables can be found that, when applied, makes identical (except for being opposite in sign) pairs of literals, one literal from the nucleus with one from a satellite. The conclusion is yielded by, ignoring the paired literals, applying the unifier simultaneously to the nucleus and the satellites and taking the union of the resulting literals.
See Also: hyperresolution.

utility

The utility of an action is a numeric measure of the value of the outcome due to taking that action. Typically, many systems act to maximize their utility. Many Machine Learning systems assume that all actions (predictions, classifications) can be evaluated with a single score and act to maximize that value. Alternate terms include rewards, payoffs, cost, and losses. The latter two are more common in game and economic theory (e.g., minimax methods).

A related term, often used when discussing maximization and minimization routines, is objective function. It is also a measure of worth and is a (usually additive) combination of the utilities of model for a set of cases.
See Also: Machine Learning, minimax procedures.

Uttley Machine

An Uttley machine is a special type of Perceptron, suggested by A. M. Uttley. By comparing the activations of "adjacent" channels in a network, and using Bayesian techniques to update the weights, he was able to limit the number of input channels required in a Perceptron network. He also demonstrated that incorporating local feedback between perceptrons reduced the number of perceptrons required active classification of patterns.

V

vague logic

See: fuzzy logic.

validation set

When training neural network, Classification And Regression Trees (CART) and other models, a portion of the data is often held out and used to select some of the overall parameters of the model, such as the number of layers in an Artificial Neural Network (ANN) and the depth of the tree in a CART model. These data are often referred to as the validation set or the design set, where the chosen model is fitted using the training set.
See Also: test set, training set.

valuation network

A graphical representation of a belief network that introduces different types of nodes to portray a wider variety of multivariate relationships than can be done in a standard Directed Acyclic Graph (DAG).
See Also: belief net.

valuations

Valuations are a generalization of the ideas of belief and probability functions, and provide a mapping from a set of outcomes over a frame of discernment to numeric values. A valuation has three properties. It supports combination, so that two valuations over the same frame can be combined. It allows projection (extensions and marginalizations) so that the frame of discernment can be changed. It meets certain requirements under which the combination and projection operations can be interchanged. A function meeting these conditions can be manipulated using the Shafer-Shenoy fusion and propagation algorithm.
See Also: Shafer-Shenoy Architecture.

Vapnik-Chervonenkis dimension

The Vapnik-Chervonenkis dimension is a measure of the complexity of a concept in Machine Learning and is used to put lower bounds on the learnability of a concept. Basically it describes the size of the largest set such that the concept class realizes all possible dichotomies of the sample. In other words, for a sample of size **d**, there are 2^d possible subsets of that sample. If every subset can be made positive for some example of the concept, then the concept class will have dichotomized the sample.
See Also: Machine Learning.

variational inference

Variational inference is an approximation technique that can be used when exact or Monte Carlo computation is infeasible. In the case of a network model with hidden variables **h** and observed (visible) variables v, a variation solution would approximate $Pr(h|v)$ with some tractable $Q(h|v)$, where $Q(h|v)$ minimizes some distance measure (e.g., relative entropy) with respect to $Pr(h|v)$.
See Also: Helmholtz machine, Markov Chain Monte Carlo Methods.

vague logic

See: fuzzy logic.

vector optimization

An optimization problem where multiple objectives must be satisfied (or maximized).

Vector-quantization networks

Vector-Quantization networks are a form of unsupervised Kohonen neural networks similar to k-means cluster analysis. Each unit corresponds to a cluster. When a new case is learned, the closest code book vector (cluster center) is moved a certain proportion along the vector between it and the new case, where the proportion is determined by the learning rate of the algorithm.
See Also: http://www-uk.hpl.hp.com/people/ewc/list-main.html.

VentEx

VentEx, currently under evaluation, is a knowledge-based decision-

support and monitoring system applied in ventilator therapy.
See Also: http://www-uk.hpl.hp.com/people/ewc/list-main.html.

Vienna Expert system for Parental Nutrition of Neonates (VIE-PNN)

VIE-PNN is an Expert System for the design of nutritional feeding regimens for newborn infants.
See Also: http://www-uk.hpl.hp.com/people/ewc/list-main.html.

VIE-PNN

See: Vienna Expert system for Parental Nutrition of Neonates.

vigilance

ART networks use a vigilance parameter to define how well an input case must match a candidate prototype. It is used to change the number and size of the categories the the network develops.
See Also: ftp://ftp.sas.com/pub/neural/FAQ2.html, http://www.wi.leidenuniv.nl/art/.

virtual attribute

A virtual attribute is one whose values are not observed or counted but are computed from other attributes. They are often computed as proxies for concepts or to simplify analysis. As an example of concept proxies, other models might suggest that a particular function of observable attributes represents the wealth of a person, and the wealth function can be computed for all cases in the database for later analysis by, say, a Data Mining algorithm looking for purchase patterns. An example of the latter would be the collapse of the discrete attribute containing years of schooling into a nominal variable with a small number of categories.
See Also: Knowledge Discovery in Databases, Machine Learning.

Virtual Reality Modeling Language (VRML)

VRML is a language used to store the specifications of a three-dimensional space. The VRML description of a scene would be used by, for example, a World Wide Web (WWW) browser to render the scene and to change the image or perform other actions in reaction to a person's input.

voxel

A voxel, analogous to a pixel (q.v.), is the smallest unit in a computer rendering of a volume, for example, in an image generated from a VRML file.

VRML

See: Virtual Reality Modeling Language.

W

wake-sleep algorithm

The wake-sleep algorithm is a form of generalized EM algorithm that can be used to train Helmholtz machines. During the "sleep phase," the recognition network is trained to recognize random output from the generative network. During the "wake phase," the generative network is adjusted to maximize the log-likelihood of the visible variables and the hidden variables produced by the recognition network. The sleep phase is analogous to an Expectation step in the EM algorithm, while the wake phase generalizes the Maximization step.
See Also: Expectation-Minimization (EM) algorithm, generalized forward-backward algorithm, sum-product algorithm.

Walker

Walker was an early 1980s prototype ambulatory robot, which demonstrated an ability to use insectile (six-legged) locomotion.
See Also: Ambler.

weakly learnable

A concept class is weakly learnable by a Machine Learning algorithm L if the algorithm L returns, with a least a fixed probability, a learning rule that has less than a fixed maximum for any distribution over the attribute space. This assumes that the learning algorithm L can access a statistical oracle that returns the average concept for any X.

This differs from the Probably Approximately Correct (PAC) learning models, which require the learning algorithm to be able to return a rule for any arbitrarily large confidence and/or arbitrarily small error rate. Schapire and Freund have demonstrated that a weakly learnable concept class can be converted to a PAC learnable concept class using boosting.
See Also: Probably Approximately Correct (PAC) learning model.

wearable computer systems

As the term implies, these are computer systems that are designed to be worn or easily carried about. A wearable system allows the user to circumvent the usual limitations of a workstation, server-based expert system, or intelligent agent. They are currently under active development and have been employed primarily in vertical applications, such as aircraft maintenance or stock analysis. The systems can range from the simple "palm" computer, such as the Palm Pilot, with specialized databases and decision programs (e.g., options analysis) to systems that are worn on a "hip pack" and have head mounted monitors, as well as specialized input devices (e.g., a "twiddler"). The newer systems can include wireless modems to allow continuous access to the Internet and other specialized information sources, such as stock market feeds or patient databases.

weight decay

A form of penalized minimization used to reduce overfitting in modeling techniques such as neural networks. Rather than attempt to minimize just the error term of the model, the technique attempts to minimize a weighted sum of the errors and the model complexity. Weight decay is a specialized form of complexity penalty, usually a sum of the squared weights in the model. This form of penalty tends to shrink the large coefficients in favor of smaller coefficients. The amount of shrinkage depends on the parameter that controls the tradeoff between error minimization and the penalty term. This is sometimes referred to as the decay constant.

weight elimination

An alternative to weight decay in neural networks. Rather than penalize the model for large coefficients, which tends to cause large numbers of small coefficients, weight elimination uses the sum of the ratio of each squared weight divided by its square and a constant, $sum(w^2/(w^2+c))$. This term tends to shrink small coefficients more than the larger coefficients, which are unaffected by the constant. This technique is also useful for subset models or for pruning predictors.

weight of evidence

The weight of evidence is a generic name for measures that score data and hypotheses. Several examples include:

- log-likelihood ratio
    The weight for a proposition H provided by evidence E is $W(H:E)=log(P(E|H)/P(E|!H))$. The latter term is the log of the likelihood ratio. It can also be rewritten as the difference between the log(posterior odds) and the log(prior odds).
- belief odds
    The weight of evidence for a hypothesis H in a belief function is *log(Plausibility(H)/Vagueness(H))*. When two hypotheses are being compared, the weight of evidence for H_1 against H_2 is $log(PL(H_1|E)/PL(H_2|E))-log(PL(H_1)/PL(H_2))$, which generalizes previous definition to include belief functions.

See Also: likelihood ratio, plausibility.

weighting restriction strategies

Weighting restriction strategies are used in automated reasoning systems to limit the complexity of clauses or equations that can be used to perform the reasoning. When a formula's complexity exceeds a specified complexity, it is removed from further consideration.
See Also: OTTER.

WER

See: Word Error Rate.

width

See: radial basis function.

Winbugs

See: BUGS.

windowing

Windowing is a term that can have multiple meanings in a Machine Learning context. It has been used in the ID3 and C4.5 context to refer to the process of selecting a sub-sample of the original data and developing a model. The model is tested against the remaining data, and, if its performance is not satisfactory, a portion of the test data "failures" are included with the original sub-sample and the model refit. This selection procedure can be repeated until the model fits well enough. The effectiveness of this technique depends on the domain and the data.

An alternative use of the same term is in time series and techniques derived from "local" models (e.g., smoothing regression models). In this context, the window describes an area around the prediction point, and only cases that fall within that window are used to make the local prediction. These windows often differentially weight the observations within the window so that observations that are "close" to the target are weighted more heavily than those that are "far away." The size of the window can be chosen by resampling techniques such as Cross-validation.

Wise Wire

Wise Wire is a commercial development of the machine-learning technology demonstrated in the News Weeder software. This latter software was able to predict a readers interest in various news articles. The Wise Wire corporation was founded to extend and exploit this technology, offering tools to automatically screen and sort articles for their interest in various categories.

WNG re-ranking

See: Word N-Gram re-ranking.

Word Error Rate (WER)

A commonly used performance measure in speech recognition, the Word Error Rate (WER) is the ratio of the number of incorrectly recognized or unrecognized words to the total number of actually spoken words.

Word N-Gram (WNG) re-ranking

Word N-Gram (WNG) re-ranking is a re-ranking technique that chooses the set of candidate words that has the highest pairwise succession probability. Given a set of candidates for word1, word2 and word3, a WNG model would choose the triple that maximized $P(word1)P(word2|word1)P(word3|word2)$.
See Also: n-gram.

word sense disambiguation

One of the important sub-tasks in semantic analysis of natural language is word sense disambiguation, in which a program needs to determine which of several possible meanings of a phrase is the correct one. As an example, in the sentence "The pigs are in the pen," the word pen could mean an enclosure or a writing device. A program performing a semantic analysis would need to determine that the sentence referred to an enclosure for animals.

Wordnet

Wordnet is a manually constructed lexical ontology. Lexical objects are organized semantically, with the central object being a set of synonyms. There are currently about 70,000 synonym sets. Each is organized in a hierarchy. Wordnet provides a taxonomy but does not include any concepts or axioms.
See Also: ontology, ftp://clarity.princeton.edu/pub/wordnet.

Word-Tag Model (WTM)

A Word-Tag Model (WTM) is a generalization of the Word N-Gram (WNG) model. It assigns syntactic tags to each of the candidate words and treats the word sequence as a Hidden Markov Model (HMM). The probability of the word is now a function of only the tag, and the system searches for the word-tag sequence that has maximum probability.
See Also: Hidden Markov Model, Word N-Gram re-ranking.

Work Envelope

The area around an (immobile) robot that can be reached by its work arm(s). Depending on the robot's configuration, this can be rectangular, cylindrical, or spherical. Its ability to move and manipulate in this envelope is defined by its degrees of freedom.
See Also: degrees of freedom, Robotics.

WTM

See: Word-Tag Model.

wxCLIPS

wxCLIPS is an extension to the C Language Integration Production System (CLIPS) Expert System, modified to work in an event-driven environment. It supports the development of multi-platform graphical shells.
See Also: C Language Integrated Production System, http://web.ukonline.co.uk/julian.smart/wxclips/.

X

xbaies

A freely available program for building Bayesian belief networks. The models can have a chain-graphical structure, including both a Directed Acyclic Graph (DAG) and undirected graphs. It can include priors and can do evidence propagation.

See Also: Bayesian Network, Directed Acyclic Graph, http://web.ukonline.co.uk/julian.smart/wxsin/xbaise.htm.

Z

zero

See: partially ordered set.

Zero-Sum Games

A game (or other situation) where there is a fixed amount of resources, so that players can only increase their share (or decrease their losses) by taking some from the other players.
See Also: minimax.

Appendix
Internet Resources

Not surprisingly, a wide variety of resources exist on the Internet. This chapter provides a pointers to various general sites we found useful when writing this book, in addition to the many specific sites mentioned in the body. As always, the Uniform Resource Locators (URLs) were current at the time this was written, and can have changed by the time you read this.

OVERVIEW SITES

The following sites have general collections of information about AI, usually collections of links.

- Yahoo!

- Links2go
  http://www.links2go.com/.....
  An example of AI in action, this site uses AI techniques to sweep the net and topically organize the net.

- NRC-CNRC Institute for Information Technology
  http://ai.iit.nrc.ca/ai_top.html

- The AI repository
  http://www.cs.cmu.edu:8001/Web/Groups/AI/html/air.html
  A wide-ranging collection of software for AI and related materials. It does not appear to have been updated since 1994.

- AI Intelligence
  http://aiintelligence.com/aii-home.htm

AI Intelligence provides a monitoring, reporting, and analysis service on Artificial Intelligence.

- AFIT AI Resources
  http://www.afit.af.mil/Schools/EN/ENG/LABS/AI/tools3.html

DATA MINING SOFTWARE

The following sites maintain collections of links to commercial, research, and freeware Data Mining software.

- Knowledge Discovery in Databases (KDD) Siftware
  http://www.kddnuggets.com/siftware.html
  An active and up-to-date software site. This is one of many pages covering the KDD field.

- Data Mining Software Vendors
  http://www.santefe.edu/~kurt/dmvendors.shtml
  A list of Data Mining software companies, current to late 1997. Also provides information on software patents and database marketing.

- The Data Mine
  http://www.cs.bham.ac.uk/~anp/software.html
  Part of an entire site devoted to Data Mining.

- The Data Miner's Catalogue of Tools and Service Providers
  http://www.dit.csiro.au/~gjw/dataminer/Catalogue.html
  This page provides links to Data Mining tool vendors and service providers.

DATA MINING SUITES

Many large software suites are beginning to enter the market. This list, adapted from a KDD-98 presentation (http://www.datamininglab.com), presents some of the larger multi-tool vendors.

- Classification And Regression Trees (CART)
  http://www.salford-systems.com/

- Clementine
  http://www.isl.co.uk/clem.html

- Darwin
  http://www.think.com/html/products/products.htm

- DataCruncher
  http://www.datamindcorp.com/

- Enterprise Miner
  http://www.sas.com/software/components/miner.html

- GainSmarts
  http://www.urbanscience.com/main/gainpage.html

- Intelligent Miner
  http://www.software.ibm.com/data/iminer/

- KnowledgeSTUDIO
  http://www.angoss.com/

- MineSet
  http://www.sgi.com/Products/software/MineSet/

- Model 1
  http://www.unica-usa.com/model1.htm

- ModelQuest
  http://www.abtech.com

- NeuroShell
  http://www.wardsystems.com/neuroshe.htm

- OLPARS
  mailto://olpars@partech.com

- PRW
  http://www.unica-usa.com/prodinfo.htm

- Scenario
  http://www.cognos.com/

- See5/C5.0
  http://www.rulequest.com/

- S-Plus
  http://www.mathsoft.com/

- WizWhy
  http://www.wizsoft.com/why.html

OTHER RESOURCES

- Artificial Intelligence in Medicine (AIM)
  http://www.coiera.com/aimd.htm

- AFIT Bayesian Networks Resources
  http://www.afit.af.mil/Schools/EN/ENG/AI/BayesianNetworks

- Software for manipulating Belief Networks
  http://bayes.stat.washington.edu/almond/belief.html